The Narcissistic/Borderline Couple

The Narcissistic/Borderline Couple

New Approaches to Marital Therapy

Second Edition

by

Joan Lachkar, Ph.D.

Routledge
Taylor & Francis Group

NEW YORK AND LONDON

Routledge
Taylor and Francis Group
711 Third Avenue,
New York, NY 10017

Routledge
Taylor and Francis Group
2 Park Square, Milton Park,
Abingdon, Oxfordshire OX14 4RN

First issued in paperback 2015

Routledge is an imprint of the Taylor and Francis Group, an informa business

Copyright © 2003 by Taylor & Francis Books, Inc.

Library of Congress Cataloging-in-Publication Data
Lachkar, Joan.
    The narcissistic/borderline couple : a psychoanalytic perspective on marital treatment / by Joan Lachkar.— 2nd ed.
        p.   ;   cm.
Includes bibliographical references and index.
    ISBN 0-415-93471-0 (hardcover : alk. paper)
    1. Marital psychotherapy. 2. Borderline personality disorder. 3. Narcissism. 4. Psychoanalysis. 5. Couples—Psychology.
    [DNLM: 1. Marital Therapy—methods. 2. Borderline Personality Disorder. 3. Narcissism. 4. Object Attachment. 5. Self Psychology. WM 430.5.M3 L137n 2003]   I. Title.

    RC488.5.L348 2003
    616.89'156—dc21
                                                                            2003009288

    ISBN 13: 978-1-138-97670-2 (pbk)
    ISBN 13: 978-0-415-93471-8 (hbk)

Contents

Acknowledgments

I am particularly grateful to all my colleagues and friends in the field of psychoanalysis, as well as to my teachers and codancers in the artistic world of classical ballet. The latter contributed much to my efforts to understand the psychic pain and conflict that occurs in the mental lives of the conflicting couples demonstrated in this book. What better way to learn about narcissism than to have looked at myself in a mirror every day since the age of seven! I feel compelled to acknowledge the special contribution of Carmelita Maracci, Stanley Holden, and Margaret Hills, noted ballet masters of classical dance, with whom I have had the good fortune to study dance for more than 20 years. It was through ballet that I learned the importance of artistic expression, and the blending of technique and discipline. Be it at the barre or within the constraints of the consultation room, one must adapt to "the dance": Both ballet and the practice of psychoanalytic psychotherapy involve the subtle blending of scientific principles with art (offering one's unique interpretation while remaining steadfast to analytic principles).

The study of narcissism and borderline pathology would not have been possible without the mentorship and influences of the following master blenders to whom I owe much gratitude. They include Drs. Wilfred Bion, James Grotstein, Otto Kernberg, Nancy Kobrin, Albert Mason, Harvey Martz, Hindy Nobler, Marvin Osman, Florence Bienenfeld, Irene Harwood, Orli Peter, Roberta Rinaldi, Judy Warmbrand, James Weiss, Peter Berton, Peter Lowenberg, and the late Drs. Samuel Eisenstein and Alexander Rogawsky. Also, my ex-husband Robert Kahn, M.D., whom I met when I was 18, taught me more about psychoanalysis than any supervisor. I am also grateful to Lloyd deMause, Jerry Piven, Jerry Atlas, Howard Stain, and all the others at the *Journal of Psychohistory* who gave me permission to delve into the political arena, blending political and marital conflict as a new dimension in the study of cross-cultural couples.

I am indebted to my editors and the staff at Taylor and Francis—particularly George P. Zimmar, executive editor, Luciana Cassano, senior editorial assistant, Mick Spillane, senior production editor, and Shannon Vargo, assistant editor—for their patience and assistance in the rewriting of this book. In addition, I am grateful for the editorial efforts of Joanne Freeman, her patience in enduring an endless plethora of revisions, and her invaluable insights and good ear. I'm also indebted to my research assistants Nicole Lachkar, Rafi Raffee, Scott Raphael, and Alexander Sokhis.

I offer special gratitude to my family, friends, and colleagues, to my patients, who paid me to learn from them, and to my dear children—Sharon, Pamela, and Nicole—to whom this book is dedicated.

Introduction

The first edition of *The Narcissistic/Borderline Couple* abstracted concepts mainly from classical psychoanalysis, self-psychology (Kohut), and object relations (Klein, Winnicott, Fairbairn, Bion, Kernberg). At that time, clinicians, particularly classically trained psychoanalysts, looked somewhat askance at diagnosing and treating relational disorders. Many thought of self-psychology and object-relational approaches as an "odd couple" relationship. But they can indeed work together, as evidenced by the increasing number of clinicians who have begun to apply an object-relational approach to the treatment of marital conflict. Even those who for many years "avoided" couple therapy on the basis that it went against their classical orientation are now actively working within this modality.

In the first edition of this book, a number of psychoanalysts and psychoanalytically trained researchers who understand both fields were acknowledged as making major contributions to marital therapy. These include Dicks (1967); Lachkar (1984, 1985, 1986, 1989); Lansky (1981, 1987); Scarf (1987); Scharff and Scharff (1987); Schwartzman (1984); Sharpe (1981); Slipp (1984); Solomon (1985, 1986); Strean (1980, 1985); and Willi (1982). Since then, an increasing number of researchers who understand both fields have been directing their attention to marital conflict. These include Carlson and Sperry (1998); Kernberg (1995); Lachkar (1998); McCormack (2000); and Rothstein (1998).

This edition further emphasizes the contribution of object relations in the treatment of couple therapy, especially in helping couples face internal deficits, conflicts, distortions, and projections. Melanie Klein's (1957) formulations have proved invaluable in couple therapy, including her introjective/projective process, a priceless construct in helping us understand the tangled web couples weave, how one partner projects a negative feeling onto the other, and how the other then tends to identify or overidentify with that which is being projected. In applying this process to couple therapy, I have renamed it *dual projective identification*, a term that seems more suited to the codependent nature of the relationship. In conjoint treatment, we see how certain dynamic mechanisms of the narcissist (grandiosity, entitlement, guilt, withdrawal) can arouse states of unworthiness and nonexistence in the borderline (shame, blame, envy, abandonment, and persecutory anxieties).

While the first edition referenced the work of D. W. Fairbairn, it may not have sufficiently stressed his importance. Extending beyond Klein, Fairbairn, more than anyone, helps us understand why couples stay in painful conflictual relationships. His concept of splitting of the ego into multitudinous internal objects deepens our understanding of why couples remain forever loyal to their painful internal objects (rejecting, insatiable, unavailable). My training in classical ballet led to the conceptualization of "the dance of the couple" to help understand the choreography—the ongoing, circular repetitive behaviors and interactions—that takes place within the narcissistic/borderline relationship. This "psychological dance" stirs up highly charged conflict that meets the primitive needs of the individuals involved. Each partner "needs" the other to play out his or her personal relational drama. Within these beleaguered love bonds, the narcissistic/borderline couple is redefined in this volume as two developmentally arrested people who coerce each other into certain roles as each brings into their current reality archaic experiences embedded in age-old sentiments. Together they play out a drama characterized by painful, never-ending patterns of behavior. They form a parasitic bond that leads not to growth and development but to destructive and repetitive patterns of behavior. It is not really important how they find each other; more important is what makes them stay together. Two narcissists or two borderlines do not "do the dance," but when paired, these oppositional types appear to maintain a bond. It is almost as if they have some extraordinary built-in sonar system or sniffing device to find one another, like a bloodhound after a rabbit.

Why are narcissistic/borderline couples more prevalent today? Perhaps the reason many clinicians are encountering more of this kind of pathologic pairing is because of an increasing percentage of single-parent families, higher divorce rates, increased numbers of working mothers, parental unavailability to children, the near extinction of extended families, and, in general, greater social isolation.

The 10 years that have elapsed since the first edition of this book have brought the opportunity to present material on couple therapy to mental health professionals and colleagues throughout the United States and Europe. Having evolved and gained new knowledge and insights not only from colleagues and clinicians but also from my students and patients, I have come to recognize the ever-changing states of narcissistic and borderline vulnerabilities. These disorders are not clear entities; rather, narcissistic/borderline states, traits, and characteristics tend to vacillate. In addition, narcissistic vulnerabilities can be recognized in other disorders. As the first edition stressed, the confusion between narcissistic and borderline states, traits, and characteristics is further acknowledged when we consider the type of narcissist or borderline we are talking about. A Freudian narcissist? A Kohutian narcissist? A Kernbergian narcissist? A borderline narcissist, an obsessive-compulsive narcissist, an antisocial narcissist, a histrionic narcissist, a depressive narcissist, or a malignant narcissist?

Although many couples may not fit into the paradigm of the narcissistic/borderline configuration, the treatment techniques and approaches outlined in this book are useful for almost all aspects of conjoint therapy. This edition ventures beyond narcissistic and borderline vulnerabilities to explore a variety of other dyadic configurations, such as what happens when a histrionic personality hooks up with an obsessive-compulsive, a dependent with a schizoid, or a passive-aggressive with a perfectionistic/caretaking-type personality. Not only are there narcissistic borderlines, narcissistic obsessive-compulsives, narcissistic passive-aggressives, but there are many faces and phases of narcissism. Although they may all show the same pattern, they form different modes of dyadic attachments.

Since the appearance of *The Narcissistic/Borderline Couple,* a remarkable number of therapists have extended beyond narcissistic/borderline relations. Within these thematic motifs, we now have narcissistic vulnerabilities in couples (Levene, 1997), the narcissistic couple (Kalogjera et al., 1998), the passive–aggressive couple (Slavik, 1998), the dependent/narcissistic couple (Nurse, 1998), narcissistic disorders and dependent/narcissistic couples (Carlson & Sperry, 1998; Nurse, 1998), and the psychotic couple (Maniacci, 1998). Others have gone beyond this malaise to address a garden variety of maladaptive strains. Carlson and Sperry, in *The Disordered Couple* (1998), included the psychotic couple and the eating-disordered couple. Although many theorists have made contributions bridging classical theory and marital conflict, few of these authors have distinguished between narcissistic and borderline vulnerabilities within a particular dyadic relationship.

Although psychoanalysts have made significant contributions to the field of marital therapy, a review of the literature that has appeared during the last decade reveals that the most inspiring material, oddly enough, has come from non-conjoint therapists. Behaviorists are too directive and ask too many questions. The object relationists are too confrontive and too focused on the internal world. The self-psychologists are "too empathic" and focus too heavily on the external (self objects).

The difference between the psychoanalytic/psychodynamic model of therapy and the cognitive approach is that the former holds the relationship to be the number 1 priority while the latter holds the individual to be the number 1 priority. My approach begins with regarding "the relationship" as the patient, gradually weaning the couple away from the relationship to self-development. Initially the relationship stirs up many unresolved developmental issues. This new approach holds that even when the therapist is confronted with the "impossible couple," or when one partner throws up his hands at the "impossible partner," a new window of opportunity appears to explore virginal territory (the unconscious or repressed conflicts the "impossible partner" arouses).

Among the new material included in this edition is an examination of the role of psychohistory in couple therapy, a growing analytical focal point. My interest in this burgeoning field began in the 1980s with a study of the Israeli-Arab conflict, which at that time held striking similarities to the marital discord between narcissistic and borderline personalities that I had observed in my fledgling clinical practice. This confluence of psychoanalysis and psychohistory led to my doctoral dissertation, *The Arab-Israeli Conflict: A Psychoanalytic Study* (Lachkar, 1983), a marriage of psychoanalysis and psychohistory. Tragically, the situation in the Middle East has now escalated far beyond narcissistic/borderline parameters.

As my practice grew, I noticed a growing number of couples that could be classified as narcissistic/borderline, which led to the publication of the first edition of this book and elicited further questions. What is it that perpetuates conflict and makes individuals and groups sacrifice their own lives and resort to self-destructive behavior? Finding these answers requires us to analyze cultural patterns handed down from generation to generation, embedded in the very identity of the group and expressed through myths, ideology, religion, and childrearing practices—that is, the psychohistory of the group.

This edition also includes a focus on the inherent complexities of cross-cultural relationships. Since we now live in a multicultural society and our consultation rooms are beginning to resemble a mini United Nations, new material has been included on the cross-cultural narcissist/borderline relationship. An increasing number of clinicians are beginning to pay heed to cross-cultural differences. It is difficult enough to treat individuals from similar cultures, let alone those from varying cultural backgrounds, traditions, and religions. Understanding group dynamics from a global perspective helps make the conflict within cross-cultural relationships more glaringly apparent. Here we consider narcissistic and borderline vulnerabilities within the matrix of cultural and societal traditions. How much of what we see in cross-cultural couple therapy is due to cross-cultural issues and how much to pathology? Where do culture and pathology meet?

This edition introduces another new concept: the *V-spot* or "vulnerable spot" (Lachkar, 2003). The reference is to the partners' most sensitive area of vulnerability, known in the psychoanalytic literature known as the *archaic injury*, a product of early trauma that each partner relentlessly holds onto. This material delves into how each partner taps into the other's deep reservoir of early painful experiences, repeating again and again the same traumatic injury. It will emphasize how the therapist must continuously remind the partners of what stirs up the V-spot and give them techniques to avoid the repeated opening up of old wounds and painful archaic injuries.

Chapter 1 expands the domain of narcissistic and borderline personality disorders to encompass the variety of shapes and forms these two personality types can take. In addition to discussing different types of narcissists, it introduces two new models of narcissism: "the artist narcissist" and the "cultural narcissist." Heinz Kohut's pioneering work in self-psychology, along with that of other authors, broadened our understanding of the narcissist. The borderline syndrome is discussed mainly from an object relations perspective, with particular emphasis given to the theories of Bion, Klein, Fairbairn, Winnicott, Kernberg, and Grotstein. This chapter describes the narcissist and borderline personalities and elaborates on their interlocking mechanisms of defense—a most vicious link that holds narcissistic/borderline partners together as it impacts perception, reality testing, and the ability to learn from experience.

Chapter 2 outlines the theoretical constructs, drawing mainly from self-psychology and object relations. The integration of these theories into conjoint treatment has its primary focus on maternal bonding and attachment, mirroring, containment, and the unique way in which these theories seek truth (internal vs. external reality). Although many have suggested that self-psychology and object relations make strange bedfellows, this "odd couple" relationship yields a perfect merger in the treatment of the narcissistic/borderline relationship.

Chapter 3 details the dance, the drama, and the bond of the narcissistic/borderline couple. The metaphor of the dance describes the vacillating choreography of interactions and behaviors that are circular, ongoing, never-ending, and destructive. The dilemma of the narcissistic/borderline relationship is further outlined to understand how couples in these beleaguered relationships on the one hand desire an intimate love bond and on the other are weighed down by a compelling force to sabotage and destroy all that is good. Chapter 3 explores the reasons that couples stay in painful conflictual relationships—not because they are crazy, but because each partner stirs up some un-developmental issue in the other that desperately needs to be worked through.

The focus of Chapter 4 is on "marital theatrics" and psychodynamics, acknowledging the qualitative differences within narcissistic/borderline disorders and exploring the interlocking systems of guilt/shame, envy/jealousy, and omnipotence/dependency. At the core of the dynamic flow between the narcissistic/borderline partners is a duel between omnipotence and vulnerability. As noted earlier, this chapter introduces the concept of the V-spot, the area of greatest vulnerability in each partner, which, when aroused, unwittingly elicits similar early trauma in the other partner and impedes the ability to think and learn from experience.

Chapter 5 addresses dynamic positions and transference formations, including the various countertransference issues evoked in the therapist. My concept of the *couple transference* is elaborated as a device for treating couples. As in the original edition, the focus is not on teaching the partners to perform self-object functions for one another but rather on teaching them to rely on the therapist for this function.

Chapter 6 relates ideas from group psychology and psychohistory to the understanding of group fantasies and shared couple myths as a preparation for the study of cross-cultural relationships in chapter 7. Understanding group behaviors provides a backdrop for understanding the regressive/primitive nature in couples. Just as groups share collective myths, so do couples share "couple myths." Chapter 6 examines psychodynamics such as shame, guilt, and saving face, and gives examples of the part each plays in narcissistic/borderline relationships.

Chapter 7 is a completely new chapter devoted to the treatment of cross-cultural couples. It emphasizes how the entire spectrum of psychoanalytic theory takes on a different face when treating couples from various cultural and traditional backgrounds. It questions how much is a cultural phenomenon and how much is pathology in these relationships and where the boundaries between cross-cultural lines meet. Psychodynamics as experienced qualitatively from various cultures are also given consideration as a major factor in the treatment of couples from varying ethic backgrounds and origins.

Chapter 8 presents the model of treatment. A six-point treatment procedure is suggested within the paradigm of three specific developmental phases, along with therapeutic function treatment points for the therapist.

In Chapter 9, new clinical case and illustrative material has been added to demonstrate some of the points made in this revised and expanded edition.

THE THERAPEUTIC APPROACH

The psychodynamically oriented therapist learns to integrate and adapt from many differing viewpoints, including self-psychology, offering enough transitional space to allow the partners to operate within an intersubjective field. The object relations approach paves the way to help couples with their intensely interlocking systems, enabling them to take more responsibility for their actions and behaviors. This process is further facilitated by gradually weaning the patient from "the relationship" to self-development, and away from the external painful object to acquaintance with the internal one. Within these techniques, the therapist must provide enough freedom, security, and transitional space to explore the depths of the couple's internal worlds.

Chapter 1

The Narcissist
and the Borderline

Clinical Descriptions

THE NARCISSIST

Freud (1914/1957) initially conceived of narcissism as the state of self-directed libido. The word is derived from Narcissus, the Greek youth of legend who fell in love with his own image in a pond. Freud viewed narcissism as a libidinal force similar to a hormone that can be transported to different parts of the body and become fixated there. These ideas are the forerunners of the notion of self that is between the ego's relationship to its ego ideal and the ego's libidinal forces cathected to its objects. Freud referred to primary and secondary narcissism. Primary narcissism is an absolute state in which all libidinal energy is stored up until the ego gets depleted and is driven to cathect to other objects. The transformation from primary to secondary narcissism occurs when the ego does a makeover from a self-narcissistic libido to a later object libido.

Freud wrote that love consists of a flowing over of ego libido to the object. In states of passion, sexual desire coincides with the ego ideal. Love mimics a psychotic state, a reunion between highly charged emotional and bodily experiences. This state emanates from the fulfillment fantasies of infantile experiences of love, and whatever gratifies this state become highly

1

charged, eroticized, and idealized. The narcissistic person who is "in love" is highly cathected to someone who has qualities that he or she wishes to have, or had and no longer possesses (beauty, fame, success, wealth, brilliance, power). The narcissist then embarks on a lifelong journey to try to own or possess these qualities through guilt and envy. Feelings of love are not sustained and are dismissed as soon as the object is devalued or destroyed. The effort of one partner to possess and spoil becomes greater as the energy is diverted more toward the grandiose self. Freud discovered that in seeking a love relationship, one will often choose a partner who has qualities he or she lacks, hoping the love object will make them whole.

The narcissist is the "entitlement lover," the self-proclaimed special child of the universe. Narcissists have excessive entitlement fantasies and an exaggerated sense of self, with which they are entirely preoccupied. They believe the world "owes them," are obsessed with perfectionism, and have an internalized, strongly castrating, and punitive superego. Narcissists are intoxicated by their own power and are unable to use the healthy aspects of narcissism because they lack the capacity for empathy and introspection. They strive relentlessly to prove their specialness.

Narcissists are individuals who need perfect mirroring, perfect stroking, perfect responses. They value such material things as fame, physical beauty, wealth, social position, and power. They are dominated by defenses that include guilt, idealization, omnipotence, grandiosity, and pomposity. When hurt or personally injured, they will respond with narcissistic rage or withdraw, isolating themselves physically or emotionally. (One can imagine what this does to a borderline partner, who already has a thwarted sense of self.) The most common archaic injury among narcissists is the mother who usurped "His Majesty the Baby" from his high chair "throne" to make way for a new sibling. Often the narcissist will spend the rest of his life in self-absorbed nostalgia, longing to recapture the early time when mommy and baby were one, living in harmony and symbiotic bliss. Any threat or reminder of being displaced by a sibling will trigger narcissistic injury.

Another key aspect of narcissism is the "grandiose self," a part of the self that guards against dependency. Because of the inability to feel or show dependency, the narcissist unwittingly projects this intolerance onto others. "It is you who is the needy one!" Narcissists confuse healthy dependency needs with parasitic ones and bond with those who offer the promise of being the perfect "mirroring" object (often a borderline). Narcissists exacerbate feelings of inadequacy and shame in others and cannot allow themselves the kind of dependency an intimate partner yearns for because it makes them feel too vulnerable. They have internalized a harsh, punitive superego, which makes them supercritical of others. "I am as perfect as mother wanted me to be. I don't need anyone! I don't need you, and I don't need this treatment!"

Narcissists are always busy trying to prove a "special" sense of existence. They are the ones who flee from treatment when feeling personally injured or unappreciated, or when their excessive demands are not met (changing appointment times, asking for special favors, coming in only when it is convenient for them).

Different Types of Narcissists

Diagnosing the narcissist is acknowledgedly complex. Although the realm of the narcissist proper has already been described, the narcissistic personality disorder is not a clear and precise entity. There are many different kinds of narcissists. These distinctions are important for the treatment of marital therapy.

The Pathological Narcissist

The pathological narcissist is obsessed with and has an exaggerated sense of self, as well as a delusional sense of entitlement. Pathological narcissists lack the capacity for intimacy, empathy, or concern for others, and are over-powered by the excessive need for approval and admiration from others. They are in need of constant recognition, and their compulsion to maintain a "special" sense of existence and the demand for incessant attention becomes more pervasive than life itself. The maladaptive defenses severely interfere with the narcissist's capacity to maintain an intimate love bond.

Example: A man may tell his narcissistic wife that he found another woman at a party very attractive and her demeanor quite charming. Unable to tolerate this, the wife storms out of the room, refusing to speak to or have sex with him for more than 2 weeks. For months on end, she harbors this injury, something she "can never forget."

In Robert Dallek's 1991 biography of Lyndon Johnson, *Lone Star Rising*, Dallek describes Johnson as a pathological narcissist. He cites an example of a White House aide who almost drowned in the swimming pool alongside Johnson because Johnson was so absorbed with talking about himself that he did not notice the aide's distress. Another example of Johnson's pathological narcissism was his relationship with his wife, Lady Byrd Johnson. Lyndon expected her to tolerate his desire for other women, including bringing to the White House bed not just one woman but two (making Clinton look saintly in comparison). When criticized about Vietnam, Johnson refused to speak with anyone and would respond with narcissistic rage.

The Malignant Narcissist

The malignant narcissist is usually a leader, a person who uses his omnipotent, sadistic fantasies to live out a cause. Someone like Slobodan Milosevic, the Serbian war criminal, fits this description: "We killed the Albanians for a good cause." The most pervasive trait of malignant narcissists is that they always feel as though they are the victims. For example, Milosevic has denied charges of genocide, claiming that the Serbs were the victims (*Los Angeles Times*, February 2002). This is not a far cry from Osama bin Laden, who claims the September 11 attacks were in defense of his own people, and the "will of Allah" (Lachkar, 2002).

Typically, individuals are seduced to collude with malignant narcissistic leaders who offer the promise of enacting the role of the protective father, which hooks into many shared collective group fantasies. The leader that can be sadistic and cruel also can be loving and kind. Leaders who play out these fantasies form a most powerful and intimate connection with the group. Often these leaders exhibit paranoid features, which compels them to believe in their self-serving political aspirations and provides the rationale for their own destructive/sadistic acts of aggression. When Milosevic swore to the Serbs that he would protect his people and never allow the Albanians to hurt them again, he became a national hero—the protective, fantasized daddy, the messianic leader come to save the group from calamity and restore the group's pride and identity (Lachkar, 2000).

On the domestic front, the object bond between a sadistic partner and a paralyzed victim is a familiar theme (Kernberg, 1992). Although the malignant narcissist may not be a national figure or a ruthless dictator, he may be a cruel, aggressive, controlling partner. Understanding one's attachment to these kinds of leaders is important, especially when treating cross-cultural couples. Individuals from different ethnic backgrounds may play out similar behaviors with the same kind of nationalistic pride and fervor (see chapter 7 on multiculturalism). From this we might discover another variation of narcissism. Is there such a thing as a "cultural narcissist" or a "cultural borderline"? While an exploration of these concepts is beyond the scope of this text, a few noteworthy points can be made.

The cultural narcissist parallels the pathological narcissist in that he brings into the therapeutic arena the same degree of nationalistic pride and will relentlessly try to flaunt his nationalistic identity. The cultural borderline, on the other hand, will fight to the end, retaliate, become a freedom fighter or a terrorist, and go to any extreme to maintain the group's collective identity.

Example: An Israeli man married to an Irish Catholic woman insists that she give up her religion without any consideration of what is important to her. One could well ask, What's the big deal? This could happen with an American Jewish man as well. The difference is cultural. The Israeli man takes on a nationalistic Zionistic attitude, which is inculcated into the culture from childhood on. Aggression is wrapped in the flag: "This is our country! The only religion is Judaism!"

The Antisocial Narcissist

Antisocial patients typically present more serious superego pathology. The antisocial narcissist's most dominant feature is the lack of superego functioning and the lack of capacity for guilt and remorse. Antisocial narcissists still maintain the excessive attitudes of entitlement that lie within the domain of the narcissist proper; however, their sense of entitlement is so excessive that it overrides any capacity for self-reflection. They may lie, steal, cajole, get caught, even confess their crimes with no guilt, remorse, or concern. Their sense of omnipotence and their entitlement fantasies are so extreme that antisocial narcissists delude themselves into thinking they can get away with their extreme behavior and show no guilt or remorse for their actions

Example: A loving husband and father did all the "right" things. He was devoted, a hard worker, loved his family, and would do anything to make his wife happy (including providing lavish bar/bat mitzvahs, luxury autos, private schools). Secretly he embezzled money, all the while appearing to be the consummate "giver" to "good causes." Yet, when caught by the IRS for income tax invasion he was not able to experience remorse. He spent most of his time and treatment blaming his wife for all the pressure she put on him.

The Depressive Narcissist

Unlike the antisocial narcissist, the depressive narcissist is plagued by guilt, embodied by a harsh and punitive superego. Depressive narcissists are dominated by guilt and self-hatred. They are perfectionists, and when life does not go their way they blame themselves. They have a sadistic superego that runs amok, is self-denigrating and self-blaming. Yet, antisocial narcissists are high functioning on many different levels. They are highly reliable, dependable, serious, and concerned about work, although they tend to judge themselves as they do others. These are the children of parents who demanded perfection. They are totally self-absorbed and persecute themselves. They are often withdrawn and isolated from others.

Example: A depressed narcissist's grandiose self turns self-hatred inward to such an extent that it infects and invades all those around her. "I am no longer the beauty I used to be and I cannot tolerate the thought of anyone seeing me."

The Narcissist as Artist

Many artists are accused of being "too narcissistic." But are they? Although the discussion of narcissism and the artist would require another book, it is important to mention that artists (dancers, musicians, painters, writers, actors) need a certain amount of narcissism to function creatively, and they require a special form of treatment. Within the performing arts, narcissism takes on a different meaning. While clinical narcissism connotes pathology, there are also healthy aspects that one might call "aesthetic survival." To kill narcissism is tantamount to killing the artist! How, then, do we distinguish between healthy and pathological narcissism? Healthy narcissism allows room for grandiosity, pomposity, self-involvement, and an obsessive investment in perfectionism, yet there is realization of the "need" for the object. One has a sense of separateness and does not internalize or identify with the negative projections of others (e.g., envy, criticism). Instead, one's personal drive and determination are so powerful that nothing gets in the way.

There is a sense in which the artist needs some transitional space to experience his art. A good illustration of this is the pas de deux in "Après midi d'un faune," choreographed around a mirror by Jerome Robbins. The two young dancers are more preoccupied with themselves than with each other (Lachkar, 2001). The only time we need to modify or chisel away at the artist's narcissism is when narcissistic defenses no longer work in the service of the ego, or when the defenses interfere with the creative process or the capacity for healthy object relations. It is beyond the scope of this book to discuss the different kinds of "narcissistic artists," but it might be noteworthy to mention a few. First, there are the overly "entitled artists" who feel the world owes them something. Second, there are artists with delusions of grandeur, those who think they have talent but who in reality don't. (The reverse is also true; there are those who have talent but are weighed down with self-doubts and self-denigration.) Third, there are the depressive artists, those who are filled with envy, anger, envy, and competitive rage and are never "grandiose" enough to achieve any semblance of success (see Case 1 in chapter 9).

Example: An extremely narcissistic young dancer, whom I treated several years ago, rarely made eye contact with me. Whenever I tried to reach out she withdrew. When I called this to her attention, she responded with outrage. It came to a head one day when she was asked to audition for a scholarship at a prestigious school. After the audition, she returned crying and overwhelmed with emotion: "They said I danced with no expression, that I was cold and distant, and I did not relate to the audience. They said I had a blank stare on my face and that I lacked passion!!" This was a breakthrough, and the dancer was able to recognize and change her attitude.

THE BORDERLINE

Although Freud (1923) did not use the term *borderline*, he noted that there was a certain segment of patients who would become discontent when treatment was progressing. He referred to these patients as having "negative therapeutic reaction" (1923, p. 39). Seinfeld (1990) elaborated Freud's bafflement and confusion regarding the negative therapeutic transference, affirming that certain people behave in a peculiar fashion during analysis. Freud claimed that these patients are intolerant of any progression of the treatment and show signs of despair when their conditions improve. They become deviant of attempt and react adversely to any praise or appreciation. They get worse instead of better.

In his famous Wolfman case, Freud (1918) noted that the patient experienced a transitory negative therapeutic reaction every time the treatment progressed. Freud (1924) extrapolated that these patients had a certain proclivity for punishment that was related to unconscious instinctual drives and that compelled them toward what he termed the death instinct. He referred to these patients as suffering from forbidden unconscious infantile impulses triggered from a sadistic superego in conflict with a masochistic ego (1918). Rosenfeld (1987) stated that Freud believed that the sadism of the superego and the masochism of the ego complemented one another in the negative therapeutic reaction. Freud (1924) spoke of these patients as suffering from a severe sense of guilt and of the sadomasochism as derived from the death instinct.

There is still a great deal of confusion about the borderline in the literature, mainly because the term has been used to describe transitory movements between patients with neurotic and psychotic personalities. Kernberg (1975) suggested that the term should be reserved for those patients who are between neurotic and psychotic states. Much of what was previously categorized as schizophrenia is now known as borderline disorder. According to Grotstein (1986), although they share many common traits with schizophrenics, the borderline personality now has its own domain. Grotstein affirmed the borderline suffers more from privation than deprivation, boundary confusion, and the inability to "gait" the data of the object.

Grotstein's view dovetails with Kernberg's description (1975), which includes a pathological and distorted world of object relations, impairment of judgment and reality and is marked by primitive defenses. Kernberg (1992) described the severity of the borderline condition, ranging from the least to the most severe: (a) the infantile personality (histrionic), (b) the self-destructive (self-mutilating) personality, and (c) the chronically self-destructive personality (inflicting pain on themselves or others). He stressed that although borderline patients have conflicts between reality and what feels like reality, their capacity to test reality is not based on delusions and hallucinations as it is with psychotic patients.

Other important contributions in defining the borderline have come from theorists who understand the specific defense mechanisms, particularly splitting, projection, and projective identfication, including Bion (1961, 1965, 1967, 1970, 1977), Grotstein (1980, 1981, 1983, 1984a, 1984b, 1987), Kernberg, (1975, 1976), Ogden (1980, 1986), and Rosenfeld (1987).

The borderline personality is dominated by shame/blame defenses and persecutory, abandonment, and annihilation anxieties. Borderlines have defective bonding capacities and are riddled with paranoia. They are driven by such defenses as splitting, projection, projective identification, omnipotent denial, and magical thinking. "One should just know what I need without having to ask!" When threatened, they tend to lash out with retaliatory responses, self-mutilation, and self-sacrifice, even at the expense of self or others. Destruction becomes more pervasive than life in and of itself. Their splitting mechanisms and tendency to project intolerable affects onto others keep them trapped in states of victimization and shame (Lachkar, 1983, 1991). They form parasitic attachments through seduction, manipulation, victimization, and pain. Borderline patients often develop a preoccupation with pain as a means of bonding with their objects (psychosomatic illness, addictions, suicidal ideation) or form sadomasochistic attachments. Unlike narcissists, borderlines do not have a sense of self, do not feel entitled, and will do anything to establish some semblance of bonding or relatedness. The borderline is trying to prove that he or she exists as a "thing in itself." Anything is better than having to face the "black hole," the emptiness, the abyss they are constantly threatened with. The borderline thinks in the following terms: "I'll do anything; just don't leave me!" "When I mutilate myself, it hurts, but at least I know I'm alive!"

The borderline often becomes the sacrificial object, the mediator or go-between, the little adult who had to grow up much too early and much too soon. Borderlines take on caretaker roles and have been abducted from their childhoods. We often see this phenomenon in child custody cases (Lachkar, 1986). Even after the dissolution of marriage, these couples remain forever bonded, putting the child in the middle of their never-ending battles. They frequently perpetuate the cycle by enacting the victim role, bonding with their objects through pain (either self- or other-inflicted). The inability to face any internal deficits and their tendency to blame/shame keep them in an endless state of impoverishment. Along with shame comes the inability to mourn, to deal with loss. In an attempt to defend against shame and embarrassment for having needs and desires, the borderline frequently turns to self-soothing modalities in the form of foreign objects, substance abuse, addictive relationships, promiscuity, deviant compulsive behaviors, addictions, suicidal ideation, and other acts to ward off nameless dread.

The focus for the borderline is primarily on bonding and attachment issues (see Case 8 in chapter 9). Because the borderline is lacking in early maternal bonding experiences, any reminder of separation will arouse intense rage or acts of revenge. In some extreme cases, when the promise of a bond is threatened, the borderline may lash out with relentless anger and rage. Unlike narcissists, they do not seek to enact the drama of being the special child, a role that the borderline has never experienced. Because they lack experience in forming healthy bonding relationships, they form parasitic relationships by projecting their needs in hostile, demanding, controlling, and other threatening ways.

Borderlines suffer from illusion rather than delusions or hallucinations. They promise the world, but cannot live up to those promises because of their uncontrollable rage and poor impulse control. As a consequence, they do not learn from experience and will invariably repeat the same mistakes again and again. For a short while, the borderline can play-act at being the perfect mirroring object for the narcissist; however, because of the lack of impulse control and inability to contain, they cannot follow through (see chapter 3 for a description of "the dance" between narcissist/borderline partners).

Borderlines are often, in Helene Deutsch's terminology (1942), "as if" personalities or "false self" (see Case 2 in chapter 9) personalities (Winnicott, 1953, 1965), denoting a self that belies or masks the true self. Because they lack a "real self," they must insert an imaginary one to prevent the sensation of emptiness. Often they are the Don Juans, and since they operate through an exquisitely formed false self, they can be very seductive. Other borderlines are weak and compliant, but purport to be strong and omnipotent by overidentifying with others like a chameleon: "I will be whatever you want me to be."

Example: This is reminiscent of a patient who operated from an exquisite false self. He was like a chameleon, could play-act at being anyone he wanted to be. Even though he despised classical music, he would act like an impresario. He was glib and imaginative, but only to the point where he could sustain his act as he tried to meet and match the expectations of others.

In conjoint treatment, therapists often get sucked into the borderline's unwavering persuasion and seductive lures, making it difficult to keep reality straight. Typically, borderlines have been abandoned by absent parents, alcoholic parents, abusive parents, or emotionally unavailable parents. Mothers of borderline children, who lack reciprocity with the child's affective states, are unable to validate or confirm the child's experience. Their reaction: "How dare you say I never did anything for you? You know I did everything I could! How dare you blame me for not being home for you after school; you know dad was an alcoholic and I had to work. It wasn't my fault!"

Many borderlines view needs as tantamount to dirt and disgust (as do obsessive-compulsives). One borderline spouse confided to the therapist, "I'm so ashamed that I told you in front of my wife that I masturbate." The therapist who understands the need for detoxification and the need for containment responds with reassuring words: "Yes, it is hard to ask your wife for what you need, so you let her know that you don't need her to stimulate you, that you really don't need anyone. You don't have to ask; you can do it all by yourself." This description is essential to the analysis of narcissist/borderline couples because the borderline's conflict between shame and dependency is at variance with issues around the Oedipal level of development.

One of the most striking features is the borderline's tendency to distort, manipulate, and misperceive reality. When they do something bad, they claim that something bad was done to them. When they lie, they claim others have lied to them. When they betray, they claim others have betrayed them. Borderlines consistently and truly believe their lies are the "truth" and forever perceive themselves as victims. Borderline patients often develop a preoccupation with pain as a means of bonding with their objects.

Different Types of Borderlines

Just as there are different kinds of narcissists, there are different types of borderlines, depending on how the grandiose invades or infects the parameters of the borderline personality. Many borderlines are first cousins to their narcissistic counterparts and are continually prone to emotional crisis. As Grotstein (personal communication, 2002) has so aptly pointed out, "The borderline is nothing more than a failed narcissist." Although it is not possible to discuss all the variations on this theme, what follows are distinctive personality traits and characteristics found within the borderline personality structure.

The Histrionic Borderline

Histrionic borderlines exaggerate, cry easily, exhibit excessive parasitic dependency needs, and display excessive emotionalism and exhibitionistic qualities. In some instances, histrionic borderlines may appear very narcissistic (e.g., the need to be the center of attention), while on the other hand, their clinging behaviors and seductive, provocative sexuality denote very strong borderline characteristics.

The Passive–Aggressive Borderline

Although the passive–aggressive personality type no longer exists in the DSM-IV, I have resurrected it for the purposes of couple therapy. There is nothing worse than being coupled with a passive–aggressive. Passive–aggressives are the most difficult personalities to treat, since they are always trying to recreate the infant/child dyad. These are the couch-potato husbands and the forgetful wives. "I'll do it later; I'll do it tomorrow, I was going to do it today, but the car broke down." They forget, delay, avoid, cajole, make an endless barrage of excuses—in short, do anything to protect the good little child from the screaming mommy. The passive–aggressive's primary aim is to unconsciously coerce a partner to behave or respond in a certain way. Patients with passive–aggressive pathology express their rage by "silently" manipulating the object into the role of the punitive parent. "See, it is you who is the angry one; me, I'm just an innocent little guy, and you are the bad mommy picking on me!"

Passive–aggressive types often hook up with caretaking partners, those who were forced to relinquish their childhoods much too early and much too soon. These are the "little adults," the mediators, the "parentified" children. Passive–aggressive personalities unconsciously stir up anger and resentment in their partners by manipulating them into this never-ending prescripted and preprogrammed role. The rage and aggression are expressed in their most virile form: silent abuse, which is turned against their partners. In treatment, passive–aggressives are those who "have the check in the mail," get lost on the way to the session, or ask the therapist to "hold" their checks. One therapist's response was, "I will hold it only until it grows up to be a 'big check'."

Example: I asked him to go to the market to get some diapers. He waited until the last minute. I just knew it; he returned and said the market was closed. I then said, "Why didn't you go to another market?" He got annoyed with me. Whatever happens he always has a way of turning me into the punitive mommy, and he remains the passive little guy just like the baby brother I had to care for when I was a child.

The Obsessive–Compulsive Borderline

Of all the borderline types, the obsessive-compulsive is, at one level, the highest functioning. In marital treatment, obsessive-compulsives seemingly are conscientious hard-working, have a good sense of family values, and are good providers. Compared to other borderline personalities, the obsessive–

compulsive has a more developed and well-integrated ego, a better tolerance for anxiety and impulse control, as well as a harshly strict but well-integrated superego. The obsessive–compulsive may be more neurotic than other borderlines in conflicts centering around repression rather than primitive defenses.

At the lower level of functioning, obsessive–compulsives are obsessed with orderliness, cleanliness, and perfectionism. They are devoid of feelings, are workaholics, and invariably put their partners down for having emotional needs or desires. They keep their partners on hold and never have enough time for them. Because the obsessive–compulsive confuses needs and desires with dirt and disgust, he will find justification to work, work, work under the guise of efficiency or the "good cause." He will also do anything to avoid intimacy. These are the pack rats, the clutterers who can't throw anything away.

Example: I threatened my wife and told her that if she ever threw away my wires, old newspapers, strings, or the old clothing that I have accumulated over the years, I would shut her out of the house. I can't throw anything away. You never know when you will need it!

The Schizoid Borderline

The schizoid personality's primary defense is a pervasive pattern of detachment from social and interpersonal relations stemming from childhood. Schizoids take pleasure in few activities, have few close friends, and appear indifferent to the praise or criticism of others. The schizoid's defenses serve primarily to keep injurious objects at a distance and prevent intimacy (Bacal & Newman, 1990). Unlike the narcissist, who withdraws when personally injured, the schizoid detaches from his internal object world. The schizoid, to a large degree, has retreated from object relations and has developed an unconscious attachment to his internal objects. The schizoid's connection to internal objects is like Velcro, a substance that he gloms onto and cannot retreat from. The attachment to his inner world becomes so intense that it completely overshadows reality, blocking involvement with external objects and keeping new experiences from emerging. Continuation on this path can lead to schizophrenia and loss of linkage to the ego, leaving the schizoid borderline trapped and empty (Ogden, 1989).

At the onset of a relationship, schizoids with borderline features may appear to be very charming, seductive, and in some cases quite sexual. Only later is it revealed how truly vulnerable and fragmented they are. Schizoid personalities are often perceived as strange, eccentric, cold, and aloof. These are the hollow, cold, indifferent, affectless men, often referred to as "misogynists." The schizoid borderline male is often preprogrammed to fear intimacy and can feel suffocated and engulfed by women, viewing a woman's vagina as dangerous and threatening, and are unable to maintain intimate connection. Women are often shocked by these men because as soon as they become emotionally attached, they will suddenly flee without warning or notice. For example, in the midst of lovemaking, just before penetration, the schizoid might abruptly pull away, put on his clothes, and depart, leaving the woman not only frustrated but puzzled and confused. And if he does finally commit to marriage, he does it in a most aloof, cold, detached, and indifferent way.

Example: We were at a party. I introduced him to my friends. He stood there looking aloof and totally uninterested in anything going on around him. I then gave him three choices of where he wanted to go to dinner. Again the typical response "Gee, I don't know; doesn't matter to me."

The Paranoid Borderline

Borderlines often have paranoid anxieties. Paranoid defenses build a protective shield of suspicion and hostility around the self to keep potential injurious objects at a safe distance (Bacal & Newman, 1990). The most pervasive occurrence in love relations is the discontinuity between the self and the love object. Paranoid borderlines deal with conflicts around intimacy and vulnerability by projecting the "bad object" or the intolerable part of themselves onto the other. When the partner identifies with that being projected, the borderline experiences the partner as dangerous and persecutory. Expressions of love, for example, may be experienced as, "You don't really love me; you are just using me!" To guard against these fears, the borderline often resorts to schizoid and paranoid behaviors. The attempt to sabotage is impulsive and precipitous; before the ego has the ability to organize the date of experience, the paranoid borderline jumps to an immediate assumption based not on fact but on imminent fears of catastropic danger.

Example: A woman tells her husband, "I just know you are having an affair; you have been coming home later and later."

CONCLUSION

In this chapter, we have extended the definitions of narcissistic and borderline personalities to discuss the variety of forms these terms can encompass. Driven by an exaggerated sense of self and an overwhelming desire to be appreciated, narcissists are obsessed with a perfection they can never attain. Narcissists live in a kind of self-absorbed nostalgia, yearning to recapture the time when mother and baby were one, a state of "at-one-ment," in total harmony, symbiosis, and synchronicity. Borderline personalities, on the other hand, are not concerned with proving a "special" sense of existence; rather, they are preoccupied with trying to prove they exist (since they never had the good breast, they don't yearn for it as narcissists do). Feelings of self-worth elude the borderline, who perceives the world as evil, dangerous, and persecutory. Borderlines lack a sense of self, do not feel entitled, and are in constant search of reassurance and containment; when that existence is threatened, they regress into states of fragmentation, or in some cases psychosis. What both the narcissist and the borderline share in common is an intense conflict between the wish to maintain an intimate, loving bond and the wish to destroy all that contributes to a vulnerable and loving relationship.

Chapter 2 further explores these disparate personality types within the theoretical parameters of object relations and self-psychology.

Chapter 2

Theoretical Implications

INTRODUCTION

The clinical constructs underlying couples therapy are drawn mainly from self-psychology and object relations. The successful blending of these two theoretical perspectives can effectuate a new and positive therapeutic experience, as the case illustrations in chapter 9 reveal. Although both self-psychology and self-object approaches are useful in treating narcissistic/borderline relations, it has been suggested that the mirroring and empathy techniques of self-psychology are more suited to meet the narcissist's mirroring needs, while object relations are more suited to the borderline's containment needs.

Grotstein (1985) asserted that the narcissist is in greater need of the empathic mode and suggested that empathy be interwoven with interpretations that address the primitive unconscious. He maintained that the narcissist seeks perfection, whereas the borderline projects the ego ideal onto the narcissist, an invitation the narcissist cannot resist. On a more practical note, Kernberg (1975) suggested more confrontational environmental interventions or supportive psychotherapy for the borderline.

Taking into account these various perspectives, it is recommended that the techniques of mirroring, empathy, and introspection be blended with an object relations approach to help narcissistic individuals deal more directly with their internal deficits. On the other hand, because of the borderline's pervasive defense of projective identification, it is recommended that the focus be primarily on the borderline's conflict, the tendency to destroy all love and intimate thoughts, along with the desire to create a new experience to recognizing the need for the object and the object's desire. The borderline is more in need of behavioral treatment, which offers structure and management along with the psychodynamic approach (Ogden, 1986).

SELF-PSYCHOLOGY

Many authors have described the application of Heinz Kohut's pioneering work in self-psychology to the treatment of narcissistic personality disorders (Brandchaft & Stolorow, 1984; Kohut, 1971, 1977; Stolorow & Lachmann, 1980). Several have recognized the value of self-psychology, especially with respect to the self-object relationship, including narcissistic transference, idealization, empathy, approval, and its mirroring functions. The Kohutian model of narcissism depicts a more highly developed narcissist whose primary and normal narcissistic phases were inadequately met at phase-appropriate times. Clinically, Kohut viewed narcissism as a form of developmental arrest in the child's archaic grandiose self that occurred when the child's main caretakers withheld specific functions. Pathological narcissism occurs with the lack of attunement, mirroring, and other self-object functions that fringe on the idealization of parental representation, resulting in the discontinuity of the self. According to Kohutian disciples, narcissism is the formation of a self-object tie with those who mirror the self, including a narcissistic transference. Otto Kernberg (1975), on the contrary, suggested that narcissism is not a normal phase but rather a defensive operation, driven by aggressive forces of retaliation, getting even—anything to get back at the parental images for failing the child at a primitive, sadistic level (e.g., "I'll become a famous movie star in spite of you").

Of all the descriptions of narcissism, Albert Mason's (personal communication, 1988) is arguably the most workable for the treatment of couples. He described narcissism as a pathological disorder in which the object does not recognize the need for the breast, a state in which the object "has it all," and cannot take in or become excited. An illustration of this is the situation where a patient is heavily invested in trying to get the therapist sexually excited, rather than allowing the therapist's interpretations to provide the "feeding" or the excitement.

OBJECT RELATIONS

Object relations is an intrapsychic approach to understanding the internal world, including the patient's "distortions" and "misperceptions." This involves a technique whereby projections, fantasies, and split-off parts of the self are studied in order to comprehend one's inability to have healthy interpersonal relationships. Object relations theory provides us with an environmental mother, a background mother, a being/doing mother, a weaning mother, and a containing/sustaining mother to help establish different kinds of bonding experiences. The importance of therapist/mother as the container becomes more vital in object relations because the central issues revolve around persecutory anxiety, shame, guilt, confusion, and fantasies of separation.

From an object relations point of view, the borderline patient is unable to use the self-object relationship. Feeling that the admission of need is bad and shameful, the borderline has a defective capacity to learn from experience. Needs are disavowed and split off, rather than used to reach out to those who can be helpful. The borderline has never really been able to leave the mother's body; thus he has difficulty with separateness and lacks differentiation among reality, myth, self, and object.

SELF-PSYCHOLOGY VERSUS OBJECT RELATIONS

At its core, self-psychology is a theory of bonding with external objects, the interpersonal tie to a self object. Object relations, on the other hand, is a theory of bonding with internal objects—objects located within the psyche and subject to continual stimulation and irritation via the environment. Object relations examines how one interacts with others in the external world. The impact of this becomes even more profound when we examine the notion of attachment to internal objects. Fairbairn (1944), more than anyone, helped us understand why people stay forever bonded to bad internal objects. His concept of schizoid bonding and splitting of the ego into multitudinous internal objects has its precursors in disassociation. He helped us understand why people form lifelong love affairs with bad internal objects. His is a psychodynamic theory based on unconscious motivations that compel a person to form a specific dynamic interaction or attachment through the process of introjection and identification.

Object relations differs from self-psychology in that even when there is a "good self object" or the environment is nurturing, the individual may experience the world as dangerous and persecutory. Certainly, external factors are important, but if the primary focus is on the external or on "poor object failures," we are in danger of undermining the internal conflict. On the other hand, if too much emphasis is placed on the self objects or the self-object tie to the therapist, whenever fragmentation or disruption occurs it is viewed as a therapeutic empathic failure. The danger is that the therapist may equate the patient's subjective experience with truth and ignore the distortions, projections, and splitting mechanisms.

To compare the application of self-psychology and object relations in a more precise way, let us consider the case of the borderline who becomes fragmented and enraged and begins to attack the therapist, claiming, "You are just like my wife; you have too many expectations of me!" The self-psychologist might address the archaic tie to the mother, confirming that as a child the patient could not please his mother, and now he feels he is expected to fill the therapist's expectations as if she were his mother. The therapist incorporating a Kleinian view would address these deficits via the patient's projection. For example, the therapist might say, "You must be feeling pressured and upset that you cannot face these expectations and sort out which ones seem realistic; instead of relying on your own feelings, you are projecting and turning things around to make it seem that I am the one who has an expectation of you!" The therapist following Wilfred Bion's emphasis on the "truth" might ask, "What's wrong with having an expectation?"

On a more cautionary note, many therapists have misunderstood, misused, or abused self-psychology, confusing empathy with kindness. Self-psychology tends to ignore the internal world, which can lead to a form of collusion or fusion when the therapist goes along with the pathology (e.g., the tendency to blame/shame the other for all the wrongdoings or shortcomings in the relationship). Kernberg (1992) notes that self-psychologists view that all aggression is "bad." "Such a view can only reinforce the patient's own conviction that agression is 'bad' and that he must defend himself against the 'accusations'" (p. 117).

Self-psychology, including the open field of intersubjectivity, offers a variety of listening stances. Self-psychologists take the patient's reality as "truth" and do not consider that the patient's "reality" might be a distortion. In object relations, the patient's "distortions" and "misperceptions" are considered as aspects of the split-off parts and projections from within the internal world. Both self-psychology and object relations must be examined within the scope of each pathology's idiosyncratic nature, keeping in mind the specific theoretical functions as an important source for analytic inquiry (the discussion of Bion will expand this notion later in this chapter).

ROLES OF THE MOTHER AND FATHER

Although Kohut (1971, 1977) stressed the mother's vital function in providing mirroring for the exhibitionist side of the child during normal stages of the narcissistic line of development, he appeared to ignore the mother's role in terms of offering safety and protection. Kohut's emphasis tended to be on the importance of empathy in the mother–child mirroring process. However, it appears that Kohut overlooked the vital role the mother plays in offering bonding and attachment experiences, a role described more clearly by object relations theorists including Bowlby (1969), Fairbairn (1954), Grotstein (1983), Klein (1957), and Winnicott (1965a). Masterson (1981) confirmed that Kohut's ideas exclude the mother and object relations.

Melanie Klein

Klein, more than any of her followers, understood the need for the mother and the breast. Klein maintained that once the infant recognizes the whole-ness of the object (at about 6 months) and its relation to the self, the infant can begin to freely reach out beyond the breast to the environment, usually beginning with the father.

Melanie Klein was the first to shift the emphasis from the father to the importance of the mother and the infant's bond to the breast. In the para-noid–schizoid position, the infant cannot maintain that mother is both good and bad. Klein distinguished between the "good" and "bad" breast, claim-ing that if the infant internalizes a "good breast" the child will grow up to feel that the world is a warm and inviting place. If, on the other hand, the child internalizes a "bad breast" he or she will grow up experiencing the world as hostile, persecutory, and dangerous. Melanie Klein taught us how we relate to others through the reflection of the child's fantasy world as she developed the notion of projective identification. Her concept of splitting relates to ambivalence and persecutory anxieties as they occur in the para-noid–schizoid position. According to Klein, a child cannot grow or develop without the capacity to mourn, grieve, face losses, tolerate guilt, and take responsibility for past transgressions. Klein (1957) derived two positions, each having its own corresponding anxieties: (1) the paranoid–schizoid position (persecutory anxiety) and (2) the depressive position (depressive anxiety). The movements between the paranoid–schizoid and the depres-sive positions are crucial for integration, as is the infant's capacity to move from a state of fragmentation to that of wholeness. In the depressive posi-tion, one can begin to face what one believes is the unknown, to tolerate states of chaos, confusion, and the unbearable abyss. To compete with a parent then becomes tantamount to killing the parent!

Within these positions, Klein entertained us with a drama of psycho-dynamic structures comprised of many intricate, interrelated dynamics (shame, guilt, envy, jealousy, and greed) as primary forces interacting within a primitive internal world (see chapter 8 on phases of treatment).

W. R. D. Fairbairn

Fairbairn (1940) offered insights that go beyond Klein's to help us understand why people stay attached to painful internal objects. He constructed an entire cast of internal objects comprised of many different forms of attachment (see list in chapter 8). Among them are (a) the craving for a tantalizing, frustrating, sadistic, betraying object, and (b) the bond to the unloving, bankrupting, insatiable object. These dynamic structures help us understand why such individuals will not take the therapist's "good advice" and will remain forever loyal to their bad and destructive internal objects: couples identify with a bad external object and cannot separate or disidentify. Fairbairn's concepts are crucial in the treatment of couples because although it is always easy to find an external object to blame (the bad partner), we must introduce the partners to the "internal" objects that help cause the problems within the relationship without making them feel responsible for the mistreatment. We as therapists must show the partners that there may be an external abuser, betrayer, rejecter, but there may also be an internal abuser—part of yourself that also mistreats you!

I have borrowed the terms "internal abuser" and "external abuser" from Fairbairn (1940), Klein (1957), and Kernberg (1980) and applied them to couples therapy to help therapists understand how there can always be an external abuser (robber, betrayer, rejecter) but there can also be an internal one that compels partners to identify or overidentify with that which is being projected. These terms also help clinicians deal with the "impossible couple," who are resistant to change and refuse even under the best clinical conditions to relinquish their negative and destructive behaviors. Even when something "good" is offered, it will not be embraced, for one will stay interminably attached to one's internal object—not necessarily because the patient is crazy but because he or she is familiar with it. One cannot say, for example, "Yes, your husband is betraying you and he does this because he as a child was betrayed." It is more effective to point out, "Yes, your husband is betraying you, but we also have to look at the part of yourself where you betray you. So if he betrays you and you betray you, then we have a terrible mess, a collusion, a dance that we can never get out of." Table 2.1 shows the different kinds of internal/external objects that people identify with.

Donald Winnicott

Donald Winnicott (1965b) is another prominent figure whose unique ideas and language have enhanced and expanded the diversified field of object relations. Winnicott replaced Klein and Fairbairn's view of splitting of the

TABLE 2.1
Attachments to Bad Internal and External Objects

Bad internal objects
- The wronged self
- The insatiable self
- The craving self
- The lost self
- The betrayed self
- The robbed self

Bad external objects
- Rejecting object
- Depriving object
- Unavailable object
- Withholding object
- Painful object (the mother of pain)
- Idealized object
- Sadistic object

ego with the concept of splitting of the personality, mainly into that of the "true self" and the "false self." The false self is the "doing self," which must conform to mother's wishes or commands. It is the self that prevents the true self from "being" or "becoming." For Winnicott these divisions are fundamental to the development and integration of the self.

The "being mommy" is the one available to the child who facilitates and helps nurture the child's true self. This availability allows the child to express his feelings openly, knowing there is a background mother who will embrace the child's "real" feelings. When the mother lacks the resiliency or is unable to "hold" the baby's reactions, the child will grow up developing a false self. It is the noncaring mother who endorses the premature false self or doing self that the child develops in order to please her. (See the case of Abigail and Claude below.)

Doing Mommy Versus Being Mommy:
The Case of Abigail and Claude

This case illustrates the importance of the "being mother," the mother who does not try to get someone to do something, but instead provides the holding environment while allowing the patient the space and time to understand the underlying anxieties that get in the way of doing.

After several conjoint sessions, it was decided that the borderline wife, Abigail, should be seen individually. Abigail was afraid to use the couch.

She felt that she would have to conform to being the nice little girl her mother wanted her to be, and feared that I would insist that she plunge right in, as her mother used to make her do, and that I would not help her recognize the steps it takes to use the couch. Instead of becoming the doing mother who would make her simply "go ahead and try it," I sought to help her by becoming the being mother, who seeks to understand what is getting in the way of doing. I tried to help her understand that she felt anxious because this left her in a state of confusion, not knowing when it was safe to risk and when it was not. It turned out that her fear was that if she used the couch I would become a lazy doctor/husband/me and would ignore her, would eat while she was lying down, would talk on the phone, and generally would take my gaze and attention from her. Even worse, Abigail feared that I would look at her as she saw her father—drunk, lazy, and a sleepy "couch father/husband."

I responded to her projections by letting her know that she was not seeing me for who I am because she was projecting a part of herself onto me. She needed to understand that she was putting into me a "sleepy and lazy" part of herself that she wanted to get rid of (the part of the self that goes along). "You need to 'do' something rather than just allow yourself to be a little child here and to allow yourself just to 'be'. It is important for me to 'be' here to help you understand what is blocking you from staying in contact with your feelings. Before 'doing' something, we need to understand why you feel I would ignore you or would see you as you see your father or husband [states of fusion], as a lazy, sleepy 'couch patient'." I explained to Abigail that as she gets rid of the part of herself that has contact with her feelings she will not be able to turn to her feelings as a vital resource.

Acknowledging the importance of the early "mommy and me" bonding relationships, Winnicott provided us with three basic concepts: (a) the different kinds of mothering experiences, (b) the therapeutic holding environment, and (c) the importance of the transitional space. Winnicott also advanced the concepts of a "holding environment," and an environmental "being mommy," whose function is to help the child with the "being self" (as opposed to the "doing self"). The holding environment, which functions as transitional space, is crucial to the ideas in this book because couples who grew up with early traumatic experiences are deficient in their containing capacities and tend to act out these traumas.

Winnicott's belief was that the therapeutic environment becomes a re-creation of a holding environment, a new opportunity with the therapist in the role of a "good enough mother" providing a good holding environment. In couple therapy this transitional space helps partners move from states between dependency and interdependency by making use of transitional objects. Winnicott helps us understand why many borderlines want unconditional love, love for the being self rather than the doing self, love for *who* rather than *what*. He also facilitates understanding of why the person who has missed out on the early attention of the mother now wants mother not part of the time but all of the time. Borderlines have difficulty providing for themselves, engage in magical thinking ("If you love me, then you will know what I need without asking"), dress inappropriately, cannot find work, and cannot maintain relationships. In conjoint treatment, the borderline patient will often complain that a mate does not give unconditional love and finds it difficult to understand the therapist's response that unconditional love is for babies, not for adults; adults must come through with their commitments.

Winnicott's concepts of "ego relatedness," the being mommy versus the doing mommy (see Case 7 in chapter 9), and the holding, facilitating, or environmental mommy provide a new perspective on the borderline and a powerful approach to understanding the borderline's profound sense of isolation and loneliness. (See Table 2.2, which lists the different mothering/bonding experiences).

DIFFERENT KINDS OF LOVE BONDS

Love can be an elusive concept. Did Freud understand it? Did Keats? Shelley? Shakespeare? As mentioned earlier, Freud viewed love as a psychotic state, a delusional state of mind, a reunion of highly charged emotional and bodily experiences. This state emanates from the fulfillment of infantile conditions

TABLE 2.2
Different Mother and Bonding Experiences

- The good breast and bad breast mother
- The being and doing mother
- The holding, environmental, background mother
- The containing mother
- The rejecting, absent mother
- The mother of pain
- The internal mother
- The facilitating mother
- The mirroring mother
- The self-object mother
- The idealized mother
- The castrated mother
- The introjected mother
- The self-hatred mother
- The playful/creative mother

of love, and whatever gratifies this state becomes highly cathected and idealized. Freud viewed the state of love as a flowing over of ego libido to the object. In states of passion, sexual desires coincide with the ego ideal.

Love relationships in general are not simple; they are comprised of many complex and interrelated aspects including love, hate, envy, jealousy, aggression, rivalry, control, domination, submission, perversion, pre-Oedipal/Oedipal conflicts, as well as many early unresolved infantile conflicts and issues.

Otto Kernberg

Otto Kernberg delves deeply into the complexity of the love bond. Kernberg's primary focus is on how people form attachments through the use or "misuse" of aggression. Aggression is addictive and exciting. Once it starts, it is difficult to stop; people get hooked (Gay, 1988). Kernberg's understanding of the use and misuse of aggression provides a valuable guideline to understanding different kinds of regressive love bonds.

In *Aggression in Personality Disorders and Perversions* (1992), Kernberg reminded us of the complexities of relationships as he distinguishes between four different kinds of love relationships: (a) normal, (b) pathological, (c) perverse, and (d) mature. (See Table 2.3 for a capsulated explanation.) Kernberg's descriptions are not only provocative but also extremely useful in the treatment of couples. He examines the success and failure of love, taking into consideration the role of narcissism, masochism, and aggression (1995). His premise is that even though couples may fight, abuse, and hate each other, if the desire to maintain a loving relationship is the ultimate goal, the partnership is considered healthy.

Normal Love

In normal love, "love conquers all." The desire to love and have a loving relationship overcomes conflict. Internal strivings and aggression do not interfere with the capacity to maintain a long-range, intimate, passionate,

TABLE 2.3
Four Types of Love Relationships

- Normal: Relationship more important; love takes over conflict.
- Pathological: Conflict takes over the relationship; part object functioning.
- Perverse: Search for excitement; partners reverse good and bad.
- Mature: Goal/task oriented; whole object functioning.

(Kernberg, 1995)

loving relationship. In a normal relationship, individuals are able to face reality. They do not live in denial and are not threatened by the other person's emotions or truth. Erotic desire is linked to the Oedipal object and is not obliterated by the failing of internal objects. One has a strong desire for symbiotic fusion with one's mate. Normal love means the relinquishing of Oedipal rivals to the realization that one can settle down with one's partner. The desire to love one's sexual partner becomes more pervasive than the desire to "possess," own, or control the Oedipal/rival object. One now can live side by side with father without having to compete with him. Couples who experience a problem within a normal love relationship will benefit from short-term psychotherapy.

Example: A man and his wife from a small farm town in Nebraska entered couple therapy with the presenting problem that the husband had a peculiar habit of cutting off heads in photos of family members and gluing them onto porno figures. This enraged his wife. As bizarre as this may seem, their relationship still remained in the realm of "normalcy." The couple was very much in love, had great capacity for erotic intimacy, and shared common values. This strange fetish did not interfere with the couple's capacity to maintain a close and intimate relationship. The treatment consisted mainly of helping the man sort out the difference between fantasy life and reality: It is okay to fantasize but it is not okay to act on these fantasies.

Pathological Love

In pathological love, conflict overcomes the desire to love or to have an intimate relationship. Pathological relationships encourage the tendency to repeat the trauma again and again ("traumatic bonding"). This is a relationship in which aggression and internal conflicts do interfere with the desire to maintain a loving relationship.

In pathological love, emotions run high. The relationship is steamy, explosive, and alters and falters between states of distress and discontinuity to moments of harmony and bliss. It is a part object tie, in which such primitive defenses as envy, control, sadomasochism, aggression, and cruelty fester. We see this in obsessive love, addictive love, love that goes in the wrong direction. In severe pathological relations, love gets directed to sadomasochism and perversion, envy, greed, control, domination, and self-destruction). Reality testing does not offer relief; instead reality is denied, split off, and projected. Couples in pathological love relationships are in need of more intensive psychotherapy.

Example: A borderline husband falls in love with a narcissistic, histrionic woman with beautiful breasts and only later feels compelled to kill any man who looks at her. Or a borderline husband unconsciously pushes his narcissistic wife to have affairs with other men, then berates her for having betrayed and abandoned him. In this way the borderline husband recreates the idealized unavailable woman/mother who died when he was in early infancy, unconsciously recreating the fantasy with the lost object.

Perverse Love

In perverse love, excitement becomes the replacement for love. Because pain is often linked to the love object, the relationship becomes highly charged and eroticized (see Case 3 in chapter 9). This is also known as "traumatic bonding" (Dutton & Painler, 1991). Many narcissistic/borderline relationships teeter on the fringes of perversity, using excitement and eroticism as surrogates for a loving relationship. Many of these couples cannot tolerate true intimacy and instead turn to excitement. What kills or destroys a perverse relationship is, in fact, love itself. It is the confusion between good and bad, an effort to shield oneself from getting too close to the "good thing." Perversion goes beyond whips and chains. It connotes confusion around one's symbolic love objects. For example, a breast may be viewed as bad because it represents a hunger, whereas an anus is viewed as good because it represents withholding qualities (the unavailable object highly charged with libidinal energy). Eroticism then becomes the emotional insurance policy against vulnerability.

Example: A man might rationalize: "Even though I know this woman isn't right for me, I feel excited! I'm with a woman who torments me, a woman who is unavailable just like my mother." Or, he might think: "Why do I stay with a woman who torments me, someone I wouldn't wish on my worst enemy? She is exactly like my mother. She is like an albatross around my neck" (see Case 17 in chapter 9).

Mature Love

Mature love is where both partners share common goals, values, and traditions, are aware of each other's vulnerabilities, and share a willingness to work things through. Mature love implies a total commitment within the province of sex, emotions, and shared couple values (Kernberg, 1995). The desire for erotic and emotional attachment is not obliterated by the world of internal objects. Desire is an outcome of need fulfillment and does not result from part-object erotic desires or Oedipal conflict.

Wilfred Bion

It was Wilfred Bion who transformed Melanie Klein's ideas into practical conceptions. For Bion, as for Klein, a good breast connotes experiences such as warm empathic responses related to others, and not the breast as a thing in itself. Bion's immensely important contributions were based primarily on the philosophy of Immanuel Kant. Bion's epigenetic developmental theory helps explain how couples and individuals learn or don't learn from experience; why individuals repeat the same mistakes over and over again; how and why they seek out or avoid truth; and why they learn to think or to avoid thinking about the unthinkable thoughts. Bion teaches us to understand how thinking becomes distorted.

To understand Bion, it is important to know something about the special language used to describe his concepts.

The K Link

Bion's innovative construct uses the letter K (as in knowledge) to describe an emotional link between people. The K link typifies the individual who tries to find truth through introspection and psychoanalytic inquiry, and –K ("minus k") suggests the reverse. The K link is based on the search for truth and knowledge, and the –K link represents the avoidance of truth and knowledge.

Alpha and Beta Elements

Alpha elements are functions that can be used for verbal thoughts and expressions that are suitable for communication, learning, and thinking. Beta elements (or functions) are undigested facts; beta functions are not memories, but refer to intolerable affects that can be used only for evacuation, not for thinking about or learning from experience.

Detoxification

Detoxification is the nullification of the poisonous substance that the child experiences when feeling bad inside. The process involves the therapist's ability to take the toxins or poisons out of the patient's internal world and convert them into a more digestible form, suitable for thinking and understanding.

Transformations

The transformation from beta elements to alpha function requires a container, a person who can make use of the projections and who is able to provide a good breast. If the good breast has not been experienced, one cannot possibly know of its existence (–K). If you tell someone to think about snow and that person has never been in snow, there will be no reference for that experience. Of if you tell someone to think positively when he or she has had only negative experiences, the person will be unable to formulate positive thoughts.

The Quick Fix

According to Bion (1977), anxiety is useful in channeling painful affects into constructive avenues. Splitting off of important affective experiences can severely interfere with healthy object relations. Usually each partner is quick to relieve the other of anxiety by offering a quick solution or a "quick fix," because neither can hold onto painful thoughts, feelings, and affects long enough to work anything through.

Containment

Containment is a term employed by Bion to describe the dynamic relationship between the mother and the infant. Bion's model of the "container and the contained" connotes the mother's capacity for transformation of incoherent emotional experience into meaningful feelings and thoughts. The mother's capacity to withstand the child's projections, anger, frustration, and intolerable feelings are basic prerequisites for her to act as the "container" for these affects. Development of the true self can occur if the mother can sustain intolerable behaviors long enough to decode or detoxify them. Bion believed that the therapist's/mother's capacity must be deep enough to hold the projections and not abandon the child.

Containment is needed because of the borderline's tendency to externalize and to blame others; it is difficult for the borderline to use others as self-objects and to maintain them as a source of nurturance. The ability of the mother or therapist to withhold and withstand for the child the intolerable feelings long enough to understand those feelings is an aspect of containment.

Because needs are warded off by shame, borderlines have a pervasive tendency to force, intrude on, or invade their objects. The tendency to evacuate is considered tantamount to getting rid of a crucial part of the self, namely, needs and feelings. For Bion (1977), all needed objects are bad especially when one feels persecuted by them. Many borderlines experience need as shame.

Thinking

According to Bion (Grinberg et al., 1977), thinking is a function of the personality. Bion presented the development of thought from (a) preconception, to (b) conception, to (c) concept. These stages can be illustrated by the relation of the infant to the breast. A preconception occurs when the infant has an innate idea that somewhere there is a breast. However, never having experienced the breast, the infant remains hungry and frustrated without knowing why. This is called a preconception. When the infant has an experience with the breast, a mating between the nipple and the mouth, this becomes a conception. When infants are able to realize they need the breast or realize what is missing, they start to develop thoughts about the breast, a concept. Borderlines tend to disregard preconceptions; thus, they cannot proceed into the second and third stages of thought.

The therapist's use of "preconception" (as an unborn thought, like intuition) is crucial in modeling that one should not be afraid to trust one's own sensory perceptions, as is typical of the borderline partner. Preconceptions, curiosity, thoughts, needs, and feelings terrorize and persecute the borderline. Thinking never develops when psychic conflict is felt to be too threatening, as in, for example, "I can't feel like a helpless little boy." The containing therapist might respond, "Yes, but if you can depend on me, then that little boy part of you can grow; if not, you will always feel little and small." The therapist's avoidance of preconceptions may collude with the patient's own vagueness, aloofness, lack of clarity, confusion, fear of risking, fear of sounding foolish, and hopelessness.

Bion helps us explore not who is right and wrong but what is in the way of deriving at truth. Although the works of Bion dovetail Klein's theories, Bion renovated them, transforming their literal meaning and object-relational links into something far deeper. He extended Klein's idea of the good and bad breast (how the infant develops an entire object world based on its earliest experience with the breast), to view the breast as a container that functions to help nourish the mind to detoxify bad thoughts and bad feelings. Couples who exhibit primitive defenses lack the containment that would allow them to learn from their mistakes. Bion's most crucial ideas center around the previously explained K link and –K link and examine the capacity to think and learn from experience. For Bion, the worst crime is to live an analytic lie. The K link marks the patient genuinely invested in the search for truth (knowledge), while the –K link represents the avoidance of truth (knowledge). Bion's explanation for this is that when the object is not contained, thoughts become suitable only for evacuation. It is the nature of projective identification that weakens the psyche and strips the self of all resources (Ogden, 1986). This is important in couple therapy because it hinders the couple's ability to realize the mistakes they are making and thus avoid compounding the problems in their relationship. Freud (see Hall, 1954) referred to this as repetitive compulsion.

Unlike Kohut, Bion, along with Klein, is far more dubious about the patient's "truth" and does not experience the patient's subjective experience as reality or truth. Patients with narcissistic and borderline personality disorders tend to distort truth. The basic premise is that when such primitive defenses as splitting, projection, and projective identification are operative, it is hard to know what is real and what is not real. This is important in couple therapy when partners insist on asking therapists, "Tell us what to do. Should we get a divorce or should we stay?" The appropriate response from the therapist would be, "Well, while you are in a state of shame/ blame or when one partner feels excessively more entitled than the other, it is hard to know what to 'do', let alone to know what is real and what is not real."

In contrast to object relationists, self-psychologists consider the patient's reality as truth, and not as a distortion. In object relations, the partner's distortions and misperceptions are considered to be aspects of the split-off parts and projections from within the internal world. Both of these methods must be examined within the scope of each pathology while keeping in mind the specific theoretical functions as an important source for analytic inquiry. Klein argued that the perception of others is merely scaffolding for distorted projections of the child's innate internal object images that imagine how others perceive them. Let us consider man's desire of the object. According to the philosopher George Hegel (1821), "Man does not desire an object. Man desires the object's desire." Isaacs (1943) supported the explanation that desire is always covetous of something. What that "something" is can only be discovered after uncovering layers of defenses within the internal world of each partner. The implication is that the experience of wanting is inherent in an image or fantasy. Pathogenic narcissism emanating from primary and secondary narcissism can severely impair relating to other objects, particularly when these internal images are obscured by one's desiring a fantasy or an idealized image which, in reality, can never be achieved. This corresponds to Kohut's (1971, 1977) "the gleam in the mother's eye," the joy the parent receives while watching the child achieve and accomplish.

OEDIPAL ISSUES

The Oedipus myth, along with other myths such as the Garden of Eden, the Tower of Babel, and the riddle of the sphinx, suggests that seeking truth leads to peril, thus turning us away from curiosity. However, some individuals learn that curiosity can lead instead to passion, experience, and learning. Oedipus plucked out his eyes to avoid truth. This rendered him a mental cripple and occurred as a consequence of his epistemophilic curiosity. The warnings of his mother and the already blinded Tiresias were to no avail. By forfeiting his eyes, Oedipus became the paradigm of the lifelong mental invalid known as "everyman."

Self-psychologists do not view Oedipal strivings as a conflict over instinctual drives, as do Freud and his early followers. Rather, they view them as involving self-esteem, vulnerability, and threat of self-cohesion (annihilation anxieties). Self-psychologists do not believe that conflict is about the sexual possession of the opposite parent associated with castration anxieties (Bacal & Newman, 1990).

From an object-relational perspective, the development of the Oedipus complex is strongly influenced by the special relationship with the mother; when this relationship is disturbed, it stirs up rivalry with father prematurely (Oedipal rivals often involve the marital partner). The infant cannot leave the breast or turn to father until it first feels safe with mother. Somewhere, other than with mother, there is an innate preconception that beyond the breast there is an object more stimulating, challenging, and exciting. This is the place for the Oedipal father.

When one finally reaches this place, one has triumphed over one's Oedipal rivals; there is no longer a need to compete, be omnipotent, or "prove" oneself. Oedipal rivals are no longer a threat and one can live peacefully and amicably in a loving relationship. Klein refered to this movement as the depressive position. In the paranoid–schizoid position, rivalry, arrogance, and exhibitionism get in the way of overcoming. Competing with father for the desired mommy can lead to guilt turned inward, to self-persecution, self-hatred, loss of curiosity, individuality, and rational thinking.

Of all the theorists, Grotstein provides us with the most in-depth understanding of the Oedipus complex. He argues that before the infant is ready for the father, the infant must have some sense of bonding with the mother. According to Grotstein (personal communication, 1985), the analyst/father Oedipus is not a real rival but a mock one. Our patients are rehearsing with us in preparation for the "real" hunters or the "real predators." Grotstein (personal communication, 1983) recognized a social Oedipus rather than a sexual Oedipus in that mother provides safety but father shows the way to challenge, to find truth or avoid truth, to seek out or avoid curiosity. Ironically, Grotstein notes that "the narcissist is never really driven enough to acquire or get what he really needs because he has not achieved Oedipal victory over the 'mock rivals'." It is the father who prohibits, then challenges us to risk, to reach out to others, or to avoid new experiences through denial, arrogance, fear, guilt, and other defenses.

The Oedipus myth, as perceived by Bion, provides a linkage with curiosity and harmony and the child's innate epistemophilic instinct to make discoveries, leading to the quest for truth and knowledge. Bion's (1958) paper "On Arrogance" and Grotstein's publications (1981, 1983) enhance and add profound insights to Klein's concepts about the Oedipus complex. Their more expansive view transcends incest and parricide.

Freud's Oedipus may be misunderstood as a literal Oedipus. For Bion, the myth has less do with a sexual component than a precursor to knowledge via psychic reality. To rely on instincts and feelings is an essential part of the learning apparatus. If one, for example, continually evacuates or projects one's feelings because they are felt to be too intolerable, then one never has the opportunity to learn from experience. Bion's major contribution to our understanding of couple therapy centers primarily on how one discovers truth. Therapists are often duped into the dilemma of discerning who is right and who is wrong. It goes something like this: Mr. Right meets Mrs. Wrong. Mr. Right is always right even when he is wrong. Mrs. Right is always wrong even when she is right. Mr. Wrong and Mrs. Right are right and wrong, so how do we find out who is right and who is wrong?

CONCLUSION

Both self-psychologists and object relationists have made valuable contributions to the study of marital conflict. Many mentioned here are not conjoint therapists, yet they have offered us stellar, insightful ideas for an area of treatment still in its infant stages. Although many assume that self-psychology and object relations make strange bedfellows, they appear to make a perfect marriage. Both theories have proven their importance in the treatment of narcissistic and borderline couples. Fairbairn has perhaps shown us better than any other theorist how to cope with the resistance in couple treatment. This resistance emanates from the partners' unwavering loyalty and attachment to an internal object, which persist despite the therapist's best advice.

Here are some points to keep in mind when dealing with the narcissistic/borderline couple: Because of the tendency of narcissists to withdraw and isolate themselves, it is suggested that they are more in need of mirroring, and because of the tendency of borderlines to attack any link to desire and wishes for intimacy, it is suggested that they are more in need of containment and management. One would not dare "think" for the narcissist; one interprets. In contrast, because borderlines do not have the capacity to think about the unthinkable, the therapist must provide this function. We function as the mother who knows before the baby.

Chapter 3

The Couple

The Dance, the Drama, and the Bond

THE DANCE

In the first edition of this book, the interactions of the narcissistic/border-line couple were described as a "dance," a choreography of movements comprised of primitive defenses and regressive behaviors that go back and forth, round and round, without ever reaching any conflict resolution (Lachkar, 1984, 1985, 1992, 1997). Because of such primitive defenses as splitting, projective identification, and magical thinking, the narcissistic/borderline partners do not learn from experience; therefore, they repeat the same painful acts again and again. Furthermore, the dialectic tensions between the partners contribute to these vacillations. On the one hand, there is the desire for an intimate connection, and, on the other, there are the unconscious forces that compel the partners to destroy or sabotage the intimate love bond (see Case 4 in chapter 9).

Driven by the need to be desired and appreciated, the narcissist, fearing a loss of specialness, is easily injured and outraged when not properly mirrored or understood. The narcissist's exaggerated sense of entitlement causes him or her to seek out the other to confirm and justify these distortions. Meanwhile, the borderline feels left out, displaced, outcast, undeserving, worthless, and empty.

For the narcissist, the movements of the dance revolve around the major features of specialness, perfectionism, adoration, and exaggerated entitlement fantasies, accompanied by the defenses of idealization, with-drawal/isolation, omnipotence, guilt, and denial as protection against per-sonal injury to the self. Narcissists appear to operate at a higher level of functioning on the ego continuum than their borderline counterparts be-cause they are dominated more by guilt than by shame. Narcissists tend to introject more than project and have strongly punitive superegos that oper-ate in terms of self-hatred and guilt.

For the borderline, in contrast, configurations of the dance center around revenge, retaliation, getting even, manipulation, victimization, and sacrifice (self and other). Borderlines are dominated by such primitive de-fenses as splitting, projection, projective identification, and magical think-ing. Borderlines have a persecutory superego, which interminably torments them and kills off "normal" needs and desires. Needs are experienced as dangerous internal forces that invade and disrupt the psyche, leading to annihilation and catastrophic devastation. When the narcissist and the bor-derline come together in a lasting bond or "bind," these dynamics inflame and the partners find themselves engaged in an ongoing state of conflict and upheaval.

As the borderline attacks, the narcissist withdraws. Unable to with-stand the threat of abandonment, the borderline reacts with endless apolo-gies and make-believe promises orchestrated merely to woo back the narcissist. Because the borderline's exquisite false self is very believable, the narcissist returns to the borderline not only out of guilt but under the per-suasion that the borderline will fulfill his or her promises and take care of the narcissist's needs.

Paradoxically, the narcissist is never narcissistic enough to follow through to get what he or she wants. The narcissist returns to the border-line again and again, culminating in repeated failed self-object attempts. The borderline promises the world but fails to follow through because of lack of impulse control and inability to come to terms with his own needs. The borderline's "false self" allows him to play-act for a while at being a perfect mirror/self/object for the narcissist. But shame/blame defenses do not allow the borderline to maintain this act.

The narcissistic husband projects a feeling onto his wife that she is worthless, not entitled to anything, and should not need or want anything. He complains, "All you do is nag, nag, nag." Not knowing how to legiti-mately express her real needs, the borderline wife escalates her nagging and demanding. As she nags, he withdraws; as he withdraws, she attacks. When the wife attacks, she connects with her narcissistic husband's punitive, in-ternalized superego. He ends up feeling guilty and she ashamed. Thus, their relationship becomes a dance between guilt and shame.

Such oppositional movements often bring about feelings of imminent danger and threat to one's sense of existence, which is always subject to predation and outside danger. For the narcissist, facing conflict and problems is tantamount to being less than perfect. For the borderline, facing one's problem is equivalent to being bad, and thus not deserving to exist in the world. (See the case illustration that follows).

THE PROJECTIVE/INTROJECTIVE PROCESS: THE CASE OF LINDA AND BOB

This case is an example of the projective/introjective process. It illustrates how the narcissistic partner projects a negative feeling onto the borderline wife, who identifies or overidentifies with what is being projected onto her.

Linda: He's not attentive to my needs. He ignores me, ridicules me, and makes me feel like a nothing. When we wake up in the morning I ask him about our plans, and he accuses me of being a nag. "Oh, here we go again," he says, "You are such a nag! Why do you have to badger me like this?" Even on my birthday, Christmas, or Valentine's Day, he acts as if I don't exist.

Bob: See what a nag she is?! Big deal, a birthday! Besides, why should I support Hallmark cards, another commercial scam concocted by materialism? Just a gimmick for suckers!

Th: Simple. Because it's traditional and she's your wife, whom you love and care about.

Bob: But why doesn't she do the same for me? After all, I have needs too.

Th: But just last week you were telling us how you had no needs, that your wife was the needy and demanding one.

Bob: But I do have needs! I need time to myself. I need space. I need not to be badgered. I need time to be alone, time to do the things I enjoy.

Linda: This is what he always does.

Th: [Acknowledging the wife's hurt.] Of course, those things are important; we all need time alone. But within the context of this relationship, these are not needs.

Bob: If these are not needs, then what are they?

Th: That's withdrawal. Your wife may come across as too demanding, but at least she expresses the desire for intimacy, communication, wanting a connection with you, and time together.

Linda: That's exactly right. This is where I get confused. When he starts telling me about space, I start to feel a terrible sense of shame for having all these needs, while he doesn't seem to need anything! I feel as though I'm just someone who gets in his way.

Th: But your needs are important, and you have to start paying more attention to them. It's not your needs that get in the way, it is your demandingness. But I think you get demanding when you don't feel entitled and when you identify with this "nuisance" part of yourself.

Bob: This is a bunch of crap! Why do we waste our time talking about needs when we are here to try and get help with our marriage? All this talk and all these sessions, and I still can't get it up.

Th: I see that when we talk about needs, desires, and feelings, you get quite anxious.

Bob: You bet. It makes me feel like a fool to even have to bring this up.

Th: It makes you feel more like a "sucker," to "suck" or take in something, to ask for what you want. This makes you feel very small, dependent, and maybe even emotionally impotent. But this is actually the very healthy side, and I'm here to help.

Bob: [Pensively] Now you're talking. I never thought of that before— the idea that my physical impotence can connect to emotional impotence.

Th: This may sound very strange to you, but facing this dependent part of you is actually the healthy and potent part.

Linda: This happens all the time. He always has to act so macho, as if he is the one who knows everything, has everything, and never needs anything from me.

Bob: Well, I must say I have been to many therapists before but never has anyone connected my inability to "get it up" with emotional impotence.

Th: Before we stop I would like to reiterate how important your needs are here, so let's start here. Please feel free to say anything, ask anything, and I will do my best to respond [a segue into the couple transference].

Bob: Uh, I did, by the way, want to ask you if you will hold my check.

Th: Ah, sounds like you're getting healthy already.

Bob: Well, I never thought it would end up like this.

Th: Good. Look forward to seeing you both next week.

The narcissist/borderline dance is never completed. It continues like a rondo, always with the hope and yearning for harmonious experience, the fantasy of togetherness achieved through the unification of mind and body, sacrifice of the self at any cost. Any disruption in the dance may be experienced by the partners as fraught with profound danger. The interaction of the couple can dramatically emphasize and exaggerate their current perspective of reality, whereas when the partners are viewed as individuals, these behaviors may appear as subtle nuances (Lachkar, 1985). It is important to recognize that the behaviors of the partners are not purposeful; rather, they are unconscious reenactments of infantile longings and painful attempts to work through these longings.

THE DRAMA

"It's not the steps that count, but how you do them." Carmelita Marcacci (personal communication, 1977), master ballet teacher and one of the nation's most acclaimed dancers and choreographers, put it just that simply. Marcacci's theatrical approach to dance is not a far cry from the marital theatrics we encounter in couple therapy. Treatment of couples involves deep understanding of their dramatic interplay. Every dancer knows about the importance of boundaries— emotional, spatial, and physical. Invading another dancer's physical space leads to a physical collision. The dancer knows how to protect emotional space as well and to keep others from intruding, and is able to focus and balance without allowing any external intrusions. For the performing artist, the search for approval can lead to a disastrous loss of balance, timing, and focus, as well as one's sense of center.

Psychoanalytic technique and theory are meaningless unless they are artistically, emotionally, and creatively executed. Each psychological movement, like each dance step, involves an interpretation that must be poignantly expressed with purpose and a direct focus. Maracci emphasized that every movement and gesture must be understood internally, processed, and related to a feeling state or to a mode of experience before it is executed into the external experience. For instance, let us consider the parallel between art and psychological interpretation. In a dance, an arm gesture must conjure up a thought, an image, or a feeling in order to give the movement meaning; otherwise, the gesture becomes statue-like, empty, meaningless. So must the therapist speak with meaning, passion, and conviction if the offered interpretations are to carry any weight. It is not sufficient for a musician to merely play the notes. Eye contact, tone of voice, gestures, phrasing, and timing all parallel the therapeutic process.

As the pas de deux of the narcissistic/borderline couple progresses, one might conceptualize the narcissist as the soloist, always needing to be on center stage, while the borderline is part of the corps de ballet. What is it that makes them fall into these roles?

Circular Behaviors

As each new drama unfolds, so does an old scenario. This old scenario may have taken place in a different time, different space, different setting, and with different players, but the vulnerabilities of yesteryear remain deeply embedded in the script. By bringing the partners to an understanding of how the past scenario is affecting current behavior, the therapist has an opportunity to effectuate an entirely new experience. Because the interactions and behaviors of the couple are painful, circular, never ending—go round and round without ever reaching any conflict resolution, it is easy for the therapist to maintain the focus, or "the spot," as it is known in dance—a crucial technique to avoid dizziness and maintain balance and equilibrium. The following illustrates this point.

No, don't look at me to complete your sentence; look at your partner and stay with your focus. Notice how you keep turning away. But as soon your partner tells you you are crazy for wanting just a "piece of paper," you throw up your hands in frustration and then lose contact with your needs. Stay on your course. Don't look at me for approval; you don't need my approval. Keep looking him in the eye, and speak as though you mean it. Do not let him get you distracted.

The following dialogue illustrates how difficult it is to stay on "the spot." (Also see the case of Mary and Joe in chapter 8).

Girlfriend: So why can't we get married?

Boyfriend: I'm not ready.

Girlfriend: So why don't we break up?

Boyfriend: Because I don't want to break up.

Girlfriend: So why do you stay with me?

Boyfriend: Because I love you.

Girlfriend: So if you love me, why don't we get married?

Therapist: Why don't you tell your boyfriend how angry you are with him?

Ironically, the conflicts that ignite the circular behavior can contribute to a plethora of important developmental insights (issues around betrayal, entitlement, self-esteem, blame/shame, submission, control, domination, capacity or incapacity to mourn). Issues around bonding are especially important for the borderline partner. Because of the false self that aims to please or, when needy, falls into the role of the innocent victim, the borderline acts out repressed feelings through a never-ending barrage of complaints. Because borderlines cannot tolerate needing and owning up to their inner badness, they need a bad object on which to project. In this way, they can retain the good parts of themselves. Often these repressed desires are acted out in passive-aggressive ways that play out the parent/child dyad (see Case 12 in chapter 9). The borderline wishes desperately to be loved, but gets lost along the way, drifting into a wishful, dreamy, sleeplike state, frequently associated with defenses of projective identification, evacuation, and envy. These passive-aggressive features are unconsciously designed to evoke intense reactions in the narcissist, leaving the borderline feeling internally depleted.

By his or her movements in the dance, the narcissist is saying to the borderline: "I'm here because I see my own needy child in you, and if I leave, I leave behind an infantile part of myself that is yearning to grow and develop." The narcissist is seduced by the borderline's false promises over and over again. Typically, it is disappointment in the outside world that draws the narcissist back to the borderline partner. Unwittingly, the narcissist "needs" the borderline in order to project unwanted, split-off needs and to ward off shame. Because of faulty object relations, neither partner can tolerate being dependent, nor can they face up to any wrongdoing or their responsibilities in the relationship. The proclivity toward narcissistic injury compels the narcissist to flee from treatment, while the tendency to feel persecuted keeps the borderline glued to the therapist in a state of victimization (see chapter 8 on treatment).

For the borderline, the dance of the relationship takes on a different configuration—toward the object when there is hope of bonding, and away from the object (through the defenses of blaming, attacking, splitting, projection and projective identification, sadistic attacks, and evacuation) when there is a threat to that bond. The borderline stays in the dance because he or she does not learn from experience. Borderlines have a fragmented ego that cannot organize the data of experience; they project outward all their unwanted parts and feel unworthy of having needs and desires. Their lack of conviction keeps borderlines plodding on treacherous ground, not daring to step out of the circle because change is felt to be dangerous and catastrophic. The borderline can play-act for a while at being the perfect mirroring self-object for the narcissist, but then is caught off guard when the narcissist withdraws, evoking old vulnerabilities of abandonment (see chapter 4 on the V-spot; see also the Case of Kathy and Mathew in that chapter).

The narcissist withdraws either physically or emotionally, but returns out of a pervasive sense of guilt-ridden anxiety and disappointment that the external world cannot assuage. The use of transitional objects for the borderline is limited, making loneliness even more excruciatingly painful. Many borderlines continue to live in impoverished and bankrupt inner states because they quickly give up parts of themselves by fusing or aligning themselves with others as testimony to their "goodness." They schematically find witnesses to justify that all the "badness" lies in the other. The inability to tolerate any badness keeps them feeling forever empty and unfulfilled.

Thus, the drama goes on. The narcissist's search for the perfect mirroring object creates endless disappointment, while the borderline's search for the unavailable/rejecting/ ridiculing object reinforces their "badness." The narcissist usually returns to the borderline with renewed promises. But these promises cannot be maintained since the partners continue to enact their archaic roles again and again. The feelings of ridicule and abandonment anxiety are expressed by a borderline wife in the following dream:

"I was at the market with two wealthy men; both men were pushing shopping carts. I watched as they filled them up with expensive food, buying only for themselves. I left abruptly, anticipating they were not only not going to feed me but also expecting me to pay. I suddenly found myself in a store, looking at ornaments and holding a small child. One woman was buying the ornaments, looking quite at ease and obviously using her husband's credit card. On the way out I walked down a dark street holding the small child; she was heavy. The thought occurred to me that I should call the men at the market to come pick me up, but I feared they would reject me or ridicule me for being too demanding, so I continued to walk. As I walked I passed by two laughing hyenas. I felt they were laughing at me. Finally they got distracted, and I was able to walk past, still holding the child. Later they caught up with me and told me to not move. I got terrorized. Finally an authority figure came by and gave them a summons. I was grateful and was able to continue my journey home."

The laughing hyenas were the projected, split-off part of herself, the unwanted part that could not tolerate her needy state of mind (the need to be fed, taken care of, nurtured). The men were the depriving narcissistic mommies who only feed themselves, and the woman buying the Christmas ornaments was the whole person she would like to be.

THE BOND

Narcissistic/borderline couples bond through many shared couple myths that give rise to shared collective fantasies, causing the couple to play and replay their roles time after time without attaining conflict resolution. The scenario is repeated time after time through idealization, devaluation, and wishful and magical thinking. These dynamics are enacted via their shared projective identification and a mélange of characters within their internal and external object world.

Personal and shared myths can distort the partners' current perspective of reality. The personal myth for the narcissist revolves around approval and reassurance: the narcissist seeks the approval of others who are idealized and who are highly cathected with narcissistic libido. If others approve, the grandiose self will be validated and given meaning. When others do not provide the needed validation, the narcissist is left feeling frustrated and insecure and returns to the borderline for reassurance. The paradox, in my view, is that the more validation narcissists receive, the more insecure they become because it takes them further away from relying on their own experience and instincts. According to Bion, validation of the self can come only from one's own experience.

The personal myth of borderlines requires that their partner love them, be emotionally available, take care of survival needs, be self-sacrificing, and offer proof that the borderline does indeed exist. The misconception that needing is synonymous with being bad is exacerbated by the faulty ways in which needs are expressed and projected—for example, when needs become greedy (through excessive entitlement fantasies or as a result of being the "deprived child") or when one invades or intrudes into the other's physical or emotional space (the borderline living inside another object). In the personal myth of the borderline, strivings and yearning for closeness or intimacy are perceived as wrong. The borderline's defenses are obstacles to intimacy and push others away. Borderlines often become their loneliness, their neediness, their nothingness.

The borderline confirms for the narcissist that it is okay to withdraw, to avoid and turn away from problems, essentially because borderlines abandon their own experiences. The narcissist validates the borderline's personal myth (confirming that the borderline is a nothing) by disregarding the borderline's razor-sharp attacks and ruthless projections. The borderline embellishes the narcissist's indulgent schemes (of being "an everything") and reinforces the rationale to run from problems and turn to others for blame. Thus, the borderline's personal myth becomes a shared myth: that the borderline is a nothing and the narcissistic an everything.

Excessive entitlement fantasies often become shared myths that tie in unrealistic and delusional expectations. For the narcissist, grandiosity often relates to guilt, to not being able to give enough or be the idealized ultimate provider, and the narcissist will react by giving too much. For the borderline, grandiosity may be a form of projective identification to ward off feelings of shame and helplessness.

Individuals in narcissistic/borderline relationships stir up an amalgam of unconscious, unresolved infantile conflicts that keep them bonded and attached at a most primitive and regressed level. The narcissistic/borderline couple stays together not because they are crazy or sadomasochistic, but because each needs the other to play out their drama. Therapists are often quite baffled and puzzled as to why couples remain in these beleaguered love bonds, forever attached and loyal to their states of victimization or the "mother of pain." According to Kernberg (1992), relational love bonds are not simple. They are comprised of many complex and interrelated aspects including love, hate, jealousy, envy, aggression, rivalry, domination, control, entitlements. (These will be discussed further in chapter 4.) These dynamics are significant in understanding the bonding process because the conflict that gets stirred up contributes to invaluable psychodynamic insights (issues such as abandonment, entitlement, betrayal).

"I don't understand why I stay with a woman who tortures me like my mother, someone I wouldn't wish on my worst enemy."

The Case of Sara and Max

Sara ended up marrying a man exactly like her father, someone who would make promises but never keep them. When Sara was a child, her father would tell her how much he loved her and promise to come to her birthday parties, take her out, spend time with her. But he repeatedly did not show up and disappointed her. Eventually she began to feel worthless and nondeserving. Max, like her father, would also promise and disappoint. Sara claims she does not know how to get her needs met. If she expresses her needs to Max, she gets rebuffed and put down, If she nags and demands, he withdraws. Thus, she remains stuck and helpless. The bond emanates from her archaic injury: that as a child, she was helpless and beholden to an unavailable father, and as an adult she still maintains the role of the powerless and helpless little child.

The subject of bonding is complex and inextricably linked to the ability to form and maintain an attachment to an intimate partner. According to Kohut (1971, 1977) and his followers, borderline patients are not able to form self-object transference and are more subject to fragmentation than their narcissistic counterparts. Many theorists agree that the borderline operates at a far more primitive and regressed level than do narcissists and those with other personality disorders and is more susceptible to disruption. When their archaic states (see "V- Spot," chapter 4) are properly valued and their projective identifications are sufficiently contained, borderline features subside and reactions to relatively minor events become less catastrophic and severe.

"It is so hard for me to tell her I need space, time alone with my son, a prenuptial agreement, and when I do she says it makes her feel like she's not special. Then she goes for days without speaking to or having sex with me."

A recent research study by Waldinger, Moore, et al. (2000), examining 48 couples from Harvard, indicates that women with borderline stuctures exhibiting primitive defenses tend to misperceive or misread the emotions, perceptions, and motivations of their male partners. Findings support theories that early trauma, child abuse, and sexual abuse make these women more susceptible to misinterpreting their intimate partners' expressions and emotions. Because borderlines lack that resilient layer of the ego that relies heavily on reality testing, perception, and judgment, the healthy layer never develops. The study concluded that women with primitive defenses and identity diffusion were less accurate in predicting their partners' emotions than were women in whom these traits were less pronounced.

DEPRIVATION VERSUS PRIVATION

Another way narcissistic couples bond is through their "privations"—more specifically, the transaction between deprivation and privation, a distinction noted by Giovacchini (1979). Narcissists are dominated more by deprivation and borderlines suffer more from privation. For the narcissist, deprivation results in the longing for the time when mommy and baby were one. At least the narcissist is able to conjure up memory traces or images of desire when mother was able to perform as the good self-object during the crucial symbiotic phase. The major narcissistic crime arose when the mother was unable to tolerate the baby's separateness when the baby started to separate-individuate and thus abruptly disrupted the baby's symbiotic attachment. Another scenario is the birth of a sibling unexpectedly usurping the baby's position on the throne with mother. This leaves the baby in a state of forever yearning to regain the lost entitlement. These longings and strivings prevail and remain mired in idyllic omnipotence and narcissistic nostalgia.

Borderlines suffer more from privation because they never had the experience of bonding that the narcissist once had, and therefore the bond cannot be "revived." The reference is to a more primitive idea of bonding. The borderline does not have the memory of specialness that the narcissist so desperately craves to recapture.

The borderline bonds by projecting his or her intolerable mental and emotional contents inside the psychic space of the other, a defective self that the narcissist translates as being less than perfect. This unbearable state in the borderline creates a sense of disappearance or banishment into an abyss or a black hole. Borderlines are usually the products of alcoholic parents, addictive parents, parents who had to abandon their children early in life because of hospitalization or mental illness, leaving the child in a profound state of abandonment depression. The only salvation for the borderline is to resurrect the self by creating an entire drama that offers some semblance of aliveness—retaliation, victimization, psychosomatic illness, or anything else that momentarily serves to ameliorate the state of morbidity or abandonment depression that characterizes the borderline.

The bitter paradox is that the borderline is never needy enough and the narcissist is never narcissistic enough for each to get their "real" needs met. So as the narcissist aimlessly tries to recapture the lost entitlement, the borderline is busy groping for ways to bond through victimization, suicide, lateness, and so on. This is what Bion (1970) referred to as parasitic bonding,

Narcissistic/borderline partners also bond by triggering one another's V-spots. The "V-spot" is a term I created to describe the most sensitive area of emotional vulnerability, tantamount to archaic injury, that becomes aroused when one's partner hits an emotional raw spot. For the narcissist it could be a reminder of not being special, not being understood, not being listened to or properly mirrored. For the borderline, it can be any reminder of early disruption of primary "at-one-ment," abandonment, rejection, betrayal.

"You always act as though your friends are more important than I am. That's what my mother always did; my sisters and brothers always came first."

BONDING TO THE PAIN

Narcissistic/Borderline Couples and Emotional Abuse

A book of this scope cannot be complete without making reference to issues around abuse. Although when we talk about narcissistic and borderline relations we are not directly referring to abuse (domestic violence, physical or emotional), the issues around abuse must not be overlooked. Even though these couples never lay a hand on each other, they feel just as violated as those who are physically abused. The emotional pain they experience is closely aligned to what I described in my last contribution, *The Many Faces of Abuse—Treating the Emotional Abuse of High-Functioning Women,* and must not be ignored (Lachkar, 1998b, 2000). It is striking how many couples exhibiting borderline personality pathology fit within this paradigm (see Case 7 in chapter 9). Let me begin by defining emotional abuse, and then I will describe the high-functioning woman (HFW). Although the book highlights high-functioning women, it certainly has important relevance to men. It is noteworthy to mention that this book focused mainly on the victimization of women as targets of male aggression especially underscored in the section on cross-cultural issues.

Emotional abuse is defined as an ongoing process and differs from physical abuse in that one person psychologically, either consciously or unconsciously, attempts to destroy the will, needs, desires, or perceptions of the other. Although emotional abuse has been inextricably linked to physical abuse, it is insidious in nature. Physical abuse is usually cyclical and intermittent, whereas emotional abuse is continuous and omnipresent. Psychological abuse has been defined as including tactics such as ridiculing, shaming, blaming, criticizing, threatening, and neglecting the partners' emotional needs. According to Loring (1994), there are two types of psychological abuse: overt and covert. Overt abuse is openly demeaning and defacing (e.g., verbal remarks, put-downs, constant criticisms); covert abuse is more subtle, hidden, but no less devastating. Until now, we have not had a clear definition of what constitutes emotional abuse or therapeutic guidelines for treating the distinct problems it causes the HFW (or high-functioning man) who is verbally and psychologically mistreated (Lachkar, 1998b; see also Case 4 in chapter 9).

Defining High-Functioning Women

These are women (and men) who function at an exquisitely high level in many aspects of their lives (lawyers, doctors, business executives, artists, supermoms). Because she displays a superb false self, the HFW can operate at a very high level at the workplace, but as soon as she comes home there awakens the most primitive and regressed side (also known as splitting), especially in the face of an abusive spouse.

She may be aware that she is being abused, but because she has been exposed to trauma in early childhood she often denies it, feels she deserves it, or feels that everything is her fault (see Case 4). Reality and reality testing does not offer relief. "Is this really happening to me or am I imagining it?" These women often play the role of caretakers or of the overly responsible parentified child, forced in early years to relinquish their childhood to perform adult functions for their parents or their siblings.

The following is a letter received from a high-functioning university professor from France.

"I have been trying for nearly a year and a half to recover from an extremely abusive relationship with a man who I classify as a malignant narcissist. We were visiting his mother in her house in Austria. In the middle of the night I asked my boyfriend where I could use the toilet. He vehemently refused and warned me that I dare not awaken his mother [the couple was staying in a basement that had only a sink]. I got desperate and jumped on the sink and peed. He then yelled and screamed at me, blaming me for breaking the sink. As it turned out, there was no damage, but he would not stop blaming me for causing a disruption, awakening his mother, and furthermore he never apologized."

The treatment of these women stirs up many major challenges, e.g., how to remain empathic to the abuser while at the same time confronting the aggression, how to introduce the victim to their "internal abusers" without making the victim feel responsible or deserving of the abuse, and how gradually to "wean" the couple away from "the relationship" and to self-development.

We obviously cannot touch on all these challenges confronting therapists treating emotionally abusive couples, but it is important to briefly note how the same dialectics between the internal and external abuser is operative within all aspects of couple therapy.

Why is it that partners stay in painful conflictual relationships? Why is it that they refuse to heed our "good advice" and instead repeat the same destructive behaviors over and over? Why is it that even after a divorce or separation these individuals maintain a bond, albeit a destructive one? As Grotstein (1987a) has illustrated, any attachment is better than no attachment. As bad as the pain is, it is still better than facing the emptiness, the abyss, the black hole, the void. "At least when I mutilate I know I'm alive! I exist!"

There are those individuals who cannot feel a semblance of aliveness unless they are fused/bonded to another in a maladaptive attachment. In addition, the pain is familiar. It is what the child got used to. Another reason is that the disparaging partner who is cruel and sadistic can also be loving and kind. This fuels the already existing confusion and the fantasy that "If I behave, I will be loved."

INTERNAL/EXTERNAL OBJECTS

As mentioned in chapter 1, Fairbairn's (1940, 1946), notion of bonding to bad internal objects has had a major influence on couples therapy. He provided a platform for us to consider why couples stay in painful, conflictual, and destructive relationships. Fairbairn expanded Klein's notion of the good and bad breast to include the idea that the ego does not split merely into two parts but into a multitude of subdivisions (rejecting, tantalizing, tormenting, withholding, unavailable object) to help explain why people stay forever faithful to "bad" internal objects. Inspired by Fairbairn's work, I have extrapolated the concept of "internal/external" objects to illuminate the relentless propensity of narcissistic/borderline partners to hold on to their bad internal objects. As bad as the pain is, it is familiar, and it is better than facing the abyss, the black hole, the void. Because pain is inextricably linked to the love object it also becomes highly charged, sexualized, and eroticized—known as "traumatic bonding."

There can always be an internal abuser, an internal betrayer, an internal rejector, an internal abandoner/withholder, but there can also be an internal part of oneself that tends to identify or overidentify with that which is being projected.

In the narcissistic/borderline relationship, unpleasurable affective experience resulting from the intense relationship between internal and external objects is transported to the other partner via the process of projective identification. The shift is away from external reality to a magnified ego, which has severed most object ties with whole external objects. These internal roles have been assigned long ago. Ogden's book, *The Primitive Edge of Experience* (1989)—an exquisite amalgam of the contributions of Fairbairn (1944, 1946)—represents a major breakthrough in understanding how people with personality disorders "have too much glue" to their internal objects and how emotional involvement with their internal objects is so intense that it precludes almost all contact with external reality (see footnote in Odgen, p. 85).

"Why do I always end up with the narcissistic, unavailable men? My first husband was a scientist, lost in his experiments, my second, a concert violinist, and the third, a doctor on call 24 hours a day. I finally thought I would settle for an elderly retired man, but all he did was talk about his kids and grandchildren and spend all his time with them."

Internal objects refer to an intrapsychic process whereby unconscious fantasies are split off, denounced, and projected to create an inner world that strives to but cannot maintain synchronicity. When these inner compositions meet with pressure from and clash with the outer world, the response is felt to be threatening and persecutory. It is at this juncture that they are denounced and split off. Addressing the internal world enables the partners to feel more in control, less hopeless, more contained, more structured and grounded.

Klein's (1957) elaboration on Freud's unconscious fantasies includes the infant's ability to perceive the world as a good breast or bad breast—good when it feels nourished and loved, and bad when it feels deprived of nurturance and sustenance. Because of the borderline's tendency to split and project overwhelming feelings of anger and rage, it is important for the therapist to help the borderline partner get in contact with the internal object that he or she identifies with. The skilled therapist must find a way to do this without making the borderline feel responsible for the mistreatment.

"No one has the right to make you feel like a nothing, but if there is an internal part of you that feels like a nothing, then you are more inclined to identify with the negativity your partner projects onto you."

Klein has intimated that in some relationships one partner (the borderline) will act out destructive impulses while the other partner (the narcissist) holds back. Because people with narcissist and borderline disorders have withdrawn from their object world or attachment to external objects, their behaviors and communication become quite confusing. The use/misuse of aggression and the introjective/projective process not only make their behavior hard to recognize but also evoke enormous countertransference in the therapist. "They just don't get it!" This requires considerable insight and an especially attentive ear on the part of the therapist, who needs to sort out the partners' dynamic interplay with their internal objects.

Ignoring the internal world with its projections, misperceptions, and distortions may lead to a form of collusion, for example, the tendency to evacuate or blame others for all shortcomings in the relationship. I am not suggesting that environmental or external forces are to be disregarded, but if the primary focus is on the external, we are in danger of undermining the importance of the internal conflict as a vigorous source of analytic investigation.

Example: The "Exciting" Object. To offset a state of internal dullness and boredom, a borderline husband leaves his wife and four children to have an affair with an "exciting" woman. Even though the "exciting" woman cheats, lies, and cajoles, he claims he is madly in love with her and can't live without her. What needs to be addressed is the internal dullness that is defensively disavowed by turning to exciting objects (see Case 3 in chapter 9). "Even though I know she's lying and sleeping around with other guys, I still love her!"

Often narcissists and borderlines turn to the wrong self objects; this keeps the partners in a circular relationship and reinforces their delusions, boredom, confusion, anxiety, dullness, and emptiness. Internal objects have been associated with psychosomatic illness, claustrophobic anxiety, panic attacks, alexithymia, and asthma in borderline and psychotic personalities. Mason (personal communications, 1988) believed that the fragmentation leading to psychosis can result from anxiety that is the psychic equivalent of a powerful internal enemy. Grotstein (1981) confirmed this position from another perspective. He noted that an internal object is characterized by qualities of projective identification and of the epistemophilic instinct in the patient, which casts a rich clinical light on a powerful internal persecutory force. I have combined the Freudian description and the Kleinian view of an internal object with a self-psychological view of an external object to add further dimension to the explanation of how narcissist and borderline couples intertwine.

PROJECTIVE IDENTIFICATION

Klein's (1952) concept of the projective identification process, expanded by others (Bion, 1968; Grotstein, 1981), is a valuable vehicle in the treatment of marital conflict. It helps us understand the tangled web couples weave. The introjective/projective process is the transportation system in the "dance" of the narcissistic/borderline partners, the way in which their dynamics are transported back and forth. Projective identification is an unconscious process whereby both partners mutually project back and forth onto one another. It is a procedure that translocates and splits off unwanted parts of the self and unwittingly places them onto the other, where they are resurrected as bizarre and foreign objects. This mechanism provides the basis for what narcissistic/borderline couples experience as betrayal, manipulation, coercion, and trickery. Projective identification by its very nature strips the psyche of its resources. The worst side effect is the loss of self-identity. In fact, when this defense mechanism is operative, one is easily coerced into playing out certain roles cast upon one (see the Case of Linda and Bob earlier in this chapter).

In order for treatment to be effective with narcissistic and borderline patients, it is essential that the therapist understand the different forms of projective identification. Bion saw projective identification as essentially healthy, whereas Klein saw it as destructive. In his "Attacks on Linking" (1959), Bion claimed that an infant needs a container to express intolerable pain and an object onto which to project painful affects, transforming them into something useful. As we have noted earlier, projective identification unconsciously conveys feelings of helplessness, and the need to attack is a way of showing the other partner what it feels like to be misused, abused, or abandoned.

According to Brandchaft and Stolorow (1984), the application of projective identification is felt to be a detriment to the subjective experience of the patient. Self-psychologists are doubtful if this defense mechanism truly exists. They don't believe that people are deliberately trying to sabotage the self-object bond, but rather view it as a disruption in the self-object bond.

It is also important to understand the various motives behind the introjective process versus the projective process. Klein described the process of introjection and projection as a dynamic interplay of forces in relation to projective identification. In love relationships one (often the narcissist) internalizes and idealizes the love object. When the idealized person disappoints, love is gone, and feelings are turned inward to become self-hate and self-persecution (Lachkar, 1983). The self-persecution often acts to ward off annihilation. When borderlines are endangered, they try to get rid of the hostile internal object by splitting off and projecting. Klein (1975) suggested that the internalization of the breast as the first good object includes a considerable amount of narcissistic libido. When the breast is experienced as hostile, it becomes destructive and, metaphorically speaking, an adjunct to the death wish. In the above examples the projector does not see his or her partner as a whole object, someone with separate needs and feelings; instead, the partner exists solely to provide a function for the projector.

Dual Projective Identification

Projective identification is only a one-way process. I therefore developed the concept of "dual projective identification," a two-way process that is more suitable for conjoint therapy. Dual projection identification functions something like a reversal of roles, whereby one partner wants to get rid of or destroy in the other what he does not like in himself (dependency needs). Just as the narcissist shames the borderline for having needs he has long ago split off, the borderline stirs up guilt in the narcissist for being less than perfect. The borderline attacks, the narcissist withdraws, the borderline feels guilty, the dance starts all over again. These vacillating processes keep the partners in a state of confusion, chaos, and ambivalence as they struggle to work through their unresolved, unconscious conflicts. Dual projective identification expresses feelings of helplessness within both partners and underlies the need for the partners to attack to show others how it feels to be misused, abused, or displaced.

Dual projective identification is an intricate concept. In single projective identification, the projections with which one identifies are part of the self. In dual projective identification, one person may be projecting feelings of deprivation onto his partner while the other partner may be projecting guilt. We may find a narcissistic partner withdrawing from the borderline because of fear of intimacy and closeness, which to him may represent the loss of a grandiose tie with a self-object. The borderline may experience the narcissist as not caring and thus may respond with crippling defenses.

"He abandons me like my father; I then attack him like his mother. When he abandons me I feel helpless and worthless. Then when I attack him he feels guilty and wants to withdraw."

The following case illustrates how each partner identifies with the other's negative projections, and how each joins the other's pathology.

The Case of Rachel and Moses

Rachel, the insatiable narcissistic wife, and Moses, her engineer borderline husband, were engaged in a folie à deux. Rachel is a shopaholic, a deprived woman with a severely impoverished childhood. She projects onto her borderline husband feelings that he is never enough, will never amount to anything. The net result—no matter how much he does, no matter how much he gives—he is castrated and viewed as an abject failure. When he complains or attempts to stand up to her, he is viewed as a victim. "There you go, always complaining, wanting people to feel sorry for you!"

Moses then projects onto Rachel feelings of nonentitlement. "All you do is spend, spend, spend, spend. All you care about is your appearance and what others think of you!" The more he complains, the more she shops and spends. Furthermore, Moses complains that the more he defends or attempts to stand up for himself, the more she attacks. No matter how much he gives her, it is never enough. "More! More! More!" But what Moses doesn't know is that he is also insatiable, albeit in the reverse direction. He is never satisfied with himself, no matter how hard he tries to achieve, to accomplish things. He always expects more of himself. "I am never enough; I can't achieve what I want to achieve; I can never do what others can do" (insatiable display of self-persecution). "I only signed one contract today; the other engineers got at least two."

In the dance of their mutual projective identification, Rachel and Moses each project onto the other the state of nothingness. For Rachel it is her never-ending sense of entitlement; for Moses it is his never-ending, all-consuming sense of victimization. Rachel paints the more obvious picture of the perpetrator in that she is forthright and overtly displays an abundance of desires that can lead to their financial demise. His insatiability is more covert; he is a "closet perpetrator" in that he spends endless session hours complaining, describing persecution, playing the victim. His belief that he can never be enough leads to emotional bankruptcy.

The therapist can interpret: "If there is no Rachel around attacking, shaming, blaming, then there is an internal, insatiable mother/Rachel voice, part of you that persecutes and blames: 'You're not doing enough, you're not doing it right, you are never enough.' So if Rachel is insatiable and you identify with this internal insatiable object, then you have colluded in the dance (folie à deux), and this can create a terrible mess."

DIAGNOSTIC DISTINCTIONS

The profile of the narcissistic/borderline couple constantly shifts as each partner stirs up unresolved issues in the other. Since narcissistic/borderline traits, states, and characteristics are not clear entities and tend to vacillate, diagnosis can be elusive. Ironically, when the borderline progresses in treatment, he or she becomes more narcissistic (there is nothing worse than a narcissistic borderline). In addition, an individual may exhibit both narcissistic and borderline characteristics simultaneously, further confusing the issue. It is challenging enough for therapists to diagnose individual personality disorders, let alone make a "couple diagnosis." Couple therapy brings out highly charged emotions, and these dynamics help the therapist make the diagnosis. Therapy encourages the partners to bring to the forefront their most fragile and vulnerable selves. In time, the dominant themes emerge. If one partner is more inclined to exhibit a constant need for approval and to prove his or her "specialness," a tentative diagnosis of narcissistic personality disorder is assigned. If, on the other hand, the one partner has a pervasive disturbance that centers around abandonment issues, a tentative diagnosis of borderline personality disorder is assigned.

In one case I supervised, the therapist was not able to note the qualitative differences between the partner more inclined toward narcissistic pathology and the one more inclined toward borderline pathology; she treated both as if they had similar vulnerabilities. The couple initially came to treatment because the narcissistic husband was in a state of devastation over his wife's affairs. The therapeutic failure occurred because the therapist turned the focus to the "reason" the wife had the affairs, rather than the narcissistic injury and pain created by the affairs. The chapter on treatment will provide further discussion on why therapeutic bonding with the narcissist must be a first priority.

Many authors do not distinguish between narcissistic and borderline vulnerabilities (see Cases 8 and 9 in chapter 9) and simply characterize both of these disorders as "narcissistic vulnerabilities in couples" (Lansky, 1981; Solomon, 1985, 1986) or label a person with both syndromes as having disorders of the self. This infers that it is the primary task of the partners to provide self-object functions for one another. It is my view that while these couples are suffering from primary deficits and are in a primitive or regressed state, it is impossible for them to provide self-object or containing functions. It is therefore up to the therapist to perform these functions.

CONCLUSION

In this chapter, we have strived to shed additional light on what keeps narcissistic couples together and to develop a further understanding of their intricate interactions. Narcissistic/borderline couples express their pain by blindly repeating their dysfunctional behaviors without learning or profiting from experience. They are engaged in painful, ongoing, circular patterns of behavior that require the intervention of a knowledgable, sensitive therapist. The uncertainties of diagnosis have been acknowledged, as have the difficulties of differentiating between borderline and narcissist states. The partners in these beleaguered relationships are in complicity with one another as they move through their psychological dance, create their unending drama, and forge an ultimately unsatisfying bond. The narcissistic/borderline couple forms relational love bonds through attachments to internal and external objects that ignite the flame to fuel them. The local transmitter is the process of projective identification or dual projective identification, which casts the roles of the partners as designed or pre-scripted through their attachments to internal objects.

Couple therapy is an experience that occurs among three persons: the two partners and the therapist. It is a deep emotional experience involving intense communication and deep-seated feelings that starts with the profound challenges of a primitive relationship and matures into the awareness of healthy dependency needs and mutual respect. With each session the curtain opens, and the opportunity for a new script begins.

Chapter *4*

Marital Theatrics

The Psychodynamics of the Narcissistic/Borderline Couple

The dance between the narcissist/borderline partners includes complex psychodynamics that shift between guilt/shame, envy/jealousy, and omnipotence/dependency. The dynamic flow between the partners involves such defense mechanisms as idealization and devaluation, internal and external objects, splitting and projective identification, introjection and projection, which continually impact the couple's judgment, reality testing, and ability to think. At the core of the narcissist/borderline relationship is a duel between vulnerability and omnipotence. Interacting dynamically is particularly useful in treating intermarriages, ethnically diverse couples, or same sex or bisexual couples. Given that it is not up to the therapist to judge or prejudge same sex couples, even though society is preoccupied with male/female identifications, the cutting edge of the treatment lies primarily in locking into the underlying dynamics (guilt, shame, envy, control, domination), and the projections thereof. (See the case below.)

THE CASE OF NATASHA AND JERI (SAME SEX COUPLE)

Natasha and Jeri have been together for 3 years in a tumultuous on and off relationship. Natasha has two children from a previous marriage. Natasha finds Jeri far more supportive and loving to her and her children than her previous husband was, but cannot allow herself to give freely to Jeri because of an inordinate amount of shame. While Natasha experiences shame, Jeri on the other hand is plagued with guilt. This case focuses primarily on Natasha, illustrating how the therapist gradually shifts from issues around "gayness" to the surrounding issues around shame, and how shame can impede and impact the ego's capacity to function at it's highest level.

Natasha: We had great sex last night.

Jeri: Yeah, but we usually have to first have lots of drinks or get high.

Therapist: Why is that?

Natasha: I don't know, it just is.

[Silence]

Jeri: Maybe because we both enjoy each other but feel uncomfortable about breaking up our families and enjoying this kind of a relationship.

Th: You must have had some good reasons, otherwise you would not have left.

Natasha: Oh, yeah for sure, my husband was abusive, he didn't make a living, and he totally ignored our kids.

Jeri: Anyway, I feel guilty. When we talk about our relationship or when we are out with others, everyone marvels how great we are, how natural it is for us to be together. Yet, when we are together we have our doubts.

Th: Well of course, it is harder to be in a gay relationship than a heterosexual one, but the fact is that you are and our society has adjusted. It does sound as though you both may be feeling guilty.

Natasha: I don't feel guilty, I don't have any remorse. In fact, I would do it again. Being with Jeri is the best thing that ever happened to me. I just feel embarrassed sometimes like I want to hide, especially when I go to school for the kids for an open house or something like that.

Th: That is very astute on your part Natasha. Yes, I see things clearer now. You're right this is not so much about guilt.

Natasha: Then what is it about?

Th: I think you are talking about something much earlier.

Natasha: Like what?

Th: Like shame!

Natasha:	Shame?
Th:	Yes, shame has to do with the impulse to hide, to not be seen, but I don't think it is shame solely from being in a gay relationship. I think it comes from somewhere else. After all, no one is chastising or ridiculing you, or leaving you out. In fact, as you say, most everyone respects you and includes you and your daughters.
Natasha:	I don't know.
Jeri:	Of course you do! You remember when your parents got divorced how you refused to go to school? How you felt like an outsider?
Natasha:	Yes, but what has that got to do with my being with you?
Jeri:	It has everything to do with me. You can't even make love to me unless you get high as a kite.
Th:	Thanks Jeri, that is helpful, that is what I am referring to. So we are not just talking about the shame about being in a gay relationship. When your father left and you felt like an outsider, the issues were not about gayness. I can't help you with your gender choice or lifestyle, but I can help you understand how shame can interfere with your ability to enjoy a deep and meaningful relationship with one another.
Natasha:	I just can't seem to let myself go without the booze or the drugs. I feel inhibited.
Th:	Yet when you paint or draw as an artist you are very uninhibited. You let yourself go, and look at the work you produce.
Natasha:	That is different. It is a different dimension. I feel safe there.
Th:	Well, my job is to help you feel internally safe here, not to taint or intoxicate the canvas with old archaic hurts and injuries. To be as creative and free in your relationship as you are with your canvas.
Jeri:	I'm the one who suffers from guilt. I have enormous guilt being in a gay relationship, and Natasha doesn't make things better.
Th:	In what way?
Jeri:	She always criticizes me for not being perfect enough, not doing things the way they "should be done." She has a superego that has run amuck. She makes me feel guilty when I try to display my affection publicly; because of her shame, she makes me feel guilty.
Th:	Well, it is one thing for Jeri to project her shaming self onto you, but it is another for you to identify with Natasha's "negativity."

These are both good points you are raising. Natasha feels plagued by shame and you, Jeri, by guilt. It becomes then a dance between guilt and shame. These dynamics are the basis of how we will proceed in our work here, for now we are focusing on Natasha's shame and how this contributes to her holding back from you, and not allowing her to display her full range of affection, which she has grandly prohibited. We will stop now and I will look forward to seeing you next week at this time.

NEEDS

There are similarities in the way narcissists and borderlines experience needs. Both partners have difficulty expressing needs in clear, healthy, and direct ways, and both experience needs as bizarre objects intruding into their psychic worlds. The major distinction lies in how each partner experiences anxiety and unconsciously defends against needs. Narcissists are dominated more by guilt, and borderlines more by shame.

For the borderline, needs are an expression of shame dominated by persecutory anxiety and envy; they are experienced internally as bad, explosive, intrusive forces. Many borderline patients view needs as akin to malignant tumors, toxic elements, or infestations that invade the psyche. "Why should I talk about needs? It will just open up a can of worms." Borderline partners often confuse their healthy needs with aggression and impose their demands upon others to express feelings of hurt, discomfort, longing, and rejection. "It is not your needs that are unhealthy; it is the way you demand them that is!"

Many borderlines suffer from a persecutory superego as they identify with a suffocating/rejecting/abusive internal mother who programs the child to oblige by the mantra, "Don't ask; don't need anything. Enough already!" This internal mother persecutes and nags, as if to say, "It is because of you that I drink and gain weight. Each time you nag me I run straight to the bottle." The borderline learns to express feelings of hurt and discomfort through alternate routes of expression—such primitive modes as victimization, suicide, and psychosomatic illness. Another defense against the suffocating/depriving internal mother is "knowing" what others will say or believing that others will magically know what the borderline needs. "If she loves me, she will know what I need and will not have to ask," or "If he really loves me he will know what I want for my birthday." Borderlines might not get what they need because they do not express their needs directly; instead they rely on "magical thinking" to convey those needs. The borderline lives in a state of martyrdom, struggling to preserve a sense of self. "Pardon me for existing" can often sum up the borderline's attitude.

The narcissist, unlike the borderline, suffers from a harsh and punitive superego. To guard against dependency needs and feelings of vulnerability, they develop omnipotent fantasies and manic defenses. To be vulnerable is tantamount to being weak and less than perfect. The narcissist considers needs as subservient to a powerful, demanding superego that is relentless and restrictive. "You don't need to ask anyone for help; that is beneath you. You don't need anything or anybody. You are above everyone." By projecting their unwanted, needy parts onto the borderline, narcissists take delight in watching their borderline partners wiggle and squirm as they become needier and needier. "Why can't you just leave me alone and let me be with my friends?!" says the narcissist. In treatment, narcissists have unrealistic expectations and place outrageous demands upon the therapist: "Give me a diagnosis! Tell me what the outcome is! I want to know!" Aggrandizement gets in the way of learning and taking in the therapeutic breast. Instead, they want the "quick fix." They might say, "I tried it once and it didn't work!" The therapist must find a creative way of bonding with an aspect of the narcissist's life that is important to him or her:

"This problem has been going on for quite some time, and it is going to take some time to 'fix' it. It's delusional and unrealistic to think that trying something once will make things work. It's like practicing your serve when you play tennis; you may make mistakes, but as you do it again and again you get better. Expressing your needs also takes practice. It may seem odd at first, like hitting a backhand, but after a while you will play a better game!"

Narcissists typically deny their "smallness" and project feelings of superiority onto others. They cannot tolerate learning from others or allowing themselves to be vulnerable as a normal intimate partner can. Instead, they are relentless in proving their specialness. To admit to any wrongdoings or weakness is tantamount to injuring the image of perfection. One narcissistic husband was so defensive that every time talk of needs came up, he would respond, "Need? What's a need? I don't know what you're talking about!" (see the case of Linda and Bob in chapter 3).

Borderline and narcissistic disorders are entangled and symbiotically fused. As the partners play off one another, they invariably split off their needs. Narcissistic partners avoid needs by believing they have a divine right to their lavish desires and their own self-indulgent schemes. Narcissists are not empathic with the borderlines' needs. Narcissists refuse to recognize their own needs not only to their borderline partner but also to the therapist. "I don't know why I'm here!" they may say to the therapist. "I don't need you and I don't need this relationship."

As the balance of power shifts back and forth between states of om-nipotence and dependence, narcissists become increasingly intoxicated with their own power and the outrageous demands from the superego. As a re-sult, they develop manic defenses to ward off facing their legitimate needs. Ironically, the narcissist is never narcissistic enough to really get what he or she wants.

An aspect that affects the borderline's capacity to "need" is the perva-sive sense of deprivation the borderline experiences. When out of balance, the borderline's false self takes over and can for a short while play-act at being the perfect mirroring object for the narcissist. Consistent withdrawal and neglect by the narcissist provide powerful triggers for the borderline to become even more demanding, envious, and destructive. When borderlines relinquish their own needy selves, it is not uncommon for annihilation anxiety, panic, and feelings of helplessness and powerlessness to take over. To guard against this, borderlines will try to control others with their eyes and their tales of victimization. The task for the therapist is to assure both partners that their needs are vital, that wanting and needing are both healthy parts of the psyche.

APPROVAL

It cannot be emphasized too strongly how important it is for the therapist to understand the difference between what approval means for the narcis-sist and what approval means for the borderline. Narcissists need approval to validate the nascent self, to prove they are really talented and brilliant. They require constant validation and mirroring responses from self objects in order to prove their sense of specialness. The borderline, on the other hand, is trying to prove he exists as an entity in itself. Because borderlines have difficulty relying on their perceptual apparatus or their experiences, they need the other to "bear testimony."

If these differences in the need for approval are not noted, the result could be severe fragmentation not only for the relationship but for personal development. Ironically, the search for approval leads to a stripping of in-ternal resources, the part of the psyche that can realistically measure suc-cess and accomplishment. The psychological tragedy is that when one turns to others for constant recognition, validation, and approval, one cannot hold onto one's own experiences as measurements of success emanating from external reality.

Example: A very narcissistic movie producer seeks constant approval and validation from the director. In time the director fires the producer, thinking he is insecure and unable to rely on his own creative insights and instincts.

THE SUPEREGO

The literature refers to many types of superegos. The Freudian view depicts an introjected whole figure, a parental voice that judges and is strictly prohibitive. Klein believed that the infant first introjects not whole but part objects: the breast or the penis. The distinction between Freud's internal object and Klein's internal object helps one understand guilt and shame. Freud's concern about what others think is opposed to Klein's primitive persecutory superego, with its preoccupation that having needs, thoughts, and desires can destroy or invade another. Mason (1981) differentiated between Freud's more mature superego, which shadows the Oedipus complex, and Klein's more primitive and persecutory one, which contains the child's more fragmented ego at the level of the paranoid–schizoid position. Freud's superego is responsible for morals, conscience, ethics, and religion. It is the internalized image that continues to live inside the child—controlling, threatening, or punishing whenever the child's Oedipal wishes attempt to make themselves known (Mason, 1981, p. 141). According to Mason, much of the literature describes the severe, harsh, murderous nature of the superego, suggesting that the primitive superego (the fear of being destroyed or the "death instinct") begins at birth. Mason associated Meltzer's (1964–1965) description of paranoid anxiety with internalized terror (because of "dead objects" and "dead babies"). The significance of this work is the implication that the kind of anxiety emanating from the primitive superego is of an explosive nature and different from the more developed superego.

OBJECT RELATIONS

Because of their tendency to fuse with their objects, borderlines, in particular, misperceive and distort reality. I believe object relations theory best describes these dynamics within the borderline syndrome. Because of paranoid anxiety, borderlines tend to distort and misperceive who is abandoning whom. They unwittingly abandon both themselves and others (the "internal abandoner"), then turn things around so that they are regarded as the victims. Not only are they fearful of being abandoned by the narcissist, they also fear that the therapist will betray or abandon them. I am reminded of a borderline husband who confessed to me during a telephone call that he was having an affair.

In the conjoint session he was terrified that I would betray him by revealing the "secret" to his spouse, or that I would abandon him by terminating the treatment. I let him know that, unlike his mother, I would not abandon or betray him but would be available to help him understand which of his unmet needs led to his "betraying" himself. Fearful of being left by therapist and spouse, borderlines hesitate to express their needs (see Case 18 in chapter 9). Because they have poor boundaries, narcissistic/borderline partners get caught up in their own delusional system, which affects perception, judgment, and reality.

Part Objects

The beginning of the paranoid–schizoid position is marked by the infant's awareness of his mother as a "part object." The first part-object relational unit is the feeding experience with the mother, and the infant's relation to the breast, initiating both oral-libidinal and oral-destructive impulses. Klein (1957) believed that the breast is the child's first possession; because it is so desired it also becomes the source of the infant's envy, greed, and hatred, and is therefore susceptible to the infant's fantasized attacks. The infant internalizes the mother as good or bad, or, more specifically, as a "part object" (a "good breast" or "bad breast"). As the breast is felt to contain a great part of the infant's death instinct (persecutory anxiety), it simultaneously establishes libidinal forces, giving way to the baby's first ambivalence. One part of the mother is loved and idealized, while the other is destroyed by the infant's oral, anal, sadistic, or aggressive impulses. Klein referred to this as pathological splitting.

Part–object functioning refers to what the parent can provide—e.g., in infancy, the breast, in later life, money and material objects—not what the child can provide for the parent. It is a one-way process. This is crucial in couple treatment because people dominated by these primitive defense mechanisms remain forever loyal to the "good-breast mother," and never allow others to impose their "badness." Thus, "whatever happened is not my fault; I am good and you are bad!" It is baffling to most clinicians how people with personality disorders resort to part-object functioning to create an entire object world to the exclusion of external reality. The challenge we face as clinicians is to help couples understand that what they perceive as love may not be love but an addiction, or what they perceive as attachment may not be attachment but abandonment. Persons who function via part objects cannot view their mates as individuals with whole object needs. They see them only as servants to part objects.

Whole Objects

The beginning of the depressive position is marked by the infant's awareness of his mother as a "whole object." As the infant matures, and as verbal expression increases, he achieves more cognitive ability and acquires the capacity to love mother as a separate person with separate needs, feelings, and desires. This newly acquired concern for the object helps him integrate and gradually learn to control his impulses—thus the budding signs of reparation. As the infant's development continues, there is a lessening of persecutory anxiety and a diminution of splitting mechanisms. Guilt and jealousy become the replacement for shame and envy. Ambivalence and guilt are experienced and tolerated in relation to whole objects. One no longer seeks to destroy it or the Oedipal rival (father and siblings, those who take mother away), but can begin to live amicably with them. In conjoint treatment, couples who begin to see one another as whole objects are developmentally available to come to terms with guilt and make reparation for all past transgressions (see "Three Phases of Treatment," in chapter 8).

Self Objects

Narcissists often lose contact with the self and thereby with the passion inside the self. What needs to be interpreted for the narcissist is the internal mother who says, "You're too good to even bother with such a person." However, by avoiding confrontation, one also avoids passion and creativity! "I can't tell my wife [partner] she's boring!" Getting rid of something by turning to "passion" or mania paradoxically diminishes the passion and creates further disappointment and narcissistic injury to the self. The narcissist's need for self objects, the formation of positive ties, and the need to turn to a variety of external sources can help explain what the person's real self-object needs are. The formation of healthy object ties for both the narcissist and the borderline is vital and is not to be confused with fusion or immersion. Often narcissists and borderlines turn to the wrong self objects; this keeps the partners in a circular relationship and reinforces their delusions, boredom, confusion, anxiety, dullness, and emptiness.

Internal objects have been associated with psychosomatic illness, claustrophobic anxiety, panic attacks, alexithymia, and asthma in borderline and psychotic personalities. Mason (1981) believed that the fragmentation leading to psychosis can result from anxiety that is the psychic equivalent of a powerful internal enemy. Grotstein (1981) confirmed this position from another perspective. He noted that an internal object is characterized by qualities of projective identification and of the epistemophilic instinct in the patient, which casts a rich clinical light on a powerful internal persecutory force. I have combined the Freudian description and the Kleinian view of an internal object with a self-psychological view of an external object to add further dimension to the explanation of how narcissist and borderline couples intertwine.

THE PROJECTIVE/INTROJECTIVE PROCESS

One of Klein's most useful concepts for conjoint therapy is that of the projective/introjective process, how one person is inclined to project a negative feeling, and how the other tends to identify or overidentify with that which is being projected.

Klein used external objects as a means of giving concrete expression to theoretical constructs and brought to light the use of projection and introjection as defensive procedures. Underlying the borderline, in my view, is the defense mechanism of projection, while narcissistic individuals are more inclined toward introjection. Klein's theories help us understand persecutory anxiety, which is of key importance in the treatment of marital conflict.

I suggest that the study of internal objects through the process of projection is most appropriate for the borderline, whereas it is more effective for the narcissist to conceptualize feelings of idealization and self-absorption through the process of introjection. Introjection motivates the narcissist to compete for the starring role, to live up to an internal, idealized imago whose standards are almost impossible to meet. Narcissists are continually struggling to get the steps of the dance right. But no matter how hard they try, practice, or repeat the experience, the internalized imago remains elusive. Understanding the projective and introjective processes helps the therapist interpret how the partners, in their similar dynamics, glaringly reflect one another.

It is also important to understand the various motives behind the introjective process versus the projective process. Klein described the process of introjection and projection as a dynamic interplay of forces in relation to projective identification. In love relationships one (often the narcissist) internalizes and idealizes the love object. When the idealized person disappoints, love is gone, and feelings are turned inward to become self-hate and self-persecution (Lachkar, 1983). The self-persecution often acts to ward off annihilation. When borderlines are endangered, they try to get rid of the hostile internal object by splitting off and projecting. Klein (1975) suggested that the internalization of the breast as the first good object includes a considerable amount of narcissistic libido. When the breast is experienced as hostile, it becomes destructive and, metaphorically speaking, an adjunct to the death wish.

Projective Identification

To distinguish when it is more efficient to use internal objects and when to use self objects, we need to look to projective identification. This is a phenomenon that occurs in a conjoint treatment setting and perhaps approximates Klein's (1957) notion of "confusional states," in which there are blurred boundaries between what is coming from outside the psyche and what is coming from within (projective and introjective processes). In single projective identification, one partner projects onto the other and the other partner identifies with the projection.

In order for treatment to be effective, it is important that the therapist understand the different forms of projective identification. Bion saw projective identification as essential and healthy; Melanie Klein saw it as destructive. In his "Attacks on Linking," Bion (1959) claimed that an infant needs a container to express intolerable pain, as well as an object onto which to project painful affects to transform them into something useful. Projective identification is a term Klein used to describe certain communications between the mother and infant. I am using the term to express feelings of helplessness within the couple and the need to attack to show others how it feels to be misused, abused, or displaced.

Bion detailed the healthy use of projective identification as an expression of protest and outrage. He transformed Klein's theories, giving more meaning to an understanding relationship with the mother and the need for maternal bonding and attachment. For Bion, projective identification helps both to understand the pain and frustration and to put a chaotic, fragmented world in some structural order via the mother's ability to transform, decode, and provide alpha functions. In couple therapy, an intervention might be: "You are trying to engage me in an argument, and if I get into an argument then I'm not going to be available to give you back something meaningful that can feed you. At least you are letting me know what it feels like to get lost and why there is so much confusion."

According to Brandchaft and Stolorow (1984), as mentioned in chapter 3, the application of projective identification carries the real danger of depriving patients of the means to defend themselves, inducing paranoia that people are deliberately trying to sabotage the self-object bond. Self-psychologists are doubtful that projective defense mechanisms truly exist, and feel that falling back on interpretations of projection undermines the subjective experience of the patient. They tend not to believe that a person unconsciously tries to evoke a negative reaction in another person, but suggest that self-object failure occurred when normal function was disrupted at a phase-appropriate time during the child's formative years.

Klein (1957) claimed that structures within the ego are formed by aspects of the self that are projected onto interpersonal objects. Although she recognized the influence of external events, she did not attach much importance to them. She placed more emphasis on the internal world, along with its entire spectrum of distortions, delusions, and misperceptions. It is implied that no matter how the environment is changed, the fusion with interpersonal and internal objects is pervasive. A battered wife as victim, for example, can keep changing spouses but will repeat similar experiences within each new relationship if the external "beater" or saboteur is not interpreted as part of the internal world. Although Klein does not undermine the importance of the external world, she claims that unless internal issues are worked through, no matter how often the environment is changed the same configuration occurs again and again. This brings us to our next section. With projective identification, there must be an external object to project onto, but there must also be an internal object to identify with.

Dual Projective Identification

Projective identification is only a one-way process. I therefore developed the concept of *dual projective identification,* a two-way process that is more suitable for conjoint therapy. Dual projection identification occurs when one partner wants to get rid of some unwanted aspect, which is felt to be intolerable within. Just as the narcissist shames the borderline for having needs he has long ago split off, the borderline stirs up guilt in the narcissist for being less than perfect. The borderline attacks, the narcissist withdraws, the borderline feels guilty; consequently, the dance starts all over again. These vacillating processes keep the partners in a state of confusion, chaos, and ambivalence as they struggle to work through their unresolved, unconscious conflicts. Dual projective identification expresses feelings of helplessness within both partners and underlies the need for the partners to attack to show others how it feels to be misused, abused, or displaced.

Dual projective identification is an intricate concept. In single projective identification, the projections with which one identifies are part of the self, as if they are one's own characteristics. Suddenly, one may feel anger or rage, even though these affects may be vehemently denied. In dual projective identification, both partners mutually identify or overidentify with the negative projections of the other. One person may be projecting feelings of deprivation onto his partner while the other partner may be projecting guilt.

I believe that differentiating between the single and dual projective identification processes is crucial because we need to discover from whence the area of anxiety emanates. This is particularly difficult when couples are in collusion, are engulfed, and are consumed and lost in the dance. For instance, if we discover that through the process of single projective identification the borderline partner is projecting feelings of deprivation, we then have an opportunity to explore the primary feelings of deprivation and their etiology. Eventually, this can lead patients to not only identification to "need" needs and desires to tolerance of their own pain and anxiety their control over their own destiny.

In dual projective identification, while one partner may be projecting deprivation onto the other, the other partner may be projecting guilt. If we allow continued projective identification, affects of vigor and vitality would be reduced to mere states of submission and compliance—and possibly guilt, withdrawal, and isolation. Typical comments might be: "I'll just die if you ever leave me! I just can't live without you!" Or, "You're putting too much pressure on us!"

Dual projective identification might involve a narcissistic partner withdrawing from the borderline because of fear of intimacy and closeness. For the narcissist, closeness and dependency may represent the loss of a grandiose tie with a self-object. The narcissist may crave the intimacy, but may also fear that closeness would impede or destroy the omnipotent fantasy of ever connecting with and preserving the symbiotic unit: "I do love you and want to be with you, but my work comes first. Can't you understand that?" The borderline may experience the narcissist as not caring and thus may respond with crippling defenses: "He abandons me like my father; I then attack him like his mother. When he abandons me I feel helpless and worthless. Then when I attack him he feels guilty and wants to withdraw." The borderline may feel paralyzed: "I can't do anything. I wish I could be more like you and concentrate on my work, but I can't. All I can think about is being with you!"

Folie à Deux

Folie à deux is a term that extends Klein's (1957) notion of projective identification whereby two people project their delusional fantasies back and forth and engage in a foolish "dance for two." It is an example of a perverse relationship, an emotional involvement with a delusional partner (abusive, a cult leader, terrorist), who contaminates the other (usually a person of a dependent or passive nature) and who momentarily makes one "lose one's mind," especially when in a state of idealization. This happened with Freud's relationship with Fleiss when Fleiss talked Freud into believing in numerology, a very strange occurrence for two highly trained and sophisticated medical doctors.

THE ARCHAIC INJURY: AROUSING THE V-SPOT

Most clinicians are aware of the impact that the archaic injury has on treating couples. The archaic injury is a term Kohut (1971, 1977) used to refer to the child's earliest emotional injury or narcissistic vulnerability, be it the birth of a sibling, an unattuned parent, or a parent giving excessive attention

to one child over another. To punctuate the importance of continually re-
minding couples of the role their archaic injury plays in their relationship,
I devised a new concept called the "V-spot," an area of extreme vulnerability
that gets aroused when one's partner hits an emotional raw spot. In psychoanalytic terms it is the seat of the archaic injury, the epicenter of emotional
sensitivity. It is a product of early trauma that affects all relationships and
often creates inappropriate and disproportionate reactions. When the V-spot is
unwittingly aroused by one's partner, there is a loss of sensibility. Everything gets shaken and shifted in the ensuing emotional earthquake: memory,
perception, judgment, reality. The V-spot is the G-spot's emotional counter-
part. The G-spot is purely physical; the V-spot is purely emotional. I liken it
to a nuclear reactor: one strike, and it is ready to blow.

It could stem from the child who was abandoned much too early and
much too soon, or the child whose mother smothered it with too much
affection, or the child who was neglected and never touched or soothed.
Another source can be a parent, caretaker, or mother who repeats a certain
mantra, "You're not good enough, not deserving enough, too demanding,"
and so on. For men, it could be the castrating, controlling, dominating,
overwhelming mother.

"It is hard for me to give to my wife because whenever she needs something I am reminded of my mother; I feel the need to rebel and run away
from her."

Understanding the V-spot is a life-long process, but once it is discovered and tamed, the partners can function from a position of rationality
rather than one of weakness, helplessness, and vulnerability arising from
raw, tumultuous emotions.

"Should I? Shouldn't I? Should I get a divorce or should I stay? Should
I have said that or shouldn't I have? Was this my fault? Am I deserving of
the abuse or mistreatment? Did I say something wrong? Do I have the right
to ask for a raise?"

As Goethe once said, it is difficult to know what to do, especially when
so much blaming and attacking is going on!

The V-Spot: Kathy and Mathew (a Telephone Session)

This case illustrates not only how narcissistic/borderline traits tend to vacillate back and forth, but how a dysfunctional relationship can evoke old
vulnerabilities of abandonment and stir up the V-spot (archaic injuries).

Kathy met Mathew while she was a surgeon at a hospital where he was
an anesthesiologist. Subsequently they moved in together. Mathew has many
narcissistic, borderline, and schizoid characteristics, while Kathy has many
borderline and histrionic characteristics. Mathew had a very morbid child-

hood and remembers his mother abusing him whenever he asked her for something. Eventually, he stopped asking, and withdrew into a morbid depression. He remembers his mother humiliating and ridiculing him in the middle of the classroom because he forgot to take the sack lunch she had made him to school. Mathew recalled that when he was around 25, his father took him and his brothers on a ski trip. His father bought them all new ski equipment and paid for all expenses, but he asked Mathew to take care of his own costs. In the previous session Mathew complained that he felt excluded because his coworkers did not invite him to go on a group skiing trip. In the same session Kathy asked Mathew what he wanted to do for his birthday. He replied, "Nothing. I want to do nothing." What follows is from the session after that one.

Therapist:	[Greeting on phone] Good morning. This is Dr. Lachkar.
Kathy:	Hi!
Mathew:	Hi!
Kathy:	[Nervous laugh]
Th:	[Pause]
Mathew:	[Laughs and says "Hi," as though the therapist should be surprised that he's at the other end of the line.]
Th:	So, who'd like to start?
Kathy:	Mathew, you go first. Why don't you start?
Mathew:	This is the trouble. I bake like a crock pot and she like a microwave oven. Our pace is different.
Kathy:	We just got back from New York. We had some good days and some bad days, but since we got back I have been going to breeders trying to research dogs. This is something we agreed on. I discovered one breed that is low maintenance. It is at the pound, but we have to get it right away; otherwise they will put it to sleep.
Mathew:	[Silent]
Kathy:	The problem is that I can't enjoy the "joy" of getting the dog. Mathew is not involved, and I'm doing all the work, just like with everything else.
Th:	Kathy, isn't this what you have been complaining about: that you always feel you are the one that has to do everything, make vacation plans, social plans, fix the house, take care of the yard?
Mathew:	But I am the practical one and the realist. It makes me angry to see her making these quick decisions. I won't even buy a new

	jacket unless I think about it. There is a jacket that I have been wanting for a year, and I'm still deliberating.
Th:	But, that's *not* being practical; that's being anxious. After all, you did agree to get a dog and you already deliberated.
Mathew:	Yes, I did, but I have my doubts. Whenever I see other people's dogs, I enjoy playing with them. But I thank God I don't have the responsibility.
Th:	So you have ambivalent feelings? Part of you doesn't want the responsibility, but the other part of you wants to make Kathy happy. So you give in by agreeing and then you hold back.
Mathew:	I guess so. That makes sense.
Th:	That interferes with your ability to share the joys in the relationship.
Kathy:	[Feeling mirrored] But I started to worry that I was falling into the pitfall of being too critical. Mathew always feels that I'm blaming him.
Th:	You know, Mathew, I'm reminded about your concerns with your coworkers at the unit. You were telling me about the envy you feel for other physicians who have passionate interests. Maybe this is the anesthetic part of you that needs awakening, the part of you that wishes to be more like them. [Therapist is moving away from issues around "the relationship" to developmental ones.]
Mathew:	That's true.
Th:	And yet, when Kathy feels passionate about something, you seem to demean her.
Kathy:	He does that with everything.
Th:	So, Kathy has the fire and passion that you would like for yourself.
Mathew:	Yes, I do admire the way Kathy gets things done and her passion.
Th:	So although you say you're practical and realistic, maybe you are not aware that there may be some unconscious envy of Kathy's enthusiasm [detachment].
Kathy:	This is upsetting because I feel so alone, like I'm always the one who has to spark him.
Th:	Well, we will continue with this next week. And I *will* see you next week.
Mathew:	I'm not sure that I can afford next week, and I will let you know.

Th:	Mathew, now you are putting me on hold like the dog and the jacket. I'm to sit back like Kathy and wait around [couple transference]. The same thing happens here. You wait for Kathy to start the session.
Mathew:	But then I'll be a burden to you because I'm always so down and depressed.
Th:	Mathew, that's a great thing you're telling us; you're worried that you will be high maintenance like the dog. Obviously we cannot deal with that now, but for sure we will next week.
Kathy:	Sounds good.
Th:	Good. Next week, Saturday, 11 a.m.

Memory, Perception, Judgment, and Functioning

When the V-spot is triggered, the capacity to reason is affected. To use an analogy, when someone is involved in a car accident they become momentarily paralyzed and immobilized. They can't think, can't remember the name of their vehicle, can't find their wallet, forget where they put their insurance card, can't remember the make of the car. This is because perception and normal functioning are impaired by the situation. The same impairment occurs when the narcissistic/borderline couple's V-spots are triggered. They react in a similar manner. Their judgment is clouded; they are unable to function normally. Suddenly the partners feel that everything is their fault or their partner's fault. Perception becomes obscured.

Example: "Each time she storms out of the house and says she is going to divorce me, take our child away, I believe her. I always panic and feel very scared and abandoned (as I did when my mother left to go to the hospital when I was 3 years of age). Yet each time she returns. Why is my reality so askew? Why is it that I can't recognize that it is only a threat? In reality, I know she does not want to get a divorce; in fact she is Catholic and it goes against her religion."

PRIMITIVE DEFENSES

As long as the partners' primitive defenses are operative because their V-spots have been aroused, it is difficult for the therapist to discern what to do. With projection, idealization, devaluation, and splitting, one cannot get a clear sense as to what is real and what is not real in the narcissist/borderline relationship. Among the primitive defenses with which the therapist must deal are those described below.

Shame versus Guilt

Shame is inextricably linked with dependency needs. It is the virus that invades the psyche and impedes the process of reaching therapeutic success. Shame is more pronounced than guilt and occurs in the paranoid–schizoid position. Shame is the preoccupation with what others think, while guilt exists primarily between a person and his or her conscience.

Example: A narcissistic husband projects a feeling onto his wife that she is worthless, not entitled to anything, and should not need or want anything. He complains, "All you do is nag, nag, nag." Not knowing how to legitimately express her real needs, the borderline wife escalates her nagging and demanding. As she nags, he withdraws; as he withdraws, she attacks. When the wife attacks, she connects with her narcissistic husband's punitive, internalized superego. He ends up feeling guilty and she ashamed. Thus, their relationship becomes a dance between guilt and shame.

Guilt is more highly developed than shame. Related to the superego (often a harsh, critical one), guilt occurs in the depressive position and is followed by the desire to make reparation and repair damage for past acts, transgressions, or wrong-doings. Guilt is a reaction to and remorse for an act (Lansky, 1995). Shame is associated with isolation and being abandoned or shunned by the group, tribe, or society. Shame is often projected or evacuated into the other as disapproval.

Envy versus Jealousy

Envy is destructive in nature and is considered by Klein and others to be one of the most primitive and fundamental emotions. It is a two-part process, based not on love but on the intent to destroy that which is envied. Greed can fuse with envy, creating the wish to exhaust the other entirely. This stems not only from wanting to own all that is desirable, but to deplete the other so that he/she no longer contains anything enviable. Jealousy, on the other hand, is a whole-object relationship whereby one desires the object but does not seek to destroy it. Jealousy, unlike envy, has a healthy component in that there is the wish to be part of the oedipal unit, to be included in the group. Jealousy is a triangular relationship based on love, whereas envy is a two-part relationship. Jealousy is directed toward rivals (siblings/father), those who take mother away (the intruders or interlopers). Envy plagues the very thing it desires (see case study below).

Dependency/Envy (Psychodynamics): The Case of Mike and Ann

This case illustrates the importance of psychodynamics, distinguishing envy from jealousy. Mike's vulnerable self provides a perfect backdrop for Ann's display of negativity as she projects onto Mike that it is "bad" to feel jealous and want exclusivity in their relationship. Mike and Ann have been together on and off for 7 years. He wants her to give up her old boyfriends and make a final commitment to move in with him. Ann appears bewildered and shocked that he could make such a request of her.

Mike: How can you keep doing this to me? Why don't you give up your old boyfriends?

Ann: [Appears surprised] How can you ask me to give up my friends? I don't ask you to give up your friends. Of course, you don't have any anyway.

Mike: [Pleadingly] How can you keep doing this to me? Why don't you give them up? How can you expect to be in a relationship with me and still flirt with your old boyfriends?

Ann: Is it normal for him to want me to give up everything for him?

Therapist: [To Ann] Do Mike's needs seem strange to you?

Ann: These friends make me feel good, whereas with Mike I always feel guilty, as if I've done something wrong.

Mike: [Blurts out] This makes me feel that I'm not good enough for you, Ann, as if I don't exist. You seem to need all the guys even when things are going well.

[Silence]

Mike: I know her alimony is running out, and that's the only reason she will consider moving in with me.

Th: Isn't your loving Ann enough?

Mike: Well, I want to know that she loves me. Isn't that something that anyone would want to know? Look, though, what she does to me!

Ann: There he goes again. He's always so jealous!

Mike: Well, how can I stop feeling so jealous when you have all these guys?

Th: Just as you are entitled to have others appreciate, admire, and value you, as these "friends" do, then so does Mike have the right to his feelings. In this instance, Mike has the right to feel jealous.

(See also Case 6 in chapter 9.)

Omnipotence versus Dependency

The discussion of omnipotence and dependency is important because children whose formative years are deficient in maternal caretaking capacities never learn how to develop healthy dependency needs. Omnipotence is the flip side of dependency. In order to ward off intolerable feelings of smallness and helplessness, one develops a grandiose self or an omnipotent self. According to Kohut (1971, 1977), the grandiose self arises from a vulnerable self whose formative years were lacking in maternal caretaking. It is often the needy, dependent child who grows up with an omnipotent self and projects onto others, making them the needy, disgusting, dependent victim scapegoats.

"It is you that is the needy one, not me! You shouldn't have any needs. I, the narcissist, am perfect. I don't need anything."

WITHDRAWAL VERSUS DETACHMENT

Bowlby's (1969) work stressed the difference between withdrawal and detachment. Detachment is not to be confused with denial or withdrawal. Actually, withdrawal is healthier because it maintains a certain libidinal attachment to the object. When one detaches, one goes into a state of despondency. Children who are left alone, ignored, and neglected for long periods of time enter into a phase of despair. The child's active protest for the missing or absent mother gradually diminishes when the child no longer makes demands.

According to Kohut and his followers, borderline patients are not able to form self-object transference and are more subject to fragmentation than their narcissistic counterparts. Many theorists agree that borderlines operate at a far more primitive and intense level of regression than those with other personality disorders and are more susceptible to disruption. When their archaic states, their V-spots, are properly valued and their projective identification is sufficiently contained, their borderline features subside and reactions to relatively minor events become less catastrophic and severe. According to Bowlby, there is a certain segment of personalities that have completely detached from their objects. In my estimation these are the schizoid personalities with borderline characteristics. The narcissist withdraws but still maintains an attachment (the need for the object). This point is important to recognize when interacting with the couple. There is a big difference between someone withdrawing and someone detaching: "I don't care; do whatever you want. I have no opinion whatever!"

The main defense mechanisms of the narcissist are withdrawal and isolation. Narcissists will isolate themselves, leave their families, ignore others, do anything to preserve their sense of self as special. The narcissist's isolation and resulting behaviors create all kinds of fantasies in their borderline partners. Narcissists are unaware of the mortifying responses they evoke. They would rather die than face humiliation, embarrassment, or injury to the sense of self.

The most obvious withdrawal is physical, in which the narcissist walks away when feeling personally injured or misunderstood. Emotional withdrawal is covert, subtle, more insidious in nature than physical withdrawal, and more pervasive. Narcissistic withdrawal can have severe detrimental effects on individuals exhibiting emotional vulnerabilities. The state of isolation can create profound feelings of inadequacy and confusion, particularly in children. Borderlines, who are inclined towards feeling left out and undeserving, tend to identify with the withdrawal. Because of their susceptibility to the projections of others, borderlines do not recognize withdrawal as a maladaptive process. The identification is usually with a split-off aspect of the self that is shrouded in confusion. The therapist must help the couple sort out how much of the withdrawal each partner is accountable for, how much is delusional, and how much is reality based.

NARCISSISTIC RAGE VERSUS BORDERLINE RAGE

My experience as a therapist suggests that narcissistic rage is a response to being misunderstood, ignored, or hurt, especially when the hurt involves one's sense of specialness. Narcissistic rage stems from a feeling of personal injury and may sound like, "How dare you put me down in front of our friends!" or "You're always humiliating and embarrassing me; you make me look like a fool!" or "Here I have tried so hard and you never appreciate all the things I've done. I'm leaving!"

Borderline rage is a sensory response to the threat to one's existence. This rage has acting-out qualities that parallel persecutory anxiety. Borderline rage is a response to the fear of not existing, as opposed to narcissistic rage, which is an emotional outburst to a threatened self, an outcome of guilt from an indulgent self. Borderline rage is an attempt to destroy that which is envied in order to hold onto the good internal objects. Borderline rage may sound like, "Don't give me your excuses. You are nothing, deserve nothing, and therefore you shall have nothing!" (projecting the state of nothingness onto the other). Or, "There you go again, going out with your friends. Aren't I good enough for you?" (abandonment anxiety). "You'll see when you get back; I won't be here waiting around for you!" (borderline tendency to get even).

The momentary states of anger and rage are modes of communicating legitimate feelings and thus are healthy. If one waits too long to deal with feelings, however, they escalate, developing into something intolerable. Anger escalates when one does not acknowledge the internal signifiers that bring on terror. Murderous rage and retaliatory fantasies can reenter the psyche via projective identification or, as Bion puts it, as "grotesque objects" in a haunting but unrecognizable form. Using Bion's (1968) concepts on thinking, the therapist translates the language of rage and attacks in order to provide digestible meaning.

Grotstein (1987) proposed that the "states of experience" constitute the most fundamental mental events for psychotic and borderline personalities and represent the confluence of elements of meaningfulness and meaninglessness. Applying Grotstein's ideas to rage and anger in borderlines, one might conjecture that what terrorizes these individuals are the unknown elements, the "nameless dread" or states of entropy and nothingness that Grotstein eloquently described as the "black hole."

Borderlines are lacking in self-regulation mechanisms; the internal signals, signifiers, and instincts that enable them to anticipate a hurtful event are disregarded. Narcissistic rage is expressed when they perceive a direct insult to their sense of entitlement, resulting in either physical or emotional isolation. Both borderlines and narcissists feel they are innocent victims and complain vehemently about each other, "Look what has been done to me!"

BODILY SENSATIONS

Anxiety in the borderline is often expressed not by words but through bodily sensations. We need to help the borderline partner pay attention to these internal signals. Nonverbal forms of communication are conveyed through body language, somatization, suicidal ideation, and many forms of addictive behaviors that include not only addiction to drugs, alcohol, and food, but also addictive relationships. These nonverbal forms of relating can preoccupy, consume, or control the other person, most often the borderline partner. In essence, self-sacrifice, subjugation of the self, and the establishment of a false self take over in the borderline's attempt to cover needs or face the void, for which these compulsions tend to act as substitutes.

Emde (1987), in an unpublished paper presented at the International Psychoanalytic Congress in Montreal, reflected Freud's views while discussing his own findings in developmental biology and infant observation. Although he did not imply diagnostic differences in borderlines and narcissists, he inferred that borderlines have more need for safety and tend to act out from their biological states rather than from their thinking states. According to Emde, affects, regarded as composite states of both pleasurable and unpleasurable feelings, are rooted in biology and function unconsciously as well as consciously. He appeared to be taking into account certain aspects of biological theory, especially signal anxiety, in describing the regulatory role and automatic functions of affective experiences.

> Signal anxiety prevents one from becoming overwhelmed by states of helplessness which in turn are linked to specific, hierarchically arranged affective structures which were originally experienced in early development. Other psychoanalytic theorists since Freud have also portrayed a developmental sequence involving signal depression or helplessness, analogous to Freud's original developmental sequence involving anxiety. (Emde, 1987, p. 3)

The composite view of Emde's (1987) work suggests that certain states of helplessness are affectively experienced as dangerous threats to the psyche; however, signal anxiety can prevent one from becoming overwhelmed, but only by heeding the importance of these signals. This view is in sharp contrast to that of Kohut, who saw affective states not necessarily as derivatives of drives (bodily experiences and sensations) but rather as continuous aspects of our lives in relation to self objects.

One important implication of Emde's (1987) work in chronic marital conflict appears to be the recognition that certain partners are not being intentionally destructive because they lack awareness of motivational forces. It is these forces that may be felt internally as something foreign or bizarre and as intrusive and invading. The implication is that words are not enough. The therapist, like the dancer, must speak directly to their patients' bodily communications with meaning and conviction. "I believe when you hold your hand to your chest, your heart is trying to express something to me!"

PAIN AND SACRIFICE

In order to obtain a clearer picture of what makes one endure pain, one needs to understand something about group formation and the extent or extremes to which the group will go in order to preserve a sense of group identity. What occurs in the group can help us understand what occurs in the collective couple "self" or the individual self. The preservation of self and the need to protect it at any cost can be more pervasive than life itself. People in groups, as well as individuals, will strive to preserve the self or the collective group self at their own expense or that of their children. The kamikaze suicide squads are an example of this behavior. In order to preserve a national cause, a sense of pride, a group self, the kamikaze fighters were willing to die for their country.

Pain stirs up unresolved issues that need to be worked through in order for the individual to grow, develop, and face new experiences. As noted previously, both borderlines and narcissists fear new experiences and prefer to reexperience old ones, even those that are painful and destructive.

Self-sacrifice can occur within the individual as well as the group in order to preserve a self or a group identity. If a patient continually threatens suicide or makes suicide attempts, we clearly get a sense of self-sacrifice. In certain religious sects, the members will choose death over loss of a group self (Lachkar, 1991). Self-sacrifice can take more subtle forms, however, making it more difficult to discern. Narcissists will sacrifice anything that will preserve self-identity or egocentricity. The narcissistic child may become a piano player because his mother, who is exhibitionistically involved with the arts, wants her child to play the piano as a reflection of herself, even at the expense of the child's needs and desires.

Borderlines frequently sacrifice themselves, their families, and their children. In court custody cases children become the sacrificial objects, are placed in the middle of arguments, deprived, made to be go-betweens, and treated as little adults playing the role of mediators, therapists, and saviors (Lachkar, 1985). In custody cases, the narcissist may withhold (payment, child support, property, visitation) because of exaggerated entitlement fantasies, but the borderline will be the one to withhold custody payments and refuse to participate fairly in property division and child visitation out of a desire to get back at the other partner (Lachkar, 1985).

Borderlines use nonverbal language to communicate disappointment in the narcissist partners who have failed them. The borderline sees this unspoken language as providing a connection or merging, which is really the wish for the holding environment that never existed. When the potential of the holding environment is threatened, as in divorce, intense fear and the desire to retaliate dominate. It is at this point that the borderline will sacrifice self and family—paradoxically, to preserve a sense of self.

WHY COUPLES STAY IN PAINFUL CONFLICTUAL RELATIONSHIPS

Chapter 6 is devoted to group psychology addressing shared collective group fantasies and why groups perpetuate destructive relationships (domestic and global), sacrifice themselves, and live a painful existence. I began to see similar patterns in marital relationships, whereby people form painful attachments. Why do these narcissists and borderlines stay in painful conflictual relationships? How do they find each other? Are they crazy, perverse, sadomasochistic? Why do they dwell in pain? Even after a divorce or separation, these people maintain a bond. They will tie up the court system, sacrifice themselves, their time, their money, and their children. The primary reason is that being bonded to pain is preferable to the emptiness, the "black hole," the void Grotstein (1987) described. The borderline stays in painful relationships because pain is preferable to emptiness. It is the "meaningless" that epitomizes states of terror rather than deprivation itself. Patients may feel enraged, but at least they feel a "sense of aliveness instead of deadness" (Kernberg, 1989, p. 196). Bonding to the pain is not a far cry from what occurs in suicide bombers on a mission. "At least I now know I am alive. I have purpose, meaning, and can give meaning to the meaninglessness! I now have honor and can give honor to my family and to my country."

CHILD ABUSE

An important clinical implication of the information we have about the narcissist/borderline couple is the relation of that union to child abuse. DeMause (1974) compiled a wide-ranging historical survey of parental attitudes toward children and their relationship to the occurrence of infanticide and child abuse. He examined whether parents loved and cared for their children, what parents said to children, what parents fantasized about children, and how these behaviors affected children's growth. From a psychohistorical perspective, DeMause presented a fantasy analysis of child abuse, providing an overview of the history of infanticide, abandonment, nursing, swaddling, beating, and sexual abuse. In addition, he examined how widespread each practice was during each time period covered. His painstaking review of the history of childhood in America is one of the most complete studies of childrearing available.

It is important to note that we still have a significant lack of clinical knowledge on the issue of child abuse and that we have severely undermined our ability to understand the basic tenets of what contributes to the making of a child abuser. In my view, it is the projected, split-off part of one's own abused internal child that one seeks desperately to destroy. If abuse issues are avoided in marital therapy and not examined in the light of splitting, projection, and projective identification, I believe we are limiting our capacity to treat these dysfunctional individuals.

DRIVE TOWARD THE DEATH INSTINCT OR DRIVE TOWARD BONDING

Before we discuss the death instinct and the drive towards bonding, we need to consider the universal nature of cruelty and the sadistic tendencies in human beings that drive them to inflict pain on others.

In discussing the erotic nature of violence, Loewenberg (1985) cited examples from the Rat Man and Dora cases to demonstrate Freud's initial insights. It was Freud's belief that "the history of human civilization shows beyond any doubt that there is an intimate connection between cruelty and the sexual instinct" (Freud 1909/1955a). Loewenberg agreed with Freud and suggested that we cannot easily get rid of violence because it has genetic roots in the anal zone and is inextricably woven into human nature. Loewenberg stated that the psychodynamics of violence involve the desire to destroy the despised part of oneself as it is projected onto the victim. In contrast, we may also project onto others positive qualities that they do not have, making them idealized figures.

It is also important to consider Klein's (1946) concept of the death instinct and its application to marital conflict. Feelings and needs are considered as painful invasions to ward off danger. The death instinct may be a response to the black hole or other threatening life forces experienced as emptiness. What marks borderline patients is that they confuse feelings of death with real death. The persecutory experience is, for Klein, a pervasive force that is felt by the infant as an internal homicide, killing off the bad mommy breast or the bad daddy penis. "Killing off" the therapist or one's own needs may be a way for borderlines to rid themselves of impending dangers.

In the mental pain generated by the experience of separation from the object tie, the borderline reverts to the primitive experience of no breast, which is intolerable. There is a preconception that somewhere in the future there is a breast, that some mystical savior will rescue the person from the dangerous other and will lead the person along the pathway of happiness. Beyond the pain, I believe that for the borderline, there is the desire for self-development, bonding, and attachment experiences with a good parental object. Borderlines often join with pain because of the inability to hold onto the feelings of loss, deprivation, and mourning, or to identify with victims.

CONCLUSION

The complex psychodynamics of the narcissist/borderline relationship involve a continuously shifting balance between guilt/shame, envy/jealousy, and omnipotence/dependency. The process that transports these feelings is projective identification, or dual projective identification. The very nature of projective identification strips the psyche of all resources, affecting judgment, reality perception, and the ability to think. To the extent that the external world is clouded in dual projections, the narcissistic/borderline partners remain exclusively attached to their internal objects. Neither partner is able to express needs directly and appropriately or learn from experience. Instead they indulge in a variety of marital theatrics based on primitive defenses, splitting, and projective identification. These are an attempt to blame the other partner for real or perceived deficiencies in the self—deficiencies arising from injuries inflicted long ago by others that remain festering in the V-spot. When the V-spot is aroused, the present becomes a mere reenactment of archaic hurts and sentiments, a staging of internally pre-scripted roles that the partners play out in an everlasting drama that begins in infancy.

Chapter 5

Dynamic Positions and Transference Formation

In conjoint psychotherapy, we discover how certain dynamic mechanisms of the narcissist (guilt, grandiosity, idealization, withdrawal) arouse intense anxieties in the borderline and, conversely, how the dynamics of the borderline (shame, envy, splitting, massive denial, abandonment, persecutory anxieties) arouse intense feelings of guilt and self-hatred in the narcissist. Who are these characters that relentlessly invade and infect the human psyche? They are all too familiar to our clinical ears: the rejecter, the withholder, the robber, the exciter, the tormentor, the judge, and other harsh authority figures. As therapists/analysts, we have the opportunity not only to discover the type of object the partner has internalized, but also to establish a clearer sense of how they play themselves out. Once this is established, we can then open the past wounds and the torn childhoods to examine and explore the origins of the traumas (the V-spot) that have followed the narcissist and borderline into adulthood.

This chapter explores a wide range of dynamic positions as a platform to understanding the spectrum of phenomenology, starting with Klein's positions.

DYNAMIC POSITIONS

Paranoid–Schizoid Position

Klein's (1946) notion of the movement from the paranoid-schizoid position to the depressive position is one of the most helpful ideas in understanding the fragmentation that occurs in regressed couples, including the narcissistic/ borderline couple. The movement from paranoid–schizoid to depressive interfaces with Kohut's (1971, 1977) idea of transmutual internalization and Grotstein's (1980) "dual track theorem." In addition, it meshes with Mahler, Pine, and Bergman's (1975) phases of separation–individuation (including the autistic, the symbiotic, the subphases of differentiation, practicing, rapprochement, and object constancy).

In the fragmented paranoid–schizoid position, thoughts and feelings are split off and projected because the psyche cannot tolerate pain, loneliness, and humiliation. In the depressive position (which Kohut referred to as introspection), one becomes more capable of containing one's own sadness, loneliness, and emptiness, and can take more responsibility for one's actions and needs.

The paranoid–schizoid position was demonstrated by Klein to be the earliest phase of development. "It is characterized by the relations to the part objects, the prevalence of splitting in the ego and in the object and paranoid anxiety" (Segal, 1964, p. 126). If, in time, the child is to have a predominantly good and nurturing environment, it is essential for the infant in the paranoid–schizoid position that good experiences predominate and that the baby view the mother as the good breast.

Partners who are in couple treatment tend to vacillate between the paranoid–schizoid position and the depressive position. They are constantly moving from states of fragmentation to wholeness. In the depressive position they have a chance to integrate and comprehend their behavior and the events that led to the damage. Before reparation occurs, however, they must learn to tolerate the frustration and impatience of the depressive position.

Depressive Position

Grotstein's contribution, which postulates Klein's phases of adhesive identification and movement from the paranoid–schizoid position, to the depressive position, is more helpful in understanding the fusion that occurs in couples than are theories that parallel or interface with Freud's oral, anal, and genital developmental sequence. The major tenet of Klein's work is that guilt, and the manic defense against guilt, causes a level of anxiety higher than persecutory anxiety.

In the depressive position, there is the realization that there is a "no breast" or an "empty breast," and the child begins to express mourning and sadness for not having the breast. As the verbal expression of thought comes into play, the child begins to rely more excessively on sensory perceptions on which thought is based.

The depressive position begins when the infant recognizes the mother as a whole object. In this position, there is a process of integrating the dissociation caused by feelings of ambivalence. Not everything is seen as black and white; couples find that there are gray areas and begin to learn to balance the extremes. Individuals in this state will develop two defenses: manic defenses (which drive one to an opposite extreme) and reparation (Klein, 1957). Klein considered both these defenses to be based on omnipotence and denial of reality and to be characterized by mastery, control, and contempt. This position brings with it the realization that things cannot change overnight, and allowance is made for feelings of mourning.

These comments on the depressive position are applicable (see chapter 8, "Three Phases of Treatment") when treating the narcissistic/borderline couple. Both borderlines and narcissists want the quick fix, since neither realizes that getting things quickly and impulsively can actually detract from their value, thereby depriving the couple even further. Borderlines in the depressive position have a particularly hard time giving up their false selves and starting to reveal their true feelings. They are too busy trying to make things look all right. Narcissists find it difficult to wean themselves from those who gratify them with immediate excitement and approval.

If one cannot mourn, one cannot contain pain. If one does not mourn, one fails to reach the depressive position. In this position the feelings are too painful to contain, and one will continue to split off feelings or find quick replacements to ward off those intolerable affects. One must learn to hold onto the feelings of sadness and aloneness in the depressive position in order to feel truly entitled, to learn from experience, to learn to be alone, and to find inner peace.

Manic Defenses versus Integration

According to Klein, "Manic defenses are evolved in the depressive position as a defense against the experience of depressive anxiety, guilt and loss. They are based on an omnipotent denial of psychic reality and object relations as characterized by triumph, control and contempt" (Segal, 1964, p. 126).

I believe Klein was referring to behaviors that operate at the extreme sides of the split, where the aim is to ward off feelings of persecution, shame, humiliation, and danger. If one has been passive, then one becomes aggressive. And if one has been excessively submissive, then one becomes overly aggressive: "Never again shall I be taken advantage of!"

This differs from integration, which emerges from a state of remorse, understanding. or humility. Integration is a defense against something. For Klein (1948), the ability to mourn relies on a "working through" and sorting out of feelings, not on manic defenses and behaviors. In her paper "A Contribution to the Psychogenesis of Manic Defenses," Klein (1975) stressed the importance of the depressive position and reviewed the splitting mechanism in a new light. At this stage, splitting is a precursor to the unification of opposing forces and, in my opinion, is an all-important process. The implication for marital treatment is that patients in the paranoid–schizoid position who are not sufficiently integrated to sort things out might attempt to stand up for themselves in inappropriate and bizarre ways

In the light of treatment, couples learn that the desire for retribution keeps them going around in circles. Because of their defenses, neither partner is able to break from the primitive bond; nor are they able to make justifiable or rational decisions. Tit-for-tat solutions, based on manic defenses or persecutory anxiety, do not lead to a solid sense of self, let alone to an understanding of the entanglement of defenses.

In the depressive position, one of the partners may realize that he cannot punish the other partner for being emotionally unavailable. It is at this stage that the patient comes to terms with disappointment and feelings of hopelessness and despair and begins to seek out new friends, mentors, and other ways of repairing the damage.

For the narcissist, the expression of a manic defense initially may sound something like, "Never again will I do anything for you! You never appreciate anything I do!" However, for the borderline, it is, "I'll show her! How dare she treat me this way! Next time she does that to me I'll do the same thing back to her!" In the depressive position, the borderline partner might rephrase his position: "No, I'm not going anywhere with you until you and I sit down and talk this thing out. You have hurt me and let me down. Now, I'm not punishing you by not going with you, but I need you to know that you have hurt me, and I will not tolerate it!"

Separation–Individuation

Some clinicians regard separateness literally: as a physical state rather than an intrapsychic quality. Before clinicians can help individuals separate and individuate, they must first understand the psychodynamics that differentiate separation and individuation. When we speak of separation, we are clearly referring to a psychological separation and not simply a physical one. Mahler et al. (1975) have helped us to distinguish the intrapsychic fusions that occurs within couples such as the narcissistic/borderline couple.

According to Mahler and her colleagues (1975), there are four subphases of intrapsychic awareness that occur along two separate tracks. One track, separation, leads to intrapsychic awareness that one needs to be self-responsible; the other, individuation, leads to the acquisition of distinctiveness and uniqueness. Mahler and her colleagues proposed that one gains an increasing capacity to recognize mother as a special person and to (a) cathect, (b) inspect, (c) move gradually into the nonmother world, and (d) move quite deliberately away from mother.

I believe the significance of this for the couple is that running away or doing separate things is not the same as being in a state of "separateness," of differentiating needs and learning to tolerate one's own differentness or unique ways. A couple may learn to do separate things; however, this is not the same as coping, tolerating, and appreciating one's differentness (the "me" and the "not me"). The phases delineated by Mahler and her colleagues (1975) have significance within narcissistic/borderline configurations because in primitive relationships there is difficulty in distinguishing the "mother world" (sameness) from the "nonmother world" (differentness). To fuse, to intrude on, or to force the other to change is just as destructive as withdrawing, ignoring, or running away. Ironically, even when the persons are living apart, they still may have something that binds them together.

While these phases are certainly important, because we are dealing with severe pathologies in couples rather than individuals per se, we must attend to the couple as a unit and define clearly these unique intrapsychic differences before we can respond therapeutically. For instance, one might interpret: "On the surface you are able to do separate things and live a separate life; however, internally you are still very much emotionally involved."

Reparation

Applicable to the innumerable concepts that Klein has contributed to the treatment of dysfunctional couples is the idea of reparation, which occurs in the depressive position. Reparation is an ego-involved attempt to heal depressive anxieties and guilt (Klein, 1937/1975; Segal, 1964). After continually splitting back and forth between extremes, one finally comes to the realization that these fragmented behaviors cause damage to the self and to others. Then reparation can begin.

For the narcissist, the ability to repair is difficult, mainly because of excessive guilt and lack of empathy. Kernberg (1976) stated that excessive guilt impairs object relations, and that the capacity for lasting relationships has to do both with guilt and with the genuineness of the wish to repair. Winnicott (1965b) and his colleagues (1975) focused on the capacity for healthy object constancy.

I believe Klein (1975) comes closest to helping us conceptualize capacity for reparation. She based it on the capacity for guilt, which she proposed occurs in the depressive position, as opposed to primitive super-ego anxiety, which occurs in the paranoid–schizoid position. This is important for both borderline and narcissistic partners, particularly in distinguishing manic defenses against guilt and envy. For the borderline, the capacity to repair is difficult, because genuine wishes for reparation are often confused with shame or the false self. Saying one is sorry, for example, is not the same as facing pain, moving through a process of mourning, and understanding how one's own behaviors have contributed to the problem.

Dual-Track Theorem

We have observed that narcissistic/borderline states and traits vacillate widely, making it difficult to tell if the partners are narcissistic or borderline. Grotstein's (1981) dual-track theorem is similar to Klein's (1957) theory of movement between the paranoid–schizoid and the depressive positions. Grotstein suggested that the paranoid–schizoid and depressive positions occur simultaneously and that throughout life one tends to vacillate between states of wholeness and fragmentation.

The dual-track concept allows for interaction. Fantasies and reality occupy equal footing. Grotstein viewed interaction experiences as lifelong dialectical forces linking one's fantasy life and one's ability to view life more realistically. Grotstein felt that the dual-track theory was of special importance in reconciling the growing disparity between classical and Kleinian analysts.

We now think of normal maturation in the context of permanent states that exist side by side with states of separation–individuation, so that no matter what the state of development or the chronological age of the individual, maturation still continues. This is important because therapy takes place in a dynamic state; the couple interaction continues to flow from one state to another, despite the structure of the stages of development.

FORMS OF TRANSFERENCE

Transference

The concept of transference explains why some patients are not content with the analyst as a helper or mentor who merely interprets, provides insights, and offers advice. Transference has to do with the reincarnation of some important figure from childhood revisited in an analytic setting. This can be a whole representation of a person (someone the analyst represents from the past) or a split-off "part" of a person.

In couple treatment, there are three different types of transferences, all of which need interpretation. There are the transferences of the two individual partners, and there is the transference of the couple as a unit. Whatever is interpreted has to be demonstrated to the couple in terms of their relationship.

There is a certain group of patients to whom Kohut refers as being analyzable. Kohut (1977) distinguished between two aspects of the narcissistic personality's bipolar self: the "grandiose self" and the "idealized parent imago." The grandiose self is expressed in the need for mirroring, which subsumes a variety of supportive, affirming, and validating responses for the person's mastery and accomplishments. It is the grandiose part of the self that develops in the transference as invincible, invulnerable, and all-knowing, as if one were above everyone else. Kohut suggested that in the unfolding "mirror-transference," patients require primarily empathic, approving, echoing, and confirming responses; if these are not forthcoming, they become enraged.

In contrast, the idealized parent imago—experiencing others as existing solely as an extension of one's own needs—extends to the external environment. The idealized parent imago provides a source of identification. The therapist, for instance, is to be available only as an extension of the patient's needs and is not to have needs of his or her own. Often friends or marital partners exist only to serve the excessive needs and demands of the narcissist and are not acknowledged to have needs of their own.

We know from Kohut that narcissistic transference does exist. But is there such a thing as borderline transference? The consensus is that the borderline personality does not adhere to classical patterns of transference. It is generally thought that in order to form a transference relationship, one must be higher on the borderline/narcissist continuum. I suggest that many transference-like phenomena do emerge in the narcissistic/borderline relationship. It appears likely that what occurs in the couple's relationship is indeed replicated in the transference.

The borderline massively projects feelings into the therapist in a way that is quite different from that of the narcissist. For instance, in a conjoint session a borderline patient was asked by the therapist to remember to discuss a particular issue with her husband during the week. As usual, the borderline wife forgot. The analyst and the husband were left feeling discounted and ignored. If we regard the disavowal aspects of the borderline as part of the self being transferred onto the therapist, we can call this "borderline transference."

Vertical Split

The vertical split in the personality consists of two sectors. The first sector is the unbroken merger with the mother. The patient becomes the executor of the mother's grandiose wishes and the messengers of her superiority. The second sector is characterized by certain goals and idealized attitudes internalized by the father. Kohut (1977) called regression the yearning for the merger with the mirroring mother and characterized the vertical split as the part of the self without a unique self-concept. For clarification, Kohut suggested that the admiring and mirroring functions be considered the traditional maternal aspects, and the idealizations as developing out of paternal functions. The bipolar self in the transference, according to Kohut (1977), has a chance to restore itself to oneness when the patient can recognize that although we never outgrow the need for self objects, the types of self objects we need change as we grow.

Countertransference

A dramatic revision has occurred since the term countertransference was introduced into psychoanalytic theory during Freud's day. Freud viewed countertransference as resistance within the analyst that gets in the way of understanding the patient. Countertransference was originally defined as the therapist's unconscious reaction, or the analyst's transference to the patient, based on the analyst's own unresolved conflictual wishes and unconscious fantasies (Freud, 1940). Winnicott (1949, cited in Slipp, 1984) was the first psychoanalyst to expand the traditional definition of countertransference to encompass all the reactions the therapist had to the patient. Object relations theorists, especially Klein, expanded these ideas further to include even more primitive responses and reactions that were being noted by therapists.

While Samuel Slipp's (1984) clear, concise review of the changes occurring in the countertransference phenomenon recognized Paula Heimann (1950) as one of the first to appreciate countertransference as a therapeutic tool, he acknowledged Klein's richer understanding of the use of countertransference. It was Klein who first used the term projective identification, which shifted countertransference's sole focus on the analyst's resistance to a broadened role as an interactive analytical experience.

Narcissistic/borderline couples evoke reactions that convey the message that we must provide immediate solutions and that unless we do, we are disregarding the couple. In conjoint treatment, as well as in individual therapy, countertransference is an extremely crucial concept that must be handled skillfully to avoid severe acting out or premature disruption of the treatment.

The therapist who becomes confused by countertransference issues—for example, the therapist's own guilt and feelings of worthlessness or betrayal—may have difficulty sorting out the distortions. It is important to address the heart of the issues, to stay separate, and deal with the area of anxiety. Some possible interventions: "Yes, sometimes guilt is important. There is appropriate guilt." Or, "Yes, it is okay to have expectations." Or, "What's wrong with having an expectation? What's wrong with feeling pressure, discomfort, anxiety? Maybe that's part of the problem; you both have a hard time tolerating any discomfort, so as soon as you get anxious you lose yourselves or blame each other. Sometimes it is appropriate to have these feelings."

Often the narcissist projects guilt feelings that the therapist is the cause of the narcissist's vulnerability and wounded self-image. Feeling that we do not appreciate them or that we are being too critical, narcissists respond with hurt feelings. The borderline, in contrast, may project onto us that we are not doing enough. The borderline wants the quick fix and often tries to make us feel ashamed and embarrassed for having needs of our own (payment, boundaries, schedules.) This is particularly important because many borderlines suffer from alexithymia (are split off from their feelings) and are not aware of what they are trying to express.

There are many countertransference issues for the therapist, including feelings of being a failure, of guilt, anxiety, not being good enough, and despair; however, the most profound feeling is that of being abandoned. Patients will often disrupt the treatment to let the therapist know what it feels like to be left out, a form of projective identification. Many will not get well as a way of letting us know how difficult and frustrating waiting can be.

One of the most important and prevalent countertransference issues in conjoint treatment is distancing: "We decided to take a break. We don't need treatment anymore." This stems from the notion that less contact is better, when, in fact, one need more closeness and intimacy, not less. Often this is a collective couple fantasy: Now that they have had a little treatment, they are all well and can "do it themselves." Just as with individual treatment, in conjoint treatment this countertransference issue must be handled skillfully. The issue of stopping treatment must be dealt with by addressing the defenses in the couple transference and not by colluding with them.

If these defenses are not understood, or if the therapist colludes with the pathogenic elements of the relationship, the result can be decompensation. An appropriate response from the therapist would be, "Now you are distancing yourself from me as you have from one another." The patient is saying, "Look, Mommy, I'm all well, and now I can do it all by myself!"

Therapists who use a psychoanalytic approach to treating these couples must meticulously pursue understanding these defenses and how they contribute to the countertransference and the couple's recurrent drama. To be more specific, the therapist may feel guilty for "using" the couple or may feel ashamed for needing them. Therapists can begin to feel like abusive, punitive parents; harsh, noncaring parents; negligent parents; or betraying, intrusive parents.

Couple Transference

Couple transference does for the couple what transference does for the individual, but in a somewhat more complex manner. Couple transference interpretations are derived from the analyst's experience and insights and are designed to produce a transformation within the dyadic relationship. It refers to the mutual projections, delusions, and distortions, or shared couple fantasies, which become displaced onto the therapist. The notion of the "couple/therapist" transference opens up an entirely new therapeutic vista— a transitional space in which to work. It is within this space that "real" issues come to life.

Example: Both partners rebuff any attempt on the part of the therapist to be helpful. They cannot allow themselves to rely on or be dependent on another. For the narcissist it means feeling vulnerable, less than perfect; for the borderline it means abandonment/betrayal.

Transference interpretations must encompass the couple myth, addressing the infantile aspects of the relationship. The therapist who uses a psychodynamic approach has a wonderful opportunity to make transference interpretations and apply them to the couple mythology by drawing on countertransference. For example, the two partners may share a mutual fantasy that if they begin to depend upon the therapist, the therapist will "abuse" or take advantage of them.

I am reminded of a couple that made me feel as though I were trespassing every time I addressed the more mundane aspects of treatment. If I needed to be paid on time, the husband made me feel ashamed, that I was entering a space beyond the safety zone. If I asked the wife to come in for more treatment, I was trespassing on her time. How dare I intrude into her space! My transgressions were clarified when I was able to zone into a memory I had as a small infant: my parents trying to escape Nazi Germany, where I saw barbed wire fences. I dreamed I had crystallized that feeling. I dreamed that I was driving to the couple's home for an emergency visit and suddenly was stopped at the bottom of the driveway with barbed wire fences and the presence of Nazis, as if to say, "stay out."

Individual transference must be directed toward the child's relationship to the parents or to other archaic experiences (the V-spot). In conjoint treatment, transference must address the couple myth or the couple fantasy in a manner similar to group psychotherapy, always keeping in mind the group dynamics and the group myths. Many of the illustrative cases in chapter 9 not only highlight the splitting and projective aspects of the narcissistic/borderline relationship but also address the couple's shared collective ideology.

The Therapist as Self Object

Couple therapy is a deep emotional experience, with intense communication and feelings that occur among three persons. Although vignettes can describe the events and therapeutic sessions can be reported, it is impossible to teach a therapist a particular approach to conjoint therapy—what to do, how to do it, what to say. Words that are not the therapist's own may come across as empty thought or empty theories. If the therapist attempts imitation, there is a risk of mere mimicry at the expense of one's unique perception of the situation and one's own beliefs, values, and theoretical framework. The technique for couple therapy simply must be developed through the transference experience of the individual therapist.

According to Kohut (1971, 1977), psychological disturbances that lead to the feelings of dismay are caused by faulty self objects, lack of attunement, empathic failures, and lack of mirroring from idealized objects. These certainly are important; however, ignoring the internal world may lead to a form of pathological collusion. External forces are significant, but if the primary focus is on the external, we are in danger of undermining the internal conflict. Furthermore, because of the tendency in couples to blame, failure to face the internal object world can be perceived as avoiding responsibility for one's behavior, or as collusion. Object relations help patients face these internal deficits, enabling them to take more responsibility for their own behavior. The primary focus of the therapist as a self object must not be misconstrued as going along with the pathology. Self-object functions may shift from bonding and mirroring to containing and weaning as changes occur throughout the phases of treatment.

Object relations theory provides us with an environmental mother, a background mother, a being/doing mother, a weaning mother, and a containing/sustaining mother to help establish different kinds of bonding and self-object experiences. The importance of the therapist/mother as the container becomes more vital in a conjoint setting because the central issues revolve around persecutory anxiety, shame, guilt, confusion, and fantasies

TABLE 5.1
Therapeutic Functions

- Empathy
- Listening
- Understanding
- Introspection
- Therapist as the mirroring object
- Therapist as self object
- Therapist as continer (hard object)
- Therapist as the transitional object
- Therapist as the bonding/weaning mommy
- Therapist as the holding and environmental mommy
- Therapist as the "being" vs. "doing" mommy
  (remembering the patient's experience and affects)
- Therapist as interpreter
- Thinking
- Containment

of separation. The empathic mode can be most valuable in conjoint therapy as an important source of exploration, particularly in the attempt to bond and form a healthy object tie. (See Table 5.1.)

The internal world or internal deficits are not emphasized in self-psychology. In my view, if we turn to faulty self objects or to the patient's "subjective reality" as the primary focus of the couple's failings and ignore the internal world of projections and introjections, then we may join in the pathology—that is, the tendency to assign blame or find the outside enemy responsible for all the couple's shortcomings in the relationship—and we may fail to see the projections from the perspective of internal "enemies." I believe that both faulty self objects and the structural ego defects must be considered.

In sorting confusional and tangential modes of relating, the therapist should understand that although the mirroring mother certainly is crucial, she does not have the same impact as the containing/holding mother. Unfortunately, many therapists misunderstand the notion of empathy and introspection, which results in a misplaced emphasis on external circumstances (the self-object tie), and a tendency to ignore the destructive parts of the personality. Sometimes the empathic mode is not enough, and the therapist needs to turn to a more holding/containing/sustaining/ hard-object mode, perhaps stating assertively, "Of course, there is an external betrayer. Now you say it's your wife; before you said it was your brother. You need to know that there is also an internal betrayer. This internal betrayer keeps you feeling helpless and seriously impairs your judgment and the way you relate to your wife and others." This kind of response usually feels good to the borderline because it conveys a sense of having something inside and can lead to deeper emotional experiences.

The most important function, according to Grotstein (1987), is the analyst's "detoxification" of the banished elements of self that have been exiled into unconsciousness. Empathy is a crucial concept in conjoint treatment, but must be used alongside the concept of weaning. Weaning the partners from blaming and attacking defenses slowly enables contact with intrapsychical difficulties and deficits. Application of Bion's work can help the therapist understand the couple's experience, which can lead the therapist to a valid interpretation of what is really happening in the relationship.

These theories overlap and can be suitable for various stages within the conjoint setting. Many authors have written of these methods, but I wish to add that it is important to keep in mind that the more primitive the couple, the more emphasis should be placed on the mirroring and bonding needs (self-object functions). Timing and listening are the very essence of successful therapy.

"Teaching" Others to Become Self Objects

Rather than teach the narcissistic/borderline partners to be self objects, it is the job of the therapist to become the self object. We cannot teach empathy and mirroring; rather, we need to become the mirroring object. These steps must be accomplished before anything is to be achieved, before an emotional separation can occur.

Many therapists treating couples are so influenced by Kohut and the movement toward self-psychology that there is an unfortunate emphasis on teaching the partners to become self objects, to become unduly understanding. Because of their defenses, neither the borderline nor the narcissist knows how to serve as a self object or how to perform self-object functions for the other. On the contrary, the focus must be on affective experiences and the various feeling states. In conjoint treatment, just as in individual treatment, the partners cannot serve as self objects until the borderline is weaned from an internally unsafe world and the narcissist is weaned from overinvolvement with the self.

Although teaching partners in a fragmented relationship to empathize with one another is certainly a laudable aim, in most instances it is an unworkable one. While these couples are in the initial phase of conjoint treatment, empathy is an unknown entity. It seems to be a more realistic goal, then, to help the narcissistic/borderline couple slowly make a transition from pathological dependence to healthy dependency to separation. The being mommy allows the patient to feel, to be, and to experience—not to do and to act. The major thrust of the treatment is to help one relate, rather than "teach" self-object functions.

"Understanding" can often be a block or defense against taking action, standing up for one's self, holding on to one's own thoughts and beliefs, or moving toward separating oneself from confusional states (see Case 13, Dana and Bob, in chapter 9). Many partners will say, "Yes, I understand, I understand," without really understanding anything. Understanding is impossible without having experiences with a good, available, containing, sustaining breast (see Bion, 1977). To paraphrase Bion, without experience there can be no understanding. Taking something quickly from the therapist and imitating it is not the same as knowing—it is fusion! To be empathic or understanding can come across as mere mimicry or imitation; and to encourage the patient to be empathic can only replicate a false self or lead to premature development, removing one even further from one's own emotional experience. When serving as the self object and modeling self-object functions, the therapist also provides the containing and sustaining functions. Words then become empty thought, or thoughts without a thinker. Bion reminded us of how important it is to allow one to have his or her own experience. Paradoxically, "understanding" or "knowing" can be a defense against ever really understanding or knowing. Real understanding is introspective.

Transitional, Confusional, and Diversional Objects

Transitional Objects

Grotstein (1984a, 1984b, 1987) observed that the borderline adheres to the mother's body, has poor skin definition, and escapes to a state of mindlessness. Tustin (1981), Meltzer (1967), and Bion (1965, 1967) supported these ideas and added that borderlines misuse "transitional objects" as "confusional objects," make poor use of "thinking apparatus," and invade their interpersonal objects so as to become fused with those objects.

Winnicott (1953) suggested that the infant learns to wait and to control impulsivity. It is suggested that wanting unconditional love can severely interfere with relating to others. According to Winnicott, the infant assumes rights over the object. The therapist can be used as a transitional object by being used in a holding capacity from regression to dependency. The more disturbed one is, the more one uses others as transitional objects.

The concept of the transitional object was first introduced by Winnicott (1953) to designate a symbolic inanimate object that represents a momentary absence of mother objects. The transitional object serves as a familiar source of comfort and soothing as it revives the mother's image, familiarity, and touch. Often these objects are blankets, soft toys, pillows, or articles of clothing; in adult life they can become quite sophisticated, for example, computers, dance, music, clothes, as well as teddy bears (see Case 14).

Borderlines have difficulty making sufficient use of transitional objects because they may not have been able to separate from the mother's body long enough to seek self-soothing devices. When they are in primitive, pre-Oedipal relationships, patients frequently may turn to other objects to work through internal conflict. Many borderlines cannot use inanimate objects as transitional objects, instead using other persons as part objects. When the borderline is able to use them, transitional objects hold the borderline together during periods of separation and help fill the empty spaces and the black holes, especially when the breast is not available.

Transitional objects may be regarded as healthy only when the behavior is understood in relation to needs. Tustin (1981) associated a transitional object with a web of ever-changing fantasies, used in a healthy way, to help the infant make a transition away from the mother. Tustin described the "bibby" and the first treasured possession with the idea that the baby had something good inside. These transitional objects make up for what is missing. Tustin made a profound distinction between the healthy use of a transitional object and a confusional object. According to Tustin, the autistic or "confusional" child needs hard, indestructible objects in order to achieve a sense of differentiation. "Such a child never experiences 'missing'. In his concretized experience, absence of a needed person is experienced as a 'hole', which can be filled immediately with an autistic object" (Tustin, p. 107). My experience with couples has brought me to the view that, as bizarre as it might sound, affairs, alcoholism, substance abuse, or compulsive shopping and spending may be healthy if the motivation behind these behaviors is to soothe or to make up for the missing object.

Confusional and Diversional Objects

Tustin (1981) performed pioneering work on pathological autism, which she regarded as leading to childhood psychosis. She discussed the differences between children in the encapsulated state and children in the confusional state. In this book, I borrow from Tustin's work on confusional states and apply it to the narcissistic/borderline couple.

Tustin (1981) referred to the child's use of the confusional object as a way of hiding and avoiding rather than soothing, not as an object to enable the child to move to and fro. In my experience with couples, the use of cars, friends, affairs, drugs, alcohol, tears, shopping, computers, or treatment may be viewed as either transitional or confusional, depending on the motivation. I believe that most patients in marital treatment fit the "confusional" category rather than the "encapsulated" one. The confusional states of the "me" and the "not me" need to be transformed out of the biological realm and into the mind, where the patient can sort out the confusion.

I am using the terms "confusional object" and "diversional object" interchangeably to describe behaviors that occur in a conjoint setting, where the primary motivation is to block or avoid intimacy and human contact. With confusional (or diversional) objects, there is no clear evidence of what is missing or needed (as with transitional objects); rather, we find vagueness and illusionary images. For instance, an affair might be an attempt to get even (confusional), rather than an attempt to rejoin or bond with another for needed gratification. Needs are not based on memories or desire but are experienced as vague, obscure, and abstract. Alcohol or substance abuse, money, affairs, telephones, cars, or friends may be regarded as transitional or diversional, again depending on whether the motivations behind involvement with these objects are for rejoining with the longed-for object or for use as mere magical amulets to ward off dangers and obstruct intimacy. Unlike transitional objects, confusional objects do not revive memories of previous good experiences.

Language can be used in a transitional or diversional manner, depending on whether it is a vehicle to enhance communication, to convey thoughts, or to interrupt thoughts. Patients who interrupt excessively, speak quickly, speak either loudly or inaudibly, and make jokes are using language in a diversional manner. The person who uses language transitionally digests thoughts and ideas and is able to communicate and to engage in a meaningful interchange. Bion (1970) stated, "Sometimes the function of speech is to communicate experience to another; sometimes it is to miscommunicate experience to another" (p. 1). According to Bion, "The psycho-analyst must employ the language of achievement, but he must remember that the language was elaborated as much for the achievement of deception and evasion as for truth" (p. 3).

A simple example of a diversional/confusional object is a telephone answering machine. Sometimes an answering machine is a device that takes messages so the call can be returned at a later time. The receiver of the call, however, may never return the call, in which case the machine may be viewed as a diversional object whose purpose is to confuse the caller, not to enhance communication. A borderline wife called the therapist following a conjoint session and left a 45-minute message on the answering machine. At the end of the message she thanked the therapist for "listening," said that this was a "good session," and told the therapist to charge her for the time. In this context, the machine can be viewed as a transitional object, taking the place of the mommy/therapist between sessions. The machine becomes the blanket, standing in for the absent breast. Incidentally, borderlines need to know that from a developmental point of view, this can be regarded as healthy because it can lead to improved bonding relations with others.

Another example of a diversional/confusional object is an automobile. A family car with only one extra seat conveys a message of being a rejecting object, suitable for only two persons rather than for the entire family.

Tears may be confusional when they block communication, as opposed to tears that convey pain, feelings of hurt, and meaningful sentiments. Dreams may be confusional when they lock or intrude on feelings, or when used to detract from rather than to enhance understanding. Money may be confusional and diversional when withheld or functional when shared and managed. Medication may be viewed as a confusional object when used to cover up an existing problem. Sometimes it can be transitional, as when it offers relief from anxiety to bridge the gap and establish a link of understanding and introspection. Friends may be transitional or diversional, depending on whether they are used to enhance communication, intimacy, and understanding, or whether they are used as status symbols or to block intimacy with others.

TECHNIQUES

Bonding and Weaning

The concept of "weaning" the patient from infantile behavior into more mature states of development arose from the British object relations school. I view the self-psychological approach as the "bonding school," and object relations as the "weaning school." Self-psychology, with its mirroring function, is applicable in the early phases of treatment, when interpretations addressing internal deficits may be perceived as attacking. In the later phases, however, object relations provides a wider range of techniques in helping us wean patients from their destructive behaviors.

The therapist cannot make up for early loss but can help the patient learn to tolerate and contain the loss, and can describe what is needed. Therapists need to bond and wean according to the developmental needs of the partners. A systematic arrangement of special boundaries that are limited, but comfortable enough for both patient and therapist, must be developed. For example, a borderline patient may need to make spontaneous contact with the therapist with instantaneous response to telephone calls (instantaneous "feedings").

This connection to the therapist can be vital. The patient can gradually be weaned to more structured calls with definite boundaries, then further weaned when he is able to internalize the therapist as a good object (see Case 14 in chapter 9). The patient may feel threatened and may exhibit concern that the therapist will abruptly stop allowing the calls or will cut the patient off, which would leave the patient with the notion that having needs is bad. Needing can become tantamount to, and synonymous with, abandonment.

During this weaning process, the therapist has an opportunity to bond with the healthy part of the patient by interpreting that living inside somebody (intruding into mommy's private life) is like hiding, or like taking something that doesn't belong to one. There is never a chance to get fed if one lives inside another object; furthermore, one never gets the real feeding that is needed (the breast) because the breast is outside, not inside. To paraphrase Mason (personal communication, 1988), inside are the guts, blood, and other unpleasant parts, suitable only for unborn infants. "This baby part of you that was so demanding before is now able to wait and have regular arranged telephone sessions with me. This is a definite step forward and shows us that you are making progress!" If something urgent were to come up and the patient could not wait, then one could always go back to "demand feeding" calls; however, it must be explained within the context of the therapy and with interpretation that there has been a setback and that something is in the way of progress (which may correspond developmentally to Mahler's "practicing phase").

Borderline patients need to know that making contact is the healthy part of them; it is not their needs that make others turn away but their uncontrollable demands. In conjoint treatment, the process is to wean patients from blaming and attacking defenses and demanding behaviors (the infantile part of themselves), and slowly enable them to contain their own anxieties by facing their internal deficits. The therapist might say, "If you act like a baby then you will get treated like one and end up feeling more abandoned and left out."

Weaning in conjoint therapy is done in order to transform intolerable affects into containment via intrapsychic and introspective processes; it is the gradual pulling away from acting and doing to thinking about and understanding. "You want your wife to have sex with you, but she is letting you know she doesn't want to have sex with a demanding baby. Instead of facing what your wife is telling you, you are trying to force her to be different. If you do that, you will end up feeling more rejected."

During the latter part of the first year, the infant makes some fundamental steps toward working through the depressive position. The paranoid–schizoid position, however, is still in force. Klein believed that as individuals we go back and forth between these two positions. If persecutory anxiety is not too prevalent during the first stage, the infant will become more interested in the environment than in preoccupation with the availability of the breast (Klein, 1946). Klein viewed weaning as a trauma that inaugurates the Oedipus complex: frustration imposed by the feeding mother, causing the infant to turn away from the mother and move toward the father. Later Klein shifted this view, regarding the move away from the mother as an escalation of the weaning process that begins in the depressive position (Klein, 1975). Klein equated the Oedipus complex with the depressive position, in which persecutory anxiety diminishes and love feelings emerge. The realization that the child cannot possess the mother causes the child to turn away from the breast and be propelled to seek new libidinal objects.

Object relations theory provides us with an environmental mother, a background mother, a weaning mother, and a containing/sustaining mother to help establish different kinds of weaning and bonding experiences. The importance of therapist/mother as the container becomes more vital in a conjoint setting because we're dealing with very primitive disorders whose central issues revolve around persecutory anxiety, shame, guilt, confusion, and fantasies of separation.

Mirroring versus Containment

Bion's (1962) conception of the container and the contained is perhaps the most useful and all-inclusive concept of countertransference for borderlines, psychotics, narcissists, and even neurotic and normal conditions. It has been my experience that the notion of the container and contained is one of the most useful in conjoint treatment.

Bion (1962) believed that all psychological phenomena, whether normal or pathological, universally dissolve when the mind acts as receiver of communicative content, which the mother does in the state of reverie by using her own alpha function. This notion of alpha function is one of Bion's more mysterious terms for Freud's primary process period. It connotes the capacity for transformation of the data of emotional experience into meaningful feelings and thoughts.

Containment

Differences between the empathic interpretations (offering mirroring) and the sustaining functions (offering containment) are remarkable contributions to conjoint treatment. How does a psychotherapist treating couples become a self object to both partners, yet remain capable of acting as a self object to both? Being empathic by reaffirming the patients' subjective experiences alone does not distinguish between true empathic resonance and collusion.

The mother who is able to withstand the child's anger, frustrations, and intolerable and unknown feelings and who is able to translate and detoxify bad feelings becomes the container for these intolerable affects. Through her reverie and her ability to understand, sustain, and contain, the mother can feed back into the infant something that the child can take inside and hold onto. The therapist must contain these intolerable behaviors and be able to decode or detoxify things into more digestible forms. The most important function of the analyst, according to Grotstein (1981), is the detoxification of the banished elements of self that have been exiled into unconsciousness.

A step-by-step process enables the narcissistic/borderline partners to begin to see one another as real individuals with separate needs and desires who can coexist with the other's needs. Cohesiveness represents an idealized parenting model, one that includes containment, mirroring, and provision of optimal frustration (e.g., analytic boundaries and limitations), but one in which the "parent" is still warm enough and sufficiently emotionally available to work through hurt feelings and old injuries.

Mirroring

Mirroring is a term devised by Kohut that describes the gleam in mother's eye that mirrors the child's exhibitionistic display. Mirroring is a specific response to the child's narcissistic-exhibitionistic enjoyment, confirming the child's self-esteem. Eventually these responses are channeled into more realistic aims, and the child is able to validate and confirm which accomplishments were attained, to self-evaluate progress and abilities.

The concept of mirroring and the empathic mode can be most valuable in conjoint therapy as a vigorous source of exploration, particularly in the attempt to bond and form a healthy self-object tie.

Empathy addresses the painful feelings, but containment transcends feelings to reach the depths of the bottomless pit, annihilation anxiety, or the black hole, inhabited by the internal persecutors. One may continually disregard one's own needs because anxiety gets in the way of learning from experience.

For example, no matter how insulting one borderline wife was, her narcissistic husband would take it as a compliment. "You're selfish! You're inconsiderate! You're greedy. You're a pig!" The narcissistic husband's normal response to these insults would be, "Yes, I know I am. I'm entitled! I'm entitled!"

As stated previously in connection with confusional and tangential modes of relating, the mirroring mother is indeed crucial but does not have the same impact as the containing and holding mother. Because many therapists misunderstand the notion of empathy and mirroring, they focus on external circumstances (the self-object tie) and ignore the destructive parts of the personality.

Confrontation versus Empathy

Masterson (1981) suggested that borderlines respond more to confrontation, whereas narcissists are more responsive to interpretation. This is compatible with the notion that the object-relational approach is appropriate for the borderline, and self-psychology for the narcissist. Masterson, more than any other author, has clarified for us that the narcissist needs an appeal to intellectualization and seems to respond to interpretation and explanation. Masterson felt that the borderline, in contrast, responds more favorably to confrontation. While the narcissist can take confrontation to mean a personal attack or injury to the integrity of the self, the borderline tends to experience a direct statement as involvement and caring. In narcissistic and borderline pathogenesis, both approaches are important and may elicit significant responses.

Many borderline patients become confused by empathic interpretations because they misperceive them as colluding with their mythology or their own persecutory delusions. These patients need clear boundary distinctions between chaos and confusion and order and structure. A borderline wife, for example, began to feel I was continually blaming her for everything that went wrong. I tried to clarify that sometimes she was responsible for certain things she had created from her behaviors, but often there were situations that had nothing to do with her.

The therapist must be able to speak directly to the heart of the issues. Some years ago a couple came to therapy in great distress because the husband, Brian, had procured a gun and, while in a drunken state, had tried to kill their eldest son. Brian and his wife, Catherine, entered the consulting room, and within a few minutes Catherine was berating Brian, insisting that he get a thorough psychiatric evaluation because she lived in terror that someday he might do it again. Brian turned to me, "Tell her to stop badgering me. It's over, done with, and I'll never do it again." In the first session I told Brian, "What you did to your son was terrible. You must feel terrible; you must have some feelings about it yourself that you'd like to discuss."

In conjoint treatment I use interpretation similarly to help understand

and mirror feelings, but I also use confrontation to focus on the destructive or crazy behavior because feelings around that behavior are disavowed. In another case, the narcissist wife reported that her husband had recently lost the mortgage to the house that she owned from a previous marriage. The borderline husband claimed that the reason he lost the house was because the wife had not contributed to making the house payments. He felt let down and wanted to get even with her, to teach her a lesson. He distorted matters and turned the situation around to make it appear that it was all her fault. He would show her what it felt like to be in a bankrupt state or live in an impoverished, empty house.

The therapist confronted the borderline husband with his distortion of the situation, which allowed him to avoid facing his own fears and deficits. The therapist offered containment by indicating that trying to fix the blame on one partner would make the sessions a mess and relegate all partners to a bankrupt state. Confrontation, then, allowed the therapist to become a hard-enough object to push against the defenses when mirroring and empathy were not enough.

The Being Mommy versus the Doing Mommy

One of Winnicott's (1953) most vital contributions, and one I believe can be most helpful in blending the being mommy and the doing mommy (see the Case of Abigail and Claude in chapter 2) is the idea of the "environmental mother," the "background mother," the "holding mother." These mommies are not the ones who tell their children what to do. Their function lies in their being. As long as the child knows that somewhere there is a mother who is emotionally available, the child feels safe. The being mother does not do anything, but merely exists, merely is there. It is her very essence that soothes, understands, and provides meaning for the child's existence. The infant has the right to the mother's total preoccupation and feels safe simply by being in the presence of the mother. Often patients just need to know we are there in the kitchen or the office—even when they are not with us. Borderlines, in particular, need the environmental or background mother who can tolerate and accept the child's various states of mind. For the narcissist, the focus is on the beaming mother who enjoys the child for who the child is, and for what the child can do or accomplish. These mothers never tell the child what to do.

The doing mother is the mother who facilitates action and who tells the child what to expect and what is expected of him. The doing mother takes pleasure and great delight in the child's accomplishments and basks in the acclaim the child receives.

In the treatment of primitive mental disorders, the therapist must apply these two states depending on the affective experience of the moment. To become the doing mommy for the borderline may, in fact, intensify abandonment sufferings. For instance, if the borderline says, "I have a headache," and the doing mommy responds, "Well, take an aspirin," this can be experienced as further rejection. I believe these two approaches offer invaluable insights into the various listening perspectives needed to meet the overlapping and changeable modes of relatedness within the depth and scope of narcissistic/borderline disorders.

Winnicott (1965b) provided us with a holding environment and an environmental mother who helps the child with the being self as opposed to the doing self (that is, the false self that must perform) through mother's preoccupation with the child. This preoccupation with the child is what borderlines have missed. Winnicott talked about the differences between privation and deprivation. For example, the mother of the little girl in a ballet studio dressing room is totally preoccupied with dressing and fussing with her—exactly the preoccupation that the borderline has never experienced. In some of these relationships, it is important to actually say, "You are not ready to do anything yet until you understand what you are feeling." One narcissistic wife told the therapist that her mother and father waited 10 years to have her, and when they finally did, they "couldn't do enough for me. I feel so guilty because I have had everything and my parents gave me so much." This information provides a clue for the therapist to quickly become the being mommy—not the one who gives advice but the mommy who is available to hear the pain and mirror the grief and frustration.

Facing Deficits

Self-psychology does not help patients face their deficits directly because facing deficits might induce disruption, empathic failures, or disregard the patient's subjective experience. In object relations, however, through various techniques (including those of containment and reverie) attempts are made to help the patient face anxiety and tolerate or confront internal shortcomings. This enables the patient to reduce anxiety and quell the tendency to avoid feelings and blame others for all external failings. It also facilitates the development of the thinking apparatus and the ego strength necessary for conjoint treatment. The main differences between a self-psychological approach and an object-relational one with respect to deficits is that in self-psychology, one strives to understand the subjective experience of the patient, putting aside one's own preconceptions, whereas in object relations the therapist addresses the patient's distortions and misperceptions at face value.

Containment, empathy, and mirroring not only provide a model but show that the therapist is not afraid to face issues and stand up to issues directly. If the therapist cannot stand up to the patients' distortions, the patient cannot be helped to stand up to others and face conflictual issues with their own partners. Interpretations must not be crude, callous, and uncaring, but they need to be interfaced with a deep understanding of pathologies. An example would be, "You must be feeling very frightened or feeling very anxious and attacked because right now you are blaming your wife." This offers a holding and sustaining environment, enabling the patient to form an alliance with the therapist as a self object.

These ego defects must be kept in mind, particularly for the borderline, who may regard either the therapist or aspects of the treatment as an intrusive or bizarre object, interfering in the couple's relationship (e.g., costing money, taking time, and so forth). The therapist sometimes tends to make premature genetic transference interpretations. Flicker's (1988) connotation is that the therapist, often too uncomfortable to handle the assault or the attacks, then tries to get relief by putting the onus on the patient's external objects. To expand this notion further, one may speculate that to make a genetic interpretation too soon may be misperceived by the borderline as a massive projection.

FANTASY LIFE OF THE NARCISSIST VERSUS FANTASY LIFE OF THE BORDERLINE

Narcissists tend to turn toward the world of fantasy rather than the world of reality. One might speculate at this point that narcissists in general have a greater capacity to make use of fantasies than do their borderline counterparts. The narcissist has richer, more vivid early memories than those of the borderline; and, unlike the borderline, who disavows or splits off the experience, the narcissist has the ability to recall early experiences. The narcissist, therefore, seems more inclined to turn to an internal fantasy life.

The rich fantasy life of the narcissist can certainly be exciting, intriguing, and creative, and the therapist must take care not to destroy these qualities. Narcissists respond negatively when we infringe on their creative fantasy life. "It is not your creativity that is in question, but your attitude at any alternate suggestion that we must address," the therapist might say. The therapist must expand on the creative aspects of the narcissist's personality in order to bond with the narcissist. "For a short while others will make you feel unique and special, but this cannot be sustained because you haven't expanded your mind to encompass the fresh ideas that we are trying to develop. You close the doors when you push these ideas away."

The narcissist's fantasized grandiose self is reactivated and is reinvested with excessive libidinal energy, enabling a richer fantasy life to emerge. In sharp contrast, the borderline's inability to conjure up these internal images results in the individual being forced to resort to acting out impulses instead of fantasizing about them. I remember a colleague on a television talk show responding to a call about a woman who was concerned about her husband's admitting to being a transvestite. The therapist's response was, "Tell him not to wear the panties, but to fantasize about wearing them." Although it is not clear if the husband was borderline or not, this questions the borderline's capacity to make use of a fantasy life.

Kohut's (1971) theory of the etiology of perversions stimulates consideration of the possibility that narcissists may internalize a self object and that borderlines, who cannot form a narcissistic transference, cannot draw up rich internal images or fantasies.

To expand this notion further, let us review Loewenberg's (1985) account of Jacobo Timerman. Timerman, who had been an Argentinian newspaper publisher, was tortured in an Argentinian jail and became an upholder of human rights. He explained what happened to his mental life while he was incarcerated. Speaking of his surroundings, Timerman described a "conversion from a dark, gloomy place to that of a universe of spontaneous innovation and institutional beauty" (Loewenberg, 1985, p. 20). One of the most important conclusions to be drawn from Timerman's experience is the notion that the cell became a microcosm and that the peephole in Timerman's cell became an "inner world," or an "eye" looking from his cell into another world. According to Loewenberg, the role fantasy plays in the emotional life of such individuals as Timerman can be a vital force in one's survival.

Applying this notion of fantasy life to the narcissistic/borderline couple may provide further insight as to why a borderline often feels hurt and left out when in a relationship with a narcissist. Is it that the narcissist is likely to conjure up the image of the borderline partner and is more apt to fantasize and keep the image in mind? Is it also that the borderline cannot use imagery or symbolization and is bound by the dictum "Out of sight, out of mind"?

Entitlement Fantasies

Within the narcissistic/borderline configuration, reality is frequently distorted as the borderline is seduced into the narcissist's delusional world of entitlement fantasies and grandiose expectations (see Case 13, Jane and Ron, in chapter 9, and the Case of Rachel and Moses in chapter 3). The borderline is often confused by the unfairness displayed by his narcissist partner. Because of the borderline's tendency to comply, this behavior can exacerbate an already existing condition of a "no self" for the borderline and a "grand self" for the narcissist. "Why do you get to have things your way all the time?" asks the borderline. "Why?" responds the narcissist. "Because I'm entitled, that's why!" This "folie à deux" brings out the pathologies of entitlement or, to be more specific, "the entitled vs. the nonentitled."

The therapist's task is to help the narcissist face the inevitable fate: that one cannot have it all. The bitter paradox for the narcissist is that the desire to be everything and have everything produces the opposite results (getting very little and not being special). The narcissist must learn to tolerate frustration in order to develop a healthy dependency relationship with the therapist, who must constantly interpret how omnipotence can "hot dog" or destroy an interpersonal relationship. Because both the narcissist and the borderline have blurred boundaries, real entitlement needs get lost. The psychodynamic therapist must remind both the narcissist and the borderline partner of what is rightfully theirs.

Excitement

Narcissists and borderlines have their own definitions of "excitement." Paradoxically speaking, the narcissist does not need the exciting object; he/she "becomes" the exciting object, the center of the universe. Because narcissists cannot tolerate the state of neediness, they unconsciously deprive, conspire, and coerce others into hungrily needing them. Through unconscious attachments to their internal objects they stage excitement by making themselves the unavailable, unattainable, and craved object. Unable to tolerate the need for the object, "the breast," the narcissist offsets dependency by making others more important (paramours, parents, relatives, friends, colleagues, or anyone that offers the potential of maintaining the narcissist's sense of specialness). Unlike the borderline, the narcissist needs to be the center of attention to maintain a special sense of existence. Both narcissists and borderlines remain glued to their exciting internal objects because they both have long ago withdrawn and decathected from the whole-object world in which reality exists. Since narcissists are governed by a strong need for mirroring and define their self-worth based on being the center of attention, it is not unusual for them to seek out others who provide those functions. In the case of the narcissistic husband who has fantasies about other women because he craves excitement (see Case 5, Lenny and Sophia), we need to address the internal dullness and discover what's in the way of finding the real passion and excitement.

Richard Tuch, in *The Single Woman–Married Man Syndrome* (2000), offered an in-depth profile of narcissistic men who maintain their specialness by having not only one but two or more women pining over them, while each single woman has only a fraction of a man. He described two types of narcissistic men: the first is a Don Juan type who merely wants to conquer women in order to dominate and control them, while the second seeks women to fulfill and make up for a missing part of himself. Both these types manipulate women for their own interests. Although Tuch did not directly state that the vulnerabilities of the narcissist relate to the need for excitement, it is implicated that the pain they arouse in the woman creates excitement.

The borderline, on the other hand, does not need to be the exciting object, but instead latches onto others as the exciting objects to offset a dead internal world (unrequited love, obsessive–addictive love, unattainable love, insatiable love, tantalizing love), anything to obliterate barrenness, inner deadness, and boredom (see Case 18 in chapter 9). The following illustrates the dilemma of a woman who remains forever attached to the exciting object.

"Why did I do this? I had a great family, a wonderful, giving, loving husband, a beautiful home, great kids, and I run with men who offer me the excitement I crave. But in the end I am always left with nothing."

Therapists must explore these differences in the need for excitement among borderlines and narcissists. Ignoring them could result in severe regression in self-development. The challenge for narcissists is to allow others to excite them by relinquishing omnipotence, e.g., allowing the therapeutic breast to feed them by noting that the state of vulnerability is healthy, and it is their grandiosity that is pathological. Borderlines must get in contact with their inner needs and real passion to resurrect a dead and dormant inner world.

THERAPEUTIC BONDING

The success of the bonding experience between the therapist and the partners in couple therapy essentially revolves around the therapist's capacity to provide different bonding techniques to meet the ever-changing and evolving states within the narcissistic/borderline configuration. These varying bonding experiences can include the self-object bond, the mirroring mother, the containing mother, the hard-object mother, and the background object mother. Because narcissists and borderlines have different bonding needs, it is essential for the therapist to be aware of the various functions he/she can provide that will best match those needs.

Bonding, which is similar to empathy, is not to be confused with collusion or going along with the pathology. It is a specific therapeutic function that allows the patients to enter comfortably into an arena where work is to ensue. Bonding between therapist and patient essentially entails the therapist's awareness of the particular function he/she must provide at a given time and in the given situation (see Table 5.1) in order to offer containment, reverie, or empathy. The therapist does not bond with the patient's aggression, victimization, helplessness, or sadism, but with the patient's vulnerability.

"It is not acceptable for you to attack your husband and shame him or humiliate him in the presence of others, but I can understand why you do this. This is what your mother did with you, and this is your way of letting us know how humiliating this was for you as a child."

Another example is that of a borderline wife, who kept calling me away from sessions with other patients and threatening to kill herself. She had to be reminded that she didn't have to threaten her life to let me know that she had needs, albeit normal ones. She had to be reminded that her needs (the need for love, contact, and emotional connection) were reason enough for me to speak with her. All she had to do was make contact and she would be treated with the utmost respect (see "Parasitic Bonding," chapter 4).

A suicidal borderline wife, a substance abuser who had recently stopped taking drugs, wasn't sure she wanted to see me as a therapist because I didn't hug her as did her other therapist. Yet, I had other qualities she thought were vital. Especially significant was that she found me emotionally available, an experience she had not had before. She felt she needed a hug because she had never experienced a holding environment. No one had "touched" her internal world with understanding. Words were not enough; unless she was hugged, she felt she was not being cared for. The hug was like a drug, offering her a quick fix. The patient needed to understand that acting out a feeling was not the same as thinking and experiencing something new. Just as a drug can cover up real feelings, so can a hug. Only when the patient began to realize that thinking is different than "acting" and can lead to lasting and meaningful "internal hugs" was she able to wean herself from her addictive behavior. She learned she had a mouth that could talk and get fed, a mind that could think, a soul that could yearn and desire. Thinking, linking thoughts to lead to new ideas, verbal expression, containment, holding, waiting, patience, and understanding had never before been experienced (privation) by this woman.

"I always thought I was the one who had to give of myself. Whenever my husband wants sex, even when I am ill, I feel obligated to provide. For the first time, I don't feel guilty not giving in. I can stand up for myself."

The therapist who understands the importance of bonding has an opportunity to become the new self object, the holding/containing/reforming mommy therapist. This is particularly valuable in exploring the archaic injury and repeating emotional experiences of the past. The primary therapeutic task is the identification of feelings. This is not a far cry from Noah naming the animals. The transformation from nonverbal states to verbal states comes about through first identifying the feeling state and then channeling or detoxifying affective experiences into something meaningful: "There is nothing wrong with chaos, confusion, or ambivalence. These are normal states. What is wrong is how you persecute and attack yourself whenever you don't have an immediate answer or a quick fix."

The therapist here has an opportunity to bond with the healthy helpless and needy part of the borderline partner: "It sounds as though you are making progress, that you can tell me you felt helpless and not enraged. I wonder why you would want to stop now?" The therapist must bond with the patient's vulnerable part to facilitate integration, concurrently interpreting the dangerous aspects that block or disrupt ego functioning and the ability to maintain suitable object relatedness.

In bonding with the borderline, the therapist relies mainly upon containing/sustaining functions and soothing and tension-relieving functions. This allows the therapist to tap into the undiscovered area of the internal world by holding tightly to specific areas of anxiety. The therapist must make a meticulous effort to wean the borderline away from the false self and not identify with the projections. For example, a borderline spouse in conjoint therapy once heard the therapist interpret some material to her husband and was favorably impressed. Although comments like this can hook into the therapist's own grandiose self, it is important to point out how the wife's false self now wants to fuse with the therapist, become like the therapist, act like the therapist; but then she will lose herself and again end up feeling empty and depleted. She needs to know that if she becomes the therapist, she will never find her own voice or be able to experience in her own way.

Therapeutic bonding occurs when the therapist can be viewed as the feeding, holding, and providing mommy, a replacement for the empty breast, the unavailable/depriving one. Bion (1967) described a danger that presents itself in an unrecognizable form that he called the "beta shield." A simple example of this is disregarding a parking ticket and then being shocked to find out the car has been impounded. Since the borderline is unable to anticipate and plan for the future or recognize that there are consequences for actions, the therapist must be able to help organize and bring structure to the borderline's chaotic, fragmented state. Protection and safety are provided through the therapist's emotional availability. This availability is in direct contrast to the danger of the narcissistic spouse, who continually reenacts the old drama of "enough is enough."

CONCLUSION

Using Klein's paranoid–schizoid and depressive positions as a starting point, this chapter goes on to detail a wide range of clinical and technical approaches that are common to the treatment of narcissistic/borderline couples—or those exhibiting primitive defense mechanisms. In addition to outlining contrasting positions and stages of treatment, I suggest that transference be expanded to include "couple transference," which encompasses the couple's mutual projections, delusions, and distortions reconstructed by the therapist, intuitiveness, imagination, association, and countertransference reactions. Dynamic positions such as shame and guilt are incorporated into the structure of the transference to illuminate how the couple plays out their innermost dramas. The therapist who understands the importance of weaning and bonding techniques has an opportunity to become the new self object—the holding/containing/mirroring/reforming mommy who can lead the partners into a more mature stage of development that will greatly influence the outcome of therapy.

Chapter 6

⚞⚟

Group Psychology and the Narcissistic/ Borderline Couple

INTRODUCTION

Only recently has the study of group psychology gained popularity. Since psychoanalysis was intended for the individual, many psychoanalysts have looked askance at applying analytic concepts and principles to group behaviors. Individual pathology becomes even more glaringly apparent within a group than when the individual is isolated from the herd. Freud (1914/1957) was the first to recognize animal instincts within the group (Lachkar, 1993, pp. 276–287) as he looked for the forces that bind people together. In studying a group of men who banded together in a primal horde, he noted that they formed a prototype social organization. In his monograph on group psychology, Freud showed that the ego ideal is the vehicle for group formation. In *Totem and Taboo* (1912/1955), Freud recognized the existence of a collective mind, a concept that I have extended to the "couple mind." Groups, like couples, use aggression and primitive defenses to guard against painful affects through collective fantasies. Scapegoating is a common phenomenon to avoid the "enemy" (real or fantasized).

Many other theorists, including Kernberg (1976, 1980), Bion (1959), Dicks (1967), Willi (1982), and Lachkar (1984, 1985, 1986, 1998a, 1998b,

2002) share the view that group psychology can offer insights into how individuals exhibit properties similar to those in group dynamics.

Kernberg (1980, 1995) brought to our attention the way in which groups collectively guard against aggression through primitive regressive defenses, very much as an individual guards against "enemies." In the relational dyad, the real or fantasized enemy can be the affair, the mother-in-law, the friends, the money, and so forth. Kernberg's understanding of the use and misuse of aggression provides valuable guidelines for our understanding of the regressive nature of relationships. His premise is that if aggression goes in the wrong direction, primitive defenses like envy take over, infect, and dominate the relationship. Just think what happens when highly charged, eroticized, sadomasochistic relational ties are operative within political groups.

Dicks (1967) applied psychoanalytic object relations to the diagnosis and treatment of marital couples. Willi (1982) expanded Dick's view of marriage. Dicks felt that unresolved object relations foster conflict within marriage and parent–child relationships. Willi took into account Dicks, Bion, and object relations theory when he used the central term "collusion." In his book *Couples in Collusion,* his basic theme was the application of group dynamics to marital therapy. Willi's work has been most inspiring in understanding the collusive nature within marital tensions, which I refer to as *folie à deux.* This is a process whereby two parties share a common delusional fantasy. This term extends Klein's (1957) notion of projective identification. *Folie à deux* involves two people projecting their delusional fantasies back and forth, engaging in a foolish "dance for two." An abusive partner, a cult leader, a terrorist, and others who contaminate or infect the other with their delusional system (usually a victim or a person with a dependent or passive nature) can make someone momentarily "lose his or her mind," especially when in a state of idealization. This happened with Freud's relationship with Fleiss, who talked Freud into believing in numerology, a very strange occurrence for two neurologically trained medical doctors. Two people can join up in each other's delusional systems.

Many of my earlier contributions have referenced group phenomena as a means to understanding the regressive/primitive nature in couples. The more regressed a couple is, the more they withdraw into themselves and live in fear of an external enemy—and the more they are inclined to collude in each other's delusional fantasies. Similar to the group, something bonds the couple together, and that something can be explored within the context of group formation. These ideas correspond closely to those of Bion (1959).

According to Bion, every individual has an impact on the group's functioning (much like a family system). Group members share collective myths, dreams, ideologies, and fantasies that can distort their perspective of reality. The couple, like the group, needs a leader (therapist) who can put thoughts and ideas into perspective and concretize the mythology, which provides justification and gives meaning to the existence of the couple. Bion believed that helping group members decode and identify covert messages could be of great value. Using the model of the Tavistock Institute of Human Relations in London, where research and training with a model of group behaviors originated, Bion emphasized the power of the group, which he claims has the capacity to dominate, control, and intoxicate its members.

I share the view that issues within the individual become more glaringly apparent when viewed from the standpoint of the group. Plagued with group myths and shared collective group fantasies, people become intoxicated and mesmerized. Behaviors that are not easy to explain are heavily rooted and embedded in the shared group myths and fantasies. Group thinking is not motivated by rational thought, but rather by dogma, pedagogy, and primitive ideas. In the primitive mind of the group's poisonous pedagogy, split-off emotions such as shame/blame and feelings of vulnerability are projected outward, making others the victim or the scapegoat. The interaction between the victim and the perpetrator or terrorist illustrates how people in the group turn to aggressive acts to get rid of unwanted parts of the self. Be it victim or aggressor, adherents of these behaviors and group fantasies perpetuate the group myths (Lachkar, 2002).

Bion (1959) made major contributions to the study of group dynamics. In his seminal work, Bion highlighted two kinds of groups. The first is the work group, a rational-thinking group whose members are task/reality oriented. Work group members form parasitic bonds and rely more on individual thinking than dogma or group ideology. Second is the basic assumption group, a regressed group whose members function on the basis of blame/shame, fight/flight, with a heavy reliance on magical thinking and other primitive defenses (omnipotence, denial, splitting, projection, and projective identification). The basic assumption group is the regressive group that inclines more toward primitive defenses and nonrational thinking; members form parasitic bonds for the sole purpose of emotional survival. This concept can be applied to the narcissistic/borderline couple. In earlier works (Lachkar, 1984, 1985), I referred to the real relationship versus the fantasized relationship. These designations are extrapolated from Bion's groups to provide further understanding of the regressive nature of these emotional dyad configurations.

The Work Group

Task Orientation

According to Bion (1959), the work group is composed of thinking, task-oriented members whose primary concern is the achievement of goals. The group members are rational and are dominated by individuality, creative forces, and situational learning. They rely on individual thinking rather than dogma or group idealogy. The work group does not oppose new ideas, and its members can operate through the mature functioning part of the ego; that is, work group members can tolerate frustration long enough to learn from experience and are able to stand up for beliefs and ideas.

The Real Relationship

Like the work group, the real relationship operates through the mature, observing part of the ego, in which reality can be experienced via the sensory motor apparatus. Persons in the real relationship pay attention to instincts, signal anxiety, can learn from experience, search out truth and knowledge, and take the necessary steps to solve problems. They are not willing to take in the projections of others and can tolerate a reasonable amount of frustration and unknown elements. The real relationship focuses on what is, not on what ought to be. In lieu of evacuation, anxiety is contained and feelings are expressed rather than spilled out.

Joseph Campbell (1988), the late mythologist, provided one view of the real relationship. He suggested that myths help put one's mind in touch with the experience of being alive. The myth tells one what the experience is—for example, what marriage is:

> The myth tells you what it is. It is the reunion of the separated dyad. Originally you were one. You are now two in the world, but the recognition of the spiritual identity is what marriage is. It's different from a love affair. It has nothing to do with that. It's another mythological plane of experience. When people get married because they think it's a long-time love affair, they'll be divorced very soon, because all love affairs end in disappointment. But marriage is the recognition of a spiritual identity. If we live in a proper life, if our minds are on the right qualities in regarding the person of the opposite sex, we will find our proper male or female counterpart. But if we are distracted by certain sensuous interest, we'll marry the wrong person. By marrying the right person, we reconstruct the image of the incarnate God, and that's what marriage is. (Campbell, p. 6)

To expand further on Campbell's (1988) ideas, I believe he was saying that when one considers the realistic aspects of marriage, one has to face that marriage is a sacrifice, not only each to the other but also to the unity in a relationship. Campbell saw a realistic relationship as existing in two phases:

First is the youthful marriage following the wonderful impulse that nature has given us in the interplay of the sexes biologically in order to produce children. But there comes a time when the child graduates from the family and the couple is left. I've been amazed at the number of my friends who in their forties or fifties grow apart. They have had a perfectly decent life together with the child, but they interpreted their union in terms of the relationship through the child. They did not interpret it in terms of their own personal relationship to each other. (Campbell, p. 7)

The Basic Assumption Group

The basic assumption group opposes new ideas, demonstrates primitive behaviors, and uses unconscious defense mechanisms to get rid of anxiety and discourage change. Group members are dominated by irrational, delusional thinking, group myths, and group fantasies. A basic assumption couple fantasizes that repetition of painful experiences or finding fault in the projected "enemy" will lead to conflict resolution. The couple may, for example, try to force change through attempts to get the other to change or through other primitive modes or expressions rather than through acceptance of reality.

There is a tendency for members of the basic assumption group to depend on the leader and not to challenge what the leader says, which provides a false sense of safety. Group psychology explains why individuals who adhere to certain mythic origins need to form an identification with a leader who can concretize their mythology. Somewhere in the group lies an enemy who is to blame, and the leader is the messiah, the one who will save the group from calamity. There is always the wish for a new ending; however, the savior never comes, and the therapist is often the last hope (Bion, 1959, 1962; Lachkar, 1984). Each basic assumption group earmarks a different leader. The dependent parasitic group, the most regressed, chooses the most malignant or pathological leader, like Hitler or Milosevic.

Scapegoating

A familiar scenario is that the group leader singles out someone to be the group's scapegoat. The group members go along because they need an object to project onto or because they idealize the leader, whom they are afraid to challenge or confront. The group then isolates the "enemy," splitting the person off as the bad object. The problem quickly mushrooms into a vicious circle. The more outcast the scapegoat becomes, the more negative the scapegoat's behavior. The magnification of the bad elements serves to preserve the group fantasy that the group is good, and that any badness must lie in the outcast, isolated member. Scapegoats and victims feed the delusional systems by taking in the projections and identifying with them.

FANTASIZED RELATIONSHIPS

Persons in fantasized relationships cannot learn from experience and cannot tolerate pain or frustration. They lose sight of the task at hand, adhere to "quick fixes," and confuse their healthy dependency needs with parasitic ones. They pair off with others who justify these psychopathologies, and they form collusive bonds with those who offer testimony to the "other's" craziness. A diminution of reality testing and judgment occurs because couples in fantasized relationships are in a constant search for approval. The narcissistic partner may seek to pair up with others who collude with exaggerated entitlement fantasies, whereas the borderline may seek justification for attacking and blaming impulses. The collective fantasized image of the relationship then becomes prey to disintegration because neither partner has a strong enough sense of self.

Understanding group formation helps to discern why regressive couples stay in the "dance" or engage in circular behaviors. In conjoint treatment, our task must focus on helping these couples face the realistic aspects of their relationships and continually remind them of why they have entered treatment.

The Affair: Real or Fantasized

No book about conjoint treatment can be complete without addressing the proverbial affair; questions about this arise at every seminar or course on couple treatment. It is my belief that the issue is not the affair, but rather the betrayal. If one betrays the other or oneself, it is likely that self-betrayal will be a theme that will recur in the couple transference, one that may manifest itself in such ways as coming late to sessions, nonpayment, unfulfilled promises, forgetfulness, and guilt.

Group dynamics theories can further our understanding of relationships occurring outside the marital unit. The affair, viewed within the context of the basic assumption group, is a collusion of betrayal with another person, stimulating such primitive defenses as wishful thinking, splitting, projection, and envy. The affair is often manifested as the split-off part of the self to ward off persecutory anxiety and envy. It may be considered a form of "pairing off" or fight/flight (terms described by Bion as a form of joining with others who share common myths and distortions of reality).

An affair is a fantasy and is not based on reality. In some instances, it is also the highest form of betrayal, not only because of the lies and deceit to the partner, but also because of those to the self. The act indicates a lack of commitment not only to a legal document but to that which is considered by most as a sacred oath. Although this realization may evoke great guilt or shame, patients need to face this.

The notion of the affair can create considerable anxiety both for the couple and, because betrayal and abandonment tend to be projected, for the therapist. Patients often feel very embarrassed and very anxious upon admitting they have been unfaithful. One does not have to be an analyst or psychotherapist to recognize the destructive nature of an affair. The affair is not indicative of a whole-object relationship, but of a part-object one. That feelings and conflictual issues get stirred up may sometimes be viewed as constructive, although only if understood in relation to the development of the self.

These comments are not moral judgments; they are not intended either to condone or to criticize but rather to enhance understanding of individuals who engage in such betrayals. These external relationships need to be examined in order to determine what internal issues get stirred up within the context of narcissistic and borderline disorders. In my view, narcissistic and borderline individuals who engage in outside relationships often do so for reasons connected to their specific disorders and qualitative differences. According to Scarf (1987):

> The discovery, by one partner, that the other is involved in an affair is a disaster, like a death—which, in an important sense, it actually is. It is the death of that marriage's innocence, the death of trust, the death of naïve understanding of what the relationship itself is all about. (p. 128)

Scarf's (1987) research corroborates the views expressed here, that affairs are often a product of internal conflict and guilt feelings on the part of the one engaging in such acts. Getting caught can vary from being infuriating to being a disruption of one's whole life. The trauma upon discovery of the partner's infidelity can be an earth-shattering experience, one that leaves the other partner finding it extremely difficult to think, to work, or to function at all. The betrayed person's mind begins to wander; the person feels split off, confused, empty, depressed, and even suicidal when not in the presence of the deceiving lover. "They ruminate and get distracted by thoughts of the affair and the betrayal!" (Scarf, 1987, p. 129).

A borderline wife was so emotionally demolished upon the breakup of the relationship with her lover that she described her experience as totally paralyzing. "I could not function. I would sit home all day, stare out the window or gaze at the answering machine, just waiting for him to call. He decided to stay with his wife. I feel so hurt and rejected, as if I don't even exist or I don't count" (borderline vulnerability).

A narcissistic husband described the experience as so unbelievably upsetting that he kept driving by his ex-lover's house just to get a glimpse of her: "She represents all the excitement in the world. She possesses all the qualities I have ever dreamed up. When I am with her, I feel passion! If feel that I am truly alive! She makes me feel so good about myself! She appreciates me, and makes me feel that I am the most wonderful man in the world!" (narcissistic vulnerability).

It is clear that taking into account narcissistic and borderline diagnostic distinctions and the qualitative differences of their individual needs can be helpful in viewing these complex and often varied situational circumstances. For instance, the narcissistic partner may enter the affair to seek out others for approval and admiration and to stir up exciement and passion as a stimulus to evoke the "real passion" yearning within the self. The borderline may seek an outside relationship to get back at the narcissistic partner. In addition, the envious qualities of the loved partner may stir up deficits lacking in both partners; however, for the borderline these deficits evoke the need to possess and control, while for the narcissist they may evoke the need to get excitement from an external force.

In short, the affair has elements similar to those in basic assumption groups. The therapist must be careful not to join up with the collusional part of the affair because in the attempt to hold onto the secret the therapist becomes the betrayer. A patient making it appear that the therapist is the betrayer can take away from the real issues and focus of the conflict.

Intimacy and Closeness: An Emotional Distancer

Many authors have described the affair as an emotional distancer, a vehicle through which couples play games vacillating between closeness and distancing. A partner might say, "I wait at least two days after he calls and then I call him because I don't want him to think I am overly anxious or needy."

To view the issues as merely a process of intimacy/closeness or separateness/distancing is, in my view, an oversimplification of the dynamic process. Rather, the focus should be on the deficiencies within the personality seeking to emerge. It is not the affair that is the issue, but it is the affair that stirs up the issues, the desires and fears, and brings them to the individual's attention in such a manner that they cannot be ignored.

Narcissistic and borderline patients often resort to play-acting or game playing because they are not truly grounded in their own sense of themselves. For instance, a borderline lover may play-act at being busy when the lover or admirer calls, as an expression of a wish to have a more fulfilling life: "I distance myself from him because when he doesn't call I feel so left out. I feel awful, as if there is no me, or as if I don't count; so I'd rather be the one to avoid seeing him than have him rejecting me." The feeling of not counting is typical for borderlines, and affair relationships with narcissistic partners, perpetuating this feeling of not existing, are quite common.

In other instances, the affair can stir up issues of control: "I feel so frustrated. I never know where she is or what she is doing. I wonder if she is making love to her husband, if she would betray me when she tells me I am the one she really cares about." This borderline patient is trying to resolve old issues of being controlled or dominated by his mother and now is wishing magically to control his lover, a situation seen frequently with borderline patients. In the case of this affair, the therapist might interpret, "Yes, now you are wishing to live in someone else's house; then you will never have a chance to face what belongs to you and what belongs to someone else."

A borderline unmarried woman involved with a narcissistic married man states, "He possesses all the qualities I have always wanted in a man. When I am not with him, I feel like a nothing, as if I'm going to die." Further investigation revealed that this woman is unconsciously seeking the lover's qualities for herself; however, the borderline defense of not feeling worthy gets in the way of fulfilling her need. The desire to attain must be viewed, in this case, as the healthy part of the relationship, and not as the destructive part.

Things are different for the narcissist, who will cling to the love object in order to gain approval and revive the fantasy of being the admired one. Admiration temporarily distracts the narcissist from facing the distorted view of what he or she is truly entitled to and from acquiring the ability to attain admirable traits of one's own. Through the idealization process, the narcissistic partner attributes to the other the role of the provider of passion and excitement. Viewing the affair in this way helps repair the split between the good and bad internal objects. Not feeling deserving enough to attain them forces the narcissist to join up, fuse, or become engulfed with another who possesses these admirable qualities. It is the split-off parts of the self that experience desire through the painful bodily sensations associated with envy, annihilation, anxiety, and primitive superego functioning. These split-off parts of the personality are then reintrojected into the psyche as the external enemy, as persecutory and retaliatory anxiety, resulting in such responses as, "Someone out there is out to get me; I'm too needy!"

Neither the intimacy nor the distancing aspects of the affair are as related to the fear of closeness as they are to the parasitic bond. The affair is a flight into fantasy, an escape, or a joining up with a messiah who will rescue one from facing one's shattered world. The real fears of the affair are related to such concepts as boundary confusion, as intrusiveness into the space of another's persecutory anxiety, a state in which one becomes overwhelmed with feelings of envy, greed, jealousy, and primitive defenses of sadistic rage, shame, guilt, magical thinking, denial, idealization, and devaluation.

The fear of loss of the lover, then, is not so much the fear of actual loss of the other as of the more important loss of contact with the defective parts of the undeveloped self. Both closeness and distancing are used in the affair to avoid this loss.

ROLE OF SOCIETY

The role played by society in the drama of the couple as a function of the group is perhaps best revealed as the couple comes to litigation and the courts. Florence Bienenfeld (1980, 1983, 1986, 1987) interviewed thousands of families during her 10 years as senior marriage and family counselor-mediator for the Conciliation Court of Los Angeles County. Bienenfeld observed that many divorcing couples who litigate child custody and financial issues through the court systems were shockingly similar to the paradigm of the narcissistic/borderline couple:

> Mediators are very accustomed to working with difficult problems and disputes and with upset divorcing and divorced parents. There are, however, some parents who continually sabotage the possibility of ever reaching an agreement or of getting things settled. It is both fascinating and often frustrating to observe the way these parents see the other parent as causing all the problems. Both parents appear blind to how they themselves made the situation worse and how they each sabotage their own children. . . .
>
> The saddest part about these intensely emotional, non-ending parental conflicts is the way their children are hopelessly trapped in the middle. (Bienenfeld, 1986, pp. 39–42)

When asked why there are so many divorces, Bienenfeld (personal communication, 1987) responded as follows:

> Statistically there are over one million marriages in California alone and at least one out of two get divorced. There are many reasons: People get married for the wrong reason. They feel pressured that it is time to get married, or that no one else came along. . . . They bring in old unresolved issues from the past or they live with the idea that someone else

will fulfill them or make them happy and when this fails they feel disappointed and blame the other. . . . Frequently, one partner will put the other partner on hold (often the narcissist), while working or raising children. . . . People cannot be put on hold. The best thing is to help couples be accountable for their lives, even victims or abusers.

Bienenfeld (personal communication, 1987) suggested that society should take more responsibility, that "there is not enough support from extended family, or neighbors, nor is there enough education from an early age teaching people how to communicate, how to settle disputes, how to mediate, how to get along with other people."

These days most children are reared by single parents and working mothers, left with babysitters from an early age. In addition, one-third of children of divorce lose one of their parents as a result of the divorce. Divorces are detrimental to family life, but are not nearly as destructive as the proceedings the family must endure during and after the dissolution process. In short, the implication is that children are never able to mourn the loss of the parent. Without being able to mourn, the child tends to get rid of the parent, and thereby is unable to introject the parent as an important and meaningful internal representation.

PSYCHOHISTORY

Psychohistory is currently crystallizing as an important method of historical research. According to Loewenberg (1985), psychoanalysis is to the individual what psychohistory is to the culture's mythology. Psychohistory offers a broader range from which to view cross-cultural differences. Many psychohistorians recognize undiscovered, primitive territory that lies in the study of group psychology. They have discussed collective group fantasies alluding to shame, blame, guilt, projection, persecution, and paranoid anxieties as fundamental concepts in understanding behaviors within groups and nations. For decades critics questioned whether psychologists had any business considering moral and political issues. Many continue to feel there is insufficient justification for analyzing groups in individual terms and that it is difficult enough making distinctions between individuals let alone tackling group diagnoses. Thus, psychotherapists have long shied away from psychohistory, claiming that it will lead to dramatic, wildly speculative interpretations. After all, psychotherapy was originally intended for the individual.

Psychohistory offers two important venues to explore as we delve into conflicts involved in cross-cultural relations. First is the role psychohistory plays in helping us understand cultural patterns handed down from generation to generation, embedded in the very core of the group's identity. These are expressed through mythology, ideology, religion, childrearing practices, and the treatment of women. These ongoing behaviors and characteristics are strikingly similar to those of couples with different ethnic backgrounds. Second is the exploration of the role that group fantasies play and the way they are enacted through identification with group leaders who best play out the group's myths, ideology, and omnipotent fantasies. These venues can help us understand how the architecture of a culture can shape certain personality types. The purpose of this analysis is not so much to assign a "diagnosis" but to explore how the structural design of a culture can engender certain personality types, which I refer to as the "cross-cultural" narcissist ("cultural" narcissist) and "cross-cultural" borderline ("cultural" borderline).

In addition to Loewenberg, other theoreticians have made significant contributions to the field of psychohistory. DeMause (1974, 2002a, 2002b) referred to group formation as a product of the abused child syndrome—what he terms the "poison container" (2002b, p. 83), the evolutionary symbol of failed childrearing practices. From a psychohistorical perspective, DeMause showed how groups shape the political, religious, and social behaviors from vestiges of early traumas. To further his analysis, he explores how groups go to war to revenge their childhood trauma and rid themselves of feelings of sinfulness and shame, hoping to cleanse their emotions, to be reborn by sacrificing victims. The child becomes the receptacle for the bad, unwanted, projected, split-off parts of themselves. "It's all the child's fault!" Children become the scapegoats for the frailties of the adult, a method of relieving anxiety by not facing the realistic aspects of the conflict. In the chapter "War as Righteous Rape and Purification," DeMause (2002b) stated how traumas from war get repeated as a "re-staging of early traumas of war and social violence" (pp. 210–217). Inspired by DeMause's analysis, many of my psychohistorical contributions (Lachkar, 1983, 1993a, 1993b, 2002) have described groups in conflicts as having similar properties to couples, and collectively sharing early trauma that is revisited during times of emotion and conflict (V-spots).

DeMause (2002, p. 344) maintained that the roots of group fantasies are inextricably linked to childrearing practices. He offered a chilling account of life in Islamic fundamentalist societies filled with violence, cruelty, and sexual exploitation of children. These are familiar themes in countries that do not stress the importance of healthy child development.

From a psychohistorical perspective Kobrin (2002) links violence among death pilots of 9/11 as traceable to the unresolved attachment to the early mother, and the act of blowing themselves up as a narcissistic/omnipotent fantasy as they form the ultimate relationship with the "cockpit" of the airplane in lieu of intimacy with a woman. According to Kobrin, it is a moment in time when they can play God.

Vamik Volkan (1979) is another prominent figure who stressed the importance of mythology as a basic tool for understanding conflict between groups—in this case the Greeks and the Turks. Volkan's explanation goes beyond "the national mood" to a group or collective mind. He was one of the first to use analytic terms such as projection and externalizaton in relation to the Turks, and he described how Turkish children learn to externalize all "bad" hostile objects onto the Greeks. Volkan's arguments hold that such projections and externalizations are supported by a cultural design that colludes with these group fantasies.

In analyzing group fantasies around acts of terrorism, Robins and Post (1997) view terrorist acts as a perverse way of connecting to the world. They maintained that people are fueled by paranoid delusional leaders and glom onto a piece of reality to "justify" their causes, e.g., the enviable or "evil" American. Paranoids have enemies; they do not have rivals or adversaries. Enemies are not to be defeated or compromised, but destroyed. People who are paranoid tend to project their hatred and hostility onto others. As Robins and Post pointed out, these kinds of leaders not only lie but believe that their lies are the truth.

Howard Stein (1978) was one of the first to assign group dynamics to religious and political groups. He later discussed the conflict between the Israelis and the Palestinians as two groups locked in a mutual suicidal, masochistic embrace, each requiring the other to justify further violence. Although I may not agree with his basic premises, he was one of the first to discuss psychodynamic interactions from a psychodynamic perspective.

The first influence on my work in melding psychohistory and therapy emanated from the Walter Briehl Human Rights Organization, a group of dedicated psychoanalysts who treat torture victims. Here I learned that people who have been tortured require special treatment, as do victims who have been physically or emotionally tormented. The classical model of psychoanalytic technique and principles was not encompassing enough to cover the complexity of the treatment of torture victims, which necessitated taking into account not only the cultural differences but the varying group dynamics. For example, certain victims of torture need to be in "familiar" surroundings (which can mean ethnic foods, familiar scents—anything to assuage reminders of torturous experiences of prison cells).

I first ventured into psychohistory by delving into the Middle East, examining the historical, mythological, psychological, and religious past. I felt compelled to understand what it is that binds these groups in ongoing, circular, never-ending, painful, destructive battles that make conflict resolution virtually impossible. Paradoxically, through my compelling interest in the Middle East, I began to see the Arab–Israeli conflict (Lachkar, 1983, 1985, 1993a, 1993b) as similar to the interactions of the narcissistic/borderline couple. This paved the way to my in-depth work on marital therapy. The elements that perpetuate political/religious conflicts are the same elements that keep marital partners enmeshed in these primitive bonds.

We cannot stereotype or make sweeping generalizations about all Arabs and Jews or any other ethnic/religious group. However, just as an analyst has the right to analyze a patient's dreams, we have the right to analyze a country's mythology, religion, leaders, ideologies, child-rearing practices, shared myths, and collective group fantasies. It has been said that the people who identify with certain leaders who perpetuate a group's mythology are the ones who perpetuate the conflict. Thus, it is critical to understand the mythology, folklore, and collective ideologies that gave rise to the psyche of the group—the essence of psychohistory.

I refer to two recurring myths in the Bible and the Koran that had significance in fueling the Arab–Israeli conflict. The first myth is the belief that Jews are God's "chosen people," which led to a collective "Israeli-Jewish" narcissistic diagnosis (dominated by such defenses as guilt, grandiosity, and excessive entitlement fantasies), and the second is that Arabs are a "fatherless," orphaned society, which led to a collective "Arab-Moslem" borderline diagnosis (dominated more by shame/blame with corresponding abandonment anxieties). Stemming from these mythic origins are age-old sentiments, passions, and feelings that continually resurface, giving rise to many shared collective group fantasies.

The Arab–Israeli conflict, with its confluence of psychoanalysis and psychohistory, has striking similarities to the marital discord that I have observed in my clinical practice (Lachkar, 1983, 1998a). Where do culture and pathology meet? Where do the boundaries between aggression, cruelty, and cultural tradition interface? Chapter 7 delves deeper into these issues, describing the forces mutual to individual psychopathology and cross-cultural relationships Psychohistorians cannot ignore the psychodynamic aspects of character and culture.

Identification with Leaders

Just as individuals can identify with certain abusive and destructive partners in a domestic relationship, so people in groups can identify with destructive leaders. At the macro level, a paranoid leader may not be a far cry from a partner in a domestic relationship. Groups form a "trance," an intense identification with a delusional leader that reinforces the group's mythological fantasies. However, in reality there is a duality: the leader who can be cruel and sadistic can also be loving and kind. Aggression and cruelty reinforce the libidinal ties in the group as long as there are outsiders onto whom envy can be projected. Often these are charismatic, albeit pathologically disturbed, leaders who are paranoid and/or schizophrenic. They offer the group the fantasy of being "savior daddy." Classic examples of such leaders are Saddam Hussein and Slobodan Milosevic. Milosevic, for instance, is a pathological narcissist with antisocial features, a fascist, and a psychopath (Doder, 1999).

Leaders who play out the pervading myths express the group's dysfunctionality and form a most powerful and intimate connection with the group. The leader knows how to play on the group's omnipresent fear of imminent danger (real or imagined) from outside forces. In regressive dependency groups, the dominant features are blame, attack, retaliation, getting back at any cost. Themes such as "Drive the Jews into the sea," "Return to the land of milk and honey," "Land for Peace," and "Save Serbia," are too familiar themes. When tensions surge, members resort to shame/blame, fight/flight, and scapegoating. The group searches for an enemy to blame and a leader/messiah who will save the group from calamity.

People identify with group leaders who offer any promise or semblance of bonding (Lachkar, 1993a, 1993b) even if it means loss, death, self-destruction, or self-sacrifice. In Arab countries the projected enemy is Israel. "Israel is our enemy; we must drive the Jews into the sea!" Not all leaders reinforce aggression; Gandhi, for one, was a champion of "peace for all." Leaders who are the most likely to survive and who inflame the conflict and aggression are the ones who best perpetuate the group's ideologies, mythologies, and collective group fantasies.

Plagued by this way of thinking, the psychohistorian might ask such questions as: How can a country like Germany, so heavily invested in morality, Christian values, and orderliness, suddenly create a sea of horror, a flood of blood, diarrhea, and filth? Similarly, how can a country such as Japan, so invested in saving face, in displaying obedience and respect for elders, suddenly engage in unspeakable brutalities and atrocities with the Chinese and Koreans?

Traumatic Societies

Societies in the Middle East have created traumatic environments for children. These include children of mothers who have been abused and who have witnessed abuse; children who have been molested, mutilated, "clitorized," infibulated; children who have witnessed parental intercourse/incest; children who have been weaned too soon or weaned too late; children of mothers who have been submissive to men; children who have been trained to fight in wars; children of Holocaust survivors; products of anti-Semitism; and Diaspora babies. These are terrified children of parents who have experienced horrific, catastrophic disasters and traumatic experience through years of battling, fighting, lost homelands, displacement, abandonment, and collective abuse. This includes profound neglect in child-rearing practices. The basic tenor of these societies reflects the backlash of years of violations, including disenfranchising women and ignoring children's rights—the right to be a child, to have a mind, to have "normal" and safe developmental conditions. In essence, when both leaders and victims share a common fantasy, they begin to form perverse attachments with destructive leaders; this is a repetition of the trauma of neglect, betrayal, violence, torture, mutilation, and abuse, repeated again and again. DeMause (2002a, 2002b) offered a chilling account of life in Islamic fundamentalist societies filled with violence, cruelty, and sexual exploitation of children. These are familiar themes in countries that do not stress the importance of healthy child development.

Pain/Sacrifice/Victimization

What is it that perpetuates conflict and makes individuals sacrifice their own lives and resort to self-destructive behavior? To find these answers we need to begin by analyzing cultural patterns handed down from generation to generation, embedded in the very identity of the group, and expressed through myths, ideology, religion, and child-rearing practices. The question of why a group sacrifices its own people at the expense of the collective group self led me to me to think about emotional abuse. Understanding group phenomena and group formation have added invaluable knowledge to what occurs in marital conflict. First is the tendency for impoverished groups to identify with aggressive/dangerous leaders who play-act the role of the fanaticized daddy/leader offering false promises of hope and security. Second, when one is vulnerable, one is more inclined to identify and fuse with those who offer a semblance of bonding (Lachkar, 1993).

It is therefore the "meaningless" that epitomizes states of terror rather than deprivation itself. Patients may feel enraged, but at least they feel a "sense of aliveness instead of deadness" (Kernberg, 1989, p. 196). The borderline stays in painful relationships because pain is preferable to emptiness—to facing the loneliness, the void, the black hole. "I'll do anything, just don't leave me!" Many borderline patients are preoccupied with pain as a way of bonding with their objects, and will often resort to self-mutilation. "When I burn myself with a cigarette, then I know I'm alive. I exist!" (the Palestinians search for an existence). As bad as the pain is, it is still better than having to face the real relationship, the real issues, the internal deficits. The relationship is the transitional object to the internal world. "I'd rather die a suicide bomber to prove we as a people exist!" (Lachkar, 2002). "Now I know I am alive! I have purpose; I shall give honor and status to my family!"

CONCLUSION

Many theorists believe that group psychology can offer insights into the behavior of individuals, who exhibit properties similar to those involved in group dynamics. Perhaps this is especially true for couple therapy. Within narcissistic and borderline relationships, the shared couple myth needs to be understood in terms of the couple as a unit, as well as in terms of each person's delusions, distortions, and projections. Can we diagnose a "couple mind" in terms of the partners' collective defenses? Is it possible to understand that one partner will inflict pain upon the other to dehumanize and destroy that person? Understanding group myths and the shared emotional fantasies of couples can help objectify the highly charged passions that are so difficult for many couples to face. Successful couple therapy requires us to deal with both individual and couple transferences.

Chapter 7

Cross-Cultural Couples

Today our consultation rooms are beginning to resemble a mini-United Nations. Our offices are filled with couples from various ethnic backgrounds (multicultural couples, cross-cultural couples, interracial and interethnic couples). No longer is it unusual to see intermarriages, same-sex marriages, blended-family marriages, and stepfamily marriages. The influx of immigrants has led to many cultural and societal concerns. Living in a vast and ever-changing society, we as therapists must learn to cope with and adapt to these rapidly changing times.

A person who intermarries is not only marrying another person, they are also marrying a culture—tying religious, ethnic, and cultural knots. Treating emotional vulnerabilities must include understanding the cultural and qualitative distinctions within the dyadic unit. In this chapter, the "dance" between the couple and between their psychodynamics is extended to their impermeable and indefinable borders. This comparative cultural analysis outlines how guilt, envy, jealousy, separation, dependency, and bonding experiences are qualitatively practiced and experienced. For example, it is not enough to analyze someone's anger or rage without considering the Korean concept of *han* (rage) as having deep historical significance. And it is not enough to understand shame without encompassing the concept of "saving face" in Asian or Middle Eastern societies. What dependency represents for a Westerner is in sharp contrast to what dependency represents for the Japanese (the mother/child bonding relationship known as *amae;* Doi, 1973). Furthermore, to understand the concept of self, one must take into account the differences between an individual self and a group self. The same holds true for guilt, envy, jealousy, "true self" and

131

"false self" (*tatamae* and *honne*). There are hierarchical positions in many cultures where elders and parents come first and wives come last. One can imagine, for instance, how this might impact a narcissistic/borderline couple, especially the narcissist, who needs to come first and be considered special.

THEORETICAL IMPLICATIONS

The entire spectrum of psychoanalytic theory takes on a different shape when treating cross-cultural couples. Self-psychology, with its mirroring and empathic techniques, appears to be most suitable for the treatment of couples of varying ethnic backgrounds, ideologies, traditions, and values. Because of its emphasis on intersubjectivity, self-psychology appreciates that each society has its own unique roles and customs and that patients and the therapist have different subjective viewpoints. The intersubjective experience does not focus on right and wrong, but rather on understanding the depths of the conflict. Concepts from self-psychology provide the perfect language for empathizing with the patient's vulnerabilities.

While it is vital that we empathize with the vulnerability, we must not empathize with the aggression. In dealing with the aggression, object relations are more suitable for meeting the containment needs. This is especially true for the more disturbed, primitive, aggressive personalities, those who tend to project, distort, act out, misperceive, and fail to distinguish fantasy from reality. It is invaluable in helping couples explore the split-off, foreign, internal part of themselves (splitting, projection, projective identification, omnipotent denial, magical thinking). Behind the banner of traditionalism, culture, and religion lurks an undue amount of cruelty and sadism. Here the therapist must blend empathy with confrontation.

The question frequently asked is, Do we have the right as Western analysts to apply Western concepts to people of varying ethnic backgrounds? My contention is that we do. Kris Yi (1995) argued that Western psychotherapy deals ineffectively with other cultures, particularly Asian cultures, because of the indiscriminate use of psychoanalytic principles that claim universal application. She does not exclude psychoanalysis and its organizing principles but proposes that it has been ineffective not because of the cross-cultural differences but because of mis-attunement and discontinuity.

CULTURAL DIAGNOSIS

Although it is beyond the scope of this text to do a detailed analysis of the "cultural narcissist" and the "cultural borderline," we need expand a bit further on what we might refer to as a "cultural diagnosis." The cultural narcissist dovetails with the pathological narcissist. This patient brings into the therapeutic environment a fervent nationalistic pride and will relentlessly try to prove his nationalistic or religious identity. The cultural borderline, on the other hand, will fight to the end, retaliate, become a terrorist, or go to any extreme in order to maintain the group's collective identity. He will die for his country and will sacrifice others as well as himself. Western clinicians who do not understand Asian or Middle Eastern cultures may be shocked to hear how some individuals will sacrifice themselves, their families, or even their children for a cause or adhere obsessively to family tradition (see example below).

Example of a cultural narcissist: An Israeli man married to an Irish Catholic woman insists she give up her religion without any consideration of what is important to her. One could argue, "What's the big deal? This can happen with an American Jewish man as well." The difference is cultural. The Israeli man takes on a nationalistic Zionistic attitude which is inculcated into the culture since childhood. Aggression wears a different flag. "This is our country! The only religion is Judaism!"

Example of a cultural borderline: "I'd rather die a suicide bomber. At least we will die with honor and dignity and prove we as a people do exist! We are heroes, not terrorists. We love and will die for Allah and for the rights of our country."

Where Do Pathology and Culture Interface?

How do we find pathology? Where do pathology and culture interface? How much is cultural and how much is pathological? Where do the boundaries between aggression, cruelty, and cultural tradition interface? What are the forces mutual to marital and political relationships (Lachkar, 1993a, 1993b)? When treating cross-cultural narcissistic/borderline couples, we need to sort out how much is cultural and how much is pathological. I contend that the grandiose self is the emotional virus that infects the emotional love bond, and that it is universal to all primitive borders. These are questions therapists can no longer ignore, considering the cultural, ethical, and religious aspects.

Culture is defined as an historically derived system of implicit and explicit designs for living. Implicit in culture is an ever-evolving order that is socially transcended, a way of life that provides a blueprint on how to live. It is the organizing principal whereby values and traditions are transmitted through ideologies, religion, political beliefs, the social system, and the arts. It is a process of enculturation and socialization through which one learns a systematic pattern of behavior fundamental to emotional survival. Enculturation is learning by osmosis without specific teaching.

Socialization is the deliberate attempt to shape and mold the person to conform to beliefs that tend to be shared by all or beliefs specifically designated by the group (Greenfield & Cocking, 1994). This understanding of culture is related to our consideration of "self-identity." Implicit in culture is the corollary that cultural conditions give one a sense of self and a sense of belonging to the group.

Cross-Culture versus Transculture

Endleman (1989) described very clearly the difference between transculture and cross-culture. Cross-culture means looking at the culture from within. It attests to the notion that people from different cultures are governed psychologically by different principles and do not share the same instinctual drives of sex and aggression. Transculture means looking at the culture from without. It attests to the notion that people are culturally different but psychologically the same. It assumes that we all share basic instinctual drives of sex and aggression, basic and universal laws of developmental phases, and bonding and child development principles fundamental to all human beings. In every culture one needs to master and overcome Oedipal rivals and basic mechanisms of defense (we all have a mother and father and incest taboos). Endleman argued that in the West, healthy aggressive drives are expressed in the context of object relations; however, in Middle Eastern and Eastern cultures, cultural transgressions are enacted masochistically, with the child made to grovel in extreme subjugation to parents or the government, which becomes externalized neurotically.

In Piven's (2002) latest article, "Lord of the Flies as Parable of the Invention of Enemies, Violence, and Sacrifice" (pp. 132–158), when depicting human savagery and cruelty, he proposes that there is something inherent in human nature that drives us to violence. "Power" becomes a dominant factor and bloodlust erupts in the symbolism removing the trappings and suit of childhood innocence" (p. 134).

Aggression is an ongoing process whereby a person, group, organization, nation, or government consciously or unconsciously attempts to control or dominate by forcing its will, beliefs, and perceptions on others either physically or emotionally. According to Freud (in Gay, 1988), aggression can become a source of pleasure which human beings are reluctant to give up once they have enjoyed it. Aggression feeds upon itself and can become addictive. The libidinal ties that bind members of a group in affection and cooperation are strengthened if the group has outsiders it can hate—the projected enemy or "scapegoat" (p. 549).

Psychodynamics from a Cross-Cultural Perspective

Shame

Many Asian and Middle Eastern cultures have been described as "shame societies," while Christian societies, such as Germany, are perceived as "guilt societies." Ruth Benedict's (1946) major thesis was that in Japanese society the emphasis falls on shame rather than on guilt. Professor Peter Berton (1996), an international relations and foreign affairs scholar and psychoanalyst whose main area of expertise is East Asia and Russia, testified that the most common threat that a Japanese mother uses to discourage certain behavior from her children is to say, "*Warawareru wa yo!*" ("People will laugh at you!").

In most Christian societies in the West, people are expected to feel guilty about certain acts, whereas in Japan, where shame is a major sanction, people are chagrined. The problem is that guilt can be relieved by confession and atonement, but chagrin cannot be relieved in this manner. A man who has sinned can get relief from guilt by confessing to either a priest or a secular therapist. (This partially explains the relative lack of popularity of psychoanalysis and other psychotherapies in Japan.) In a shame society, furthermore, reprehensible acts remain hidden so long as such bad behavior is not publicized.

Shame is a matter between the person and his group. It is concerned with what others think, whereas guilt is a matter between a person and his conscience (superego). Shame is the need to hide one's true inner feelings, which are repressed. The Japanese, like many other Asian cultures, are heavily invested in "saving face." Obedience to others is of utmost importance. One must strive not to compete, show feelings, induce competition, or try to be unique. The parent will ridicule or humiliate the child to keep him or her in check.

In the West, we strive to become unique, but shame prevents us from vigorously pursuing ways to get these needs met. Further, shame interfaces with Oedipal issues. To triumph over the Oedipal father, one has to relinquish envy, competition, control, and domination (pre-Oedipal issues, defenses that thwart success or disrupt the road to success), and learn to live side by side with the Oedipal father.

Guilt

Do Germans allow themselves to mourn because they are a guilt society? Does Japan cover up its war crimes because of shame? Loewenberg (1987) discussed how Germans tried to prove their superiority by projecting their own depreciated and unwanted dirty/anal parts of themselves onto the Jews, and then relishing the anguish and humiliation they were imposing by

> debasing the Jews, and treating them as contaminants. In each case they postulated a new degradation and in fantasy placed themselves in the position of the Jew to experience how it felt. Defecation was strictly regulated; it was one of the most important daily events, discussed in great detail. During the day, prisoners who wanted to defecate had to obtain permission from a guard. It seemed as if education to cleanliness would be once more repeated. (1987, pp. 314–315)

According to Loewenberg, transforming Jews became a fecal triumphant orgy. In my analysis, this was a sadistic superego running amuck that could not possibly meet the demands placed upon it (Berton & Lachkar, 1997).

Guilt is a higher form of development than shame and is directly related to the superego formation. Guilt occurs in the depressive position followed by the desire to make reparation, to take responsibility for past acts, transgressions, or wrong-doings. Guilt is a reaction to an act of doing and the remorse for that act (Lansky, 1995). Germans have "developmentally evolved" from the state of envy and shame and have relinquished the desire to destroy and now wish to make reparation (unlike the Japanese, who have never come to terms with their war crimes).

Envy

Envy is destructive by nature. It differs from jealousy in that it seeks to destroy that which is enviable. In the West, envy is considered acceptable, because we are a competitive nation. In other cultures, envy becomes an intolerable affect, considered dangerous and harmful to the basic harmony of the group. The Japanese will go to endless extremes to avoid the envious glances of others and to maintain the harmony (*wa*). One wealthy Japanese automobile executive was compelled to park his Mercedes five blocks away from work to avoid inducing envy in his fellow employees. Envy stirs up shame.

Japanese psychoanalyst Masae Miyamoto (1994) went so far as to diagnose the Japanese as narcissistic and masochistic. Pleasure, which leads to independence, which results in individuality and creativity, is considered to be a loss of impulse control (*messhi houkou*). He reaffirmed that those who stand out and deviate from the group warrant a hostile response. To survive in a Japanese bureaucratic environment, one must follow three rules: Don't be late, don't take vacations, and don't initiate anything new.

Dependency

The Western notion is that the infant is born dependent, then goes through stages of separation and individuation, and eventually develops autonomous ego functioning. In Asian societies, the process of individuation is not encouraged. Instead, interdependence is developed. The concept of *amae* is very complex and has been the subject of debate among Japanese and American analysts. Some scholars have intimated that the need for *amae* beyond infancy is a sign of pathology in Japanese society (Iga, 1984).

Amae is a form of dependency relating to the mother's intense internalization and identification with her child's needs, especially those of her male child. It embodies the feelings that all normal infants have toward the mother: dependence, the desire to be passively loved, the unwillingness to be separated from the warm mother/child circle and cast into a world of objective "reality." It manifests itself as the desire to merge or fuse with others. Yet, this love creates extreme forms of ambivalence and hostility. Under the guise of "closeness," the mother will co-sleep, co-bathe, and in some instances engage in incest by masturbating baby boys to relieve their erections (Adams & Hill, 1997). This longing is normal in infancy but cannot be satisfied in adult life. Yet, in Japan the need for *amae* continues and manifests itself in a variety of social conventions and characteristics. The eminent Japanese psychoanalyst Takeo Doi (1973; Johnson, 1994) called *amae* a key concept for understanding Japanese personality structure.

In Japan there is a lack of differentiation between self and other that would be regarded with horror by Western psychiatrists. In Japan self-identity is organized around the group. The psychological center of gravity is embedded in the other, and what the other is feeling, thinking, or doing.

Example of Amae: A Japanese scholar came to visit the United States for the first time. He was invited as a guest to a home of a colleague. He was asked by his colleague's wife if he was hungry and would like something to eat. He responded by telling her he was not hungry, humbly bowed, and thanked her graciously for her kind offer. Shortly after, he began to feel a festering rage and realized that she (the hostess) did not offer *amae*. "If she cared about me she would just know I was hungry and would have offered me food. In Japan guests are always offered food even if they claim they are not hungry."

Amae can affect the narcissistic/borderline Japanese/American couple: An American man married to a Japanese wife complains that he feels suffocated by his wife's relationship with their son. He complains that she infantilizes him, and even though he is over 2 years old, continues to breastfeed. "I can't stand it; she's arranged to take him everywhere—to work, to social events, to bed. All she does is hold him, breastfeed him, and she doesn't let him cry. She attends to his every whim. This just isn't right! She doesn't allow her son to grow up." Here is another example.

The Case of the American Husband and the Japanese Wife

Bert: I always ask my wife what she would like to do on the weekend, where she would like to go, but she doesn't respond. Or else she tells me that anywhere I would like to go is fine.

Therapist: Then what happens?

Bert: Well, we either stay home or I take her to a movie.

[Yuki is listening attentively.]

Bert: I asked her if she is hungry after one movie, and she said she was fine, so we came home. This is when the shit hit the fan. She wouldn't have sex with me, she withdrew, and wouldn't talk to me for days. I can't take it anymore!

Yuki: But he doesn't offer me *amae*.

Bert: What is this crap about *amae*? All she talks about is *amae*! I am a red-blooded American male, and I don't need this crap about self-sacrifice. I'm not a mind reader; let her just tell me directly what she wants. Enough of this shit!

Yuki: In Japan, it is quite common for others to just "know" what the other needs without asking. To ask appears greedy, self-serving, a betrayal to our culture. We look carefully into the eyes of others, and the eyes communicate. Bert should have known I was hungry, he should know I don't like movies. This was a big insult to me!

Bert: But this is not Japan. This is America!

Another kind of dependency relationship is maternal fusion, exemplified here by the relationship between an American Jewish husband and his Italian wife: A narcissistic American Jewish husband who is a corporate executive complains that he is a busy man and that his Italian wife doesn't allow him any space to work or to go on business trips. All the complaints she experienced in the relationship became reenacted with the therapist (in the "couple transference"). Things began to climax when I confronted her about her difficulty in leaving at the end of the session. She would take an endless amount of time to get out of her chair, gather her stuff, and ask questions. At the door she would begin another barrage of complaints about her husband and her abusive father. At home she would clutter my voice mail with messages, my e-mail with downloads of endless documents and pictures. When I confronted her about our "culture clash," she said: "I'm an Italian, and in Italy people are very close. Even therapists become part of the family. They visit in the home, go out socially, and are not so stand-offish. You act like a cold fish, a complete stranger. I tell you everything about myself and you tell me nothing. I need more from you, and you aren't willing to give it."

At the end of each session, I began to feel more and more invaded and intruded upon. When I confronted her about this, her response was: "I need it! I need it! In Italy, I could stay at my appointment and talk if I wished, and my analyst would never rush me out the door as you do. In fact, he would even offer me something to drink, something to eat, help me on with my coat. You have never even offered me a cup of coffee. We are Italians. We take our time. You Americans are all crazy; you rush, rush. You are so typical of people in the States where everyone is so cold, aloof. It's just not that way in my country."

I began to show her that beyond our "cultural differences" was an internal mother she experienced as cold and indifferent. I also reminded her of a father who always brushed her aside, and who ousted her when her younger brothers were born. The hunger and yearnings to feel included drove her compulsive search to fuse with the maternal object (maternal fusion). Briefly stated, ensuing issues reached far beyond what she considered "culturally correct."

Individual Self versus Group Self

In many societies, particularly in Asian and Middle Eastern countries, the individual self is virtually nonexistent. More pervasive is the group self or the collective group self. According to Yi (1995), American culture emphasizes the autonomous self which stresses uniqueness and self-expression, whereas Asian societies lean toward interdependence that stresses heavy reliance on the group and others. But when we talk about a cultural self, what self are we talking about? An individual self? A group self? A self-actualized self? A collective group self?

Hierarchy and Obligatory Bonds

Therapists must have some knowledge of obligatory relational bonds. In Middle Eastern and Asian societies, parents and elders come first; deference and devotion to parents is a strong, long-enduring tradition. The following is an example of a narcissistic wife who went to Israel for the first time to visit her husband's parents. It was her birthday weekend: "We went to Israel to visit my husband's parents. When we arrived I found out that it was my husband's parents' anniversary. It also happened to be my birthday. When I confronted my husband and asked why he made such a fuss over his parents and ignored me, he said that parents come first."

The image of mother as self-sacrificing and all-giving becomes a strongly internalized object. In Asian societies it is based on Confucianism, where dependent and interdependent interactions are clearly delineated: parent to child, husband to wife, older brother to younger brother, employer to employee. In China and Japan, the father/son relationship is considered to be the most important dyad. The superordinate and subordinate are quite clear: boss/employee, elder/younger, teacher/student, master/servant, husband/ wife. These relationships require benevolence, authority, responsibility, and wisdom from superordinates. From subordinates they require obedience and subservience. In Japan the primary responsibility is not to the family but to the boss, although another important relationship is the mother/ child *amae* bond. Outside of the home (*soto*), women occupy subordinate positions with few individual rights and little power. Inside the home (*uchi*), women as mothers hold stable and powerful positions (unlike the Koreans, who are totally dependent on their husbands).

In Korea, the obligatory bonds start with king to subject, parent to child, husband to wife, older sibling to younger sibling. The father is highly idealized as the perfect provider, and if and when this fantasy is disrupted, it evokes profound feelings of rage or *han*. The Korean father becomes the all-encompassing king, the benevolent lord and master who is highly revered and idealized. He is viewed as an all-powerful, all-giving being whose main task is to care and provide for the family. During WWII, after the Japanese invasion, the image of the benevolent father was shattered. He "betrayed" them and let them down. Korean women had to endure the tragic losses of their husbands and fathers and had to fend for themselves by becoming aggressive and very revengeful.

Han comes out more in the United States than in Korea. When in the United States, Koreans are without the support or "holding environment." In Korea there is the support of the tribe, the group. When Koreans leave, they betray the group. Furthermore, marrying a foreigner is tantamount to marrying "a pig." One might question, Why doesn't the Koreans' subservient attitude carry over into the United States? In Korea, the family and village serve as a container or holding environment for the group's rage and feelings. The woman is supported in her compliance. Without the support of the "container," the woman is thrown into a frenzy, a state of intense fragmentation. The biggest problem Koreans face when they come to this country is feelings of profound loneliness, confusion, and powerlessness. Adaptation is especially stressful for women, as newly assigned roles such as "working mother" disrupt the child/mother symbiosis. Women not only suffered tragic losses before and after Korean War, but they now struggle with new identities as women and mothers.

Treatment of Women

Men who violate women's rights under the banner of "cultural differences" claim such behavior is an inherent component of their culture or society. However, there are many universal governing psychological principles that argue against this. From a transcultural perspective, Oedipal conflicts are universal. Societies or religious groups that cannot find healthy ways to deal with aggression or dependency needs hide under the rubric of religion to assuage their shame or guilt, a "toilet receptacle" to mask their torrid rage. The healthy way to deal with mental pain (loss, betrayal, abandonment) is through reparation and mourning of the loss, not revenge and retaliation. Absent this, women become the target for men's aggression and the sacrificial objects.

Example: the American woman and the Lebanese husband. An American woman who married a Lebanese husband described their relationship as follows.

> Our courtship was the most romantic. He was warm, kind, and thoughtful, I loved his accent, his generosity. Then suddenly there was a drastic change when we got married and had a baby. As soon as our son was born my husband wanted to go visit his parents in Lebanon. I was excited, for I have never been to the Middle East and was anxious to meet the new grandparents. When we arrived his parents cordially greeted me, kissed me on both cheeks, and for the next two weeks ignored me. They acted as if I was a fly on the wall, as if I didn't exist. All my husband's attention went to his parents and the baby. Gradually things got worse, tension mounted on all sides. I couldn't stand it anymore. I knew I had to confront him. Instead of being understanding and considerate as he was before, I saw a side to him I had never seen. He got enraged with me for threatening him and started scolding me for having very poor manners. He went on and on, lecturing how women should act, that women show respect. As he spoke he got angrier and angrier, accusing me of insulting him in front of his parents, that they were shocked and outraged by my behavior.
>
> But things didn't stop there. At first I thought he was joking, but judging by the expression on his face, I came to realize he was dead serious. He decided it would be best for our son to be raised in Lebanon, to have doting parents, meaningful traditions and values, unlike in the

United States, which is no more than a "drug society where people only think about themselves." Then the nightmare fell upon me. We returned to the States, and without my knowing he took our baby son and went to Lebanon. I spent a year screaming, "My baby, my baby! I need my baby back." But to no avail. After a long legal process, there was nothing I could do. I saw a therapist, who helped me regain a sense of self and alleviate the guilt projected on me of being a bad person.

This example has particular clinical relevance because today the majority of therapists going into the field of mental health are women. Men from male-dominated societies have difficulty allowing themselves to be vulnerable to women. Female therapists must pay special attention to the vulnerable position and be readily available to interpret this anxiety, a perfect entrée into working within the couple transference. Whether working with same-culture or cross-cultural couples, the main task is to find a way to work within the couple transference. The therapist noting the cultural narcissist's grandiose self as controlling and dominating might say: "You are having trouble allowing yourself to depend on me, even though I am not your wife. Instead you resort to trying to control and dominate both of us. Yet I am not someone you can control. I am someone here to help you adjust to all the changes that are going on in your relationship."

This brings up the concept of human rights. Such groups as Amnesty International, Human Rights Watch, Freedom House, and Defense of Human Rights and Public Liberties advocate strict guidelines in holding human rights violators accountable. So strong is this growing pressure that many nations will deny financial support to foreign governments that tolerate or promote discrimination against women. Increasing consciousness and commitment to women's' rights will be redefined to make equal treatment of women abroad a top priority.

Under the banner of religion or traditionalism, one can act out the most heinous crimes against women. Violations against women are often perpetuated by certain hostile, angry, aggressive group leaders who play out the group's unconscious collective fantasies against women. The Koran supports women being submissive to men. The guise of religion masks an undue amount of aggression. Religion and culture provide permission for men to act out their cruelest and most vicious fantasies against victims, mainly women and children. Women in the Middle East have no rights and no vote. They are submissive to men, similar to women from Japan, Central America, and India. Some therapists are blatantly shocked by the attitudes and values from varying cultural backgrounds, e.g., clitoridectomies, women having no rights, women treated as chattel, and cannot understand the difficulty women have in standing up for their rights within the relational bonds.

The "True" and "False" Self

Winnicott (1965a) established the idea of the "true self" and "false self." The false self is the defense against the true self—the creative or unique self. According to Winnicott, the false self belies the true self. It is the shield that protects the self from shame. Doi (1985) noted that in the Japanese culture there are two sides to social behavior: *tatamae* (hidden self) and *honne* (true self). In Japan women show a true self or private self in the home; here she is lord and master, particularly of children and finances. In the external world she exhibits a public self or outer self. Japanese parents convey to their children that to show emotions is dangerous, that "people will laugh at you." From an object-relational perspective, one might surmise that the Japanese have denounced their true selves by remaining faithful to their victimized/shameful selves.

When there is a highly developed private self, nonverbal empathic sensing becomes more salient, as in the case of the Japanese self (requiring more finely tuned empathic intuitive sensing). Verbal expression is then used mainly to observe proper social etiquette in the hierarchical relationships (Foster, Moskowitz, & Javier, 1986). This could easily segue into a discussion about modes of verbal and nonverbal communication. According to Roland (1988) the firmer the outer ego boundaries are, the more reliance there is on verbal communication (as in the case of North Americans), as if to safeguard the uniqueness of individuals as separate entities.

TREATMENT SUGGESTIONS

The influx of immigrants is creating a growing need to update our clinical approaches to the treatment of cross-cultural couples. To date there is no systematic methodology in the treatment of cross-cultural couples. What follows are some treatment points, along with brief examples. Some of the examples may seem a bit severe or even outlandish, but they do make a point and perhaps can open new therapeutic vistas for the treatment of cross-cultural couples within the context of narcissist/borderline relationships.

The treatment approach suggested below is designed to help therapists understand that Western principles do not encompass the large range of issues confronting us today. What might be considered narcissistic or borderline within our boundaries may be considered normal and cultural elsewhere. How much is pathological and how much is cultural? In other words, where do the borders between pathology and culture lie? Let us begin by examining the following points.

Treatment Points for Cross-Cultural Couples

- Learn the fundamental dynamics of the culture; mirror and reflect. Time takes on a different meaning in the East. "It is the Will of Allah if we will be here for our next appointment" (*inshallah*).
- Know something about the foods, holidays, and traditions. Learn a few words of the patient's language, at least "hello" and "goodbye." If the patient is Asian, serve tea and bow slightly.
- Be empathic to the cultural differences, not to the aggression.
- Be aware of the differences between the individual and group self.
- Be aware of special treatment needs. Try to bond through some common ground, e.g., "I just love Arabic music."
- Be aware of body language (with Asians, keep your distance; with Persians and Italians, stay close).
- Find pathology within the individual.
- Find pathology within the culture.
- Find pathology within the couple transference.
- Find pathology within the government.
- Use the cultural contrast hook.
- Remind the couple why they are in treatment.
- Mirror the conflict.
- Empathize with the vulnerabilities, not the aggression.

Example of pathology within the government: In the Arab world people are now obsessed with listening to Qutari, a TV satellite channel similar to CNN. Arabs, Bedouins, rich and poor, sit around for hours listening to discussions of such taboo issues as women's rights, voting, democracy, and polygamy. Many Arab countries, including Algeria and Saudi Arabia, have tried to censor programs that are critical of their regimes, but because of high technology censorship has been impossible. In conjoint therapy one can make the point that people in the patient's own culture are becoming disgruntled with how they are being treated.

Example of cross-cultural conflict: In marital treatment, the Asian partner may sit in silence, while her partner is compelled to talk. The therapist needs to be aware of how the silent partner is inwardly "culturally" aggressive and unconsciously coercing her partner to enact a certain role appropriate to her culture, i.e., the role of caretaker.

The therapist needs to know how a person functions in his or her own culture. For example, a Japanese patient was told by his analyst that his low fee would be raised. The patient became enraged with the analyst, feeling the analyst was greedy and selfish and did not offer *amae*. After several months of exploration, the analyst learned that the patient also had the same money issues with his family in Japan. Since people in Japan are most generous with money and do not withhold gifts or money, it became apparent that his "withholdingness" was not a phenomenon of culture but more likely an intrapsychic one.

Make use of the "cultural contrast hook." Emphasize the differences between the patient's culture and other cultures. For example, if a Middle Eastern man complains that his wife disobeys him and only listens when he beats her, the therapist has an opportunity to apply the cultural contrast hook: "Yes, I do understand how this is your tradition. But imagine if your wife came from a tribe in Central Africa where most of the people were cannibalistic and their tradition was to eat the body parts of their fellow human beings? How would you feel if your wife ate you and said it was customary?"

Empathize with the vulnerability and not with the aggression. The following therapeutic suggestion illustrates the point: "Just as you feel your leader in Baghdad tries to protect you from us 'evil' Americans, I feel that I have to protect you, because if you beat your wife you could get deported or sent to jail. It would be as if I stole something in your country. I would get my fingers cut off."

Find the area of conflict and mirror it. Often couples are so embedded in tradition and ideology that treating them can become a source of great frustration. In these instances, therapists must relinquish their grandiose thinking that a few sessions are going to change a lifetime of patterns. The therapist must apply "mirroring" techniques, mirroring pain and conflict again and again.

Example: "So you [the husband] feel angry and enraged when your wife wants to go out socializing without you. You feel she is being disrespectful and not acknowledging you as the man and the ruler of the house. And you [the wife] feel that though you have married a Middle Eastern man he should adjust to our ways, and you should be able to do what every American woman does: have the freedom to go and choose without being controlled and dominated. So you are both telling me about your pain and frustration in adjusting to being together. That if you adjust to your husband's way, it makes you feel like his puppet, and if you adjust to your wife's way, it makes you feel lost and abandoned, alienated from your country that you miss and long for."

Use words, food, language, and expressions from the patients' culture in order to bond with the couple. Learn to say hello, goodbye, and thank you in several languages. Ask the couple about their ethnic food preferences and customs so you can serve, for example, tea or pita and hummus. This provides background aromas that are familiar to them and helps them feel at home. If one of the partners is Asian and bows, the therapist should bow in return. Ask the partners to express themselves in their language even if you don't understand what they're saying, just to get a sense of their affect while they speak.

The following is an example of cultural empathic failure:

> I am from Israel and my wife is a fourth-generation Protestant American. When we first got married she agreed to convert to Judaism, but after we had our kids, she started to put Christian icons all over the house. Furthermore, I don't think our therapist understands where I am coming from. My wife gets upset whenever I go out alone with my family. I need to spend special time with my mother, father, and brothers. My wife yells and screams and insists she is also part of the family. But in reality, she's not. In my country, parents come first, and if my mother wants to be with "her" family and me, that has priority. Also, our therapist knows nothing about our culture. Often I say "Shalom" to her, and she responds back, "Hi, how are you today?" On Rosh Hashana, I greeted her and said, "Shana Tova," and she responded, "Hope you have a nice weekend."

The above example is obviously quite severe, and most therapists would shiver in their boots at the thought of such a situation. Although it is not the intent here to deeply delve into treatment, I would like to make three following points: First, the therapist should make use of self-psychology, a most valuable modality that enables the therapist to "mirror," empathize, and reflect the couple's differences by expressing the pain each partner experiences. Second, the therapist should make use of the cultural contrast hook, a notion I invented while treating cross-cultural couples. Briefly stated, a cultural contrast hook is a piece of cultural behavior taken from another culture to use as an example, intended to evoke feelings of extreme bizarreness (see the case below). Third, the therapist should discern how much is cultural and how much is aggression. Let us once again be reminded that under the guise of culture or religion, people can act out their most heinous and sadistic urges.

Case Illustration: The Japanese Husband and the Han-Driven Korean Wife

Taro, a Japanese businessman who worked for a well-established company in Japan, was sent to Korea to work. It was in Korea that he met Hyunh (Helen), a 39-year-old divorced woman with an 11-year-old son from a previous marriage. Taro was eventually transferred to the United States, where Hyunh found employment as a travel agent. Even though it was a stormy, rocky, and very shaky relationship, they stayed together. The conflict centered around Helen's wish for marriage and commitment "When are we getting married?" she kept asking. Taro would not respond, but would merely give a polite nod or simply remain silent. His nonresponsiveness and noncommittal attitude drove Helen into a frenzy. What Helen did not understand is that the Japanese, not wanting to offend or embarrass other people, do not openly say "no," but remain silent. What Taro didn't understand is how his silence would stir up Helen's rage and abandonment anxiety. In order to keep the harmony (*wa*) and to placate Helen, Taro would say "yes," although he really meant "no."

The silent treatment and Taro's confusing and submissive ways reminded Helen of her weak and passive father. Helen had a need to idealize her father as the Korean icon of a benevolent, all-encompassing, giving father. This is not unusual in Korean culture, where the father is king and master. When Helen experienced Taro as weak she would lose all sense of control, attack him with a barrage of insults and complaints, and resort to ridicule and shame. This brought up a plethora of cultural issues in Taro's background, mainly shame and victimization. To ensure that the child does not stir up conflict, to keep aggression at bay, to teach the child to be obedient, and to maintain or restore harmony (*wa*) at all costs, Japanese parents ridicule and laugh at the child. As the pressure from Helen mounted, Taro withdrew even more into silence. The more he remained in frozen isolation, the more Helen became the scorning/shaming parent (an old but familiar scenario for Taro).

Throughout their relationship Helen coerced Taro into the role of the weak and failed father, projecting that Taro was responsible for her physical, emotional, and financial well-being. Being a provider was a normal role for Taro, especially since Japanese men are basically the breadwinners, but even when he did "provide" it was still never enough. Whatever he did was never enough. Helen always wanted more (identification with an insatiable internal object). When things didn't go her way, she flew into an interminable rage. Helen's needs escalated to a point where she became insatiable. Taro finally succumbed to marriage, and even this brought on a great deal of rage or *han*. "Why couldn't you have done this sooner? Why can't you be like other 'normal' men?" Taro began to develop severe anxiety and psychosomatic symptoms (inability to sleep, constant stomach problems, migraine headaches). What he could not express verbally, he expressed via his body. This is when he and Helen entered into conjoint treatment.

An American-trained clinician with a Western-centered value system based on uniqueness, individualism, and separateness found it difficult to understand Taro and Helen, whose self- and collective group identities lie within the group. The double-bind and clinical issues of this couple present a familiar scenario. Has Helen internalized an insatiable object because in reality her "real" father was dysfunctional? Is her dysfunctionality stirred up when she feels betrayed and abandoned, connecting her to her group self—the idealized image of men as the all-benevolent caretakers? Why would someone like Taro join up with a woman like Helen? Can we consider Taro's passivity pathological? When Taro gives in and complies to her wishes, Helen becomes enraged with him for being too passive. Taro's passivity is "normal" within the context of his culture; what appears pathological is that he splits off the aggressive part of himself connecting him to her object world. When Taro remains silent, Helen feels betrayed and abandoned, connecting her to her group self—the idealized image of father/husband. Historically speaking, is it fair to say that Taro becomes the impotent, helpless father who cannot protect Helen from the external, "dangerous" Japanese invaders who took over their territory?

Are Taro and Helen a narcissistic/borderline couple? On the surface they appear to be remarkably similar, but given the cultural twist, they are seen from a different light. From the transcultural perspective, Helen appears borderline (aggressive, retaliatory). Taro appears narcissistic, showing very little empathy for Helen, thinking he could live with Helen forever without making a commitment. The cultural overtones certainly make diagnosis more difficult.

During the course of treatment, it was noted that any reminder of Taro not being the revered, benevolent father stirred up many narcissistic injuries. Even after they got married and Taro put some property in her name and adopted her son, Helen still demanded and complained. Things began to culminate as her son got older and she insisted he sleep in her and Taro room. This brought up many conflicts, including issues around separation/individuation, autonomy, and dependency. Many Korean children are used to sleeping with the mother, holding onto mother's elbow. In the Korean culture it is the symbolic mother who provides the "dew" to ward off dangerous spirits. The mother/child bond is of primary importance. Any threat to this bond triggers intense anxiety. Even though Taro was not able to express his desire for intimacy, it was evident that he became more and more frustrated as he was shortchanged any sexual activity.

Discussion

Through their shared projective identifications, Taro and Helen needed the other to play out their internalized dramas. In their cultural "dance," they projected onto each other their shameful parts, old hurts, and narcissistic injuries and vulnerabilities (she entitled to everything, he, to nothing). Helen came to understand how she projected her shameful and humiliated self onto Taro, making him the object of ridicule and humiliation. Unconsciously she coerced him to make up for her past by demanding that he become the fantasized benevolent father, and when that delusion got shattered, she made him into a useless, dirty, helpless, impotent being. Taro, having his own cultural and shameful past, including parents who made him feel impotent and useless, was easy prey for Helen's relentless attacks and negative projections. Working through the couple's transference brought many insights. Taro learned that being passive and timid led to far more conflict and destruction than if he expressed his needs directly. His needs would not destroy but paradoxically could lead to the love and intimacy they both desired.

Illustration of the Mistreatment of Women: The Case of the Middle Eastern Husband and the American Wife

Therapist: So why are you here?

Abdul: I really don't want to be here because I don't believe in therapy. In my country, this is unheard of. If we have a problem, we pray to Allah for forgiveness, and our will and destiny is in his hands.

Mary: This is what my children and I have to put up with all the time. I don't believe in prayer, magical thinking, wishes, dreams. I am a practical person, well educated and well informed, and can't believe I'm with someone who does all this "hocus pocus stuff." I believe in talking things over and working things out. Every time there is a problem, Abdul talks about Allah. Can't he realize he is in America now? This is not the Middle East. When there were just the two of us, I could ignore it, but now this is very difficult for our children.

Th: Yes, it does sound as though there are some real cultural differences that are causing stress and very hurtful feelings.

Mary: We went to Saudi Arabia last year and took the children to visit Abdul's parents. My daughters and I vowed we would not wear our veils [chadors], but when we arrived wearing our American garb we found ourselves being stared down. Not only were we viewed as foreign and strange, but their eyes were burning through our clothes, as if we were prostitutes.

Abdul: [laughing] Yes, and you should have seen how quick they put on their chadors and hijabs. Have you ever visited my country? There, the women don't even have a say. They aren't even allowed an opinion. My wife doesn't know how lucky she is that I am not like that.

Mary: He may not be like that, but he doesn't realize how difficult it has become to talk freely. Maybe we can do that here.

CONCLUSION

Self-psychology appears to be the most effective treatment modality in cross-cultural therapy. It offers mirroring and empathic responses to scale nearly impermeable walls of defense and object relations to contain and deal with the aggressive and destructive aspects of the relationship. Where do narcissistic and borderline pathology meet? The grandiose self of the narcissist pompously purports that his or her ways are best. How do we discover a "self" within the borderline who comes from a shame society and does not exist outside the context of the group? It is important for the therapist to probe deeply enough to find pathology within the individual and the vertex where conflict exists within his or her own culture.

Therapists cannot ignore the cultural, ethical, and religious aspects of therapy. In treating couples from various cultures, we may be dealing with societies that identify with destructive leaders, endless pain, sacrifice, and victimization. Some of these societies do not stress separation from the maternal object but instead maintain a lasting bond in a maternal fusion. The dilemma many therapists treating cross-cultural couples face and fear is that they may not be sufficiently knowledgable. However, the therapist need only be familiar with some basic customs and traditions to effectively analyze the role culture plays in strained relations between cross-cultural partners so that the healing process can begin.

Chapter 8

Model of Treatment

Treatment Techniques and Procedures

OVERVIEW

Conjoint therapy can prove to be an important precursor and/or adjunct to individual psychotherapy or psychoanalysis. A systematic approach to conjoint therapy has long been needed to treat the pre-Oedipal relationships of the narcissistic/borderline couple. I have reviewed recent developmental theories and divided them into categories based on fusion, separation, and interaction.

Bion (1970) postulated three types of interactions: commensural, parasitic, and symbiotic (healthy dependency). These concepts have been interwoven into the treatment phases. The six-point treatment steps that I initially outlined (Lachkar, 1984) is based on these three developmental phases: Phase 1, a state of oneness; Phase 2, a state of twoness; and Phase 3, the emergence of separateness. These sequences illustrate movement from a state where self and other are indistinguishable and boundaries are blurred and fused to a state of greater clarity, and, finally, to an awareness of separateness.

STRUCTURE

Using a psychodynamic or psychoanalytic approach, the therapist tries to understand not only what the problem is but how it arose. Some of these discoveries may begin in the waiting room.

The Waiting Room

The first face-to-face contact is made in the waiting room. It is here that the therapeutic boundaries are established. Some therapists allow one partner to enter the consultation room and begin the session even though the other partner has not arrived; others insist that the session should not begin until both parties are present. The decision depends largely on the outlook and the "containing" capacity of the therapist. In my view, the couple coming for conjoint therapy must be treated as a couple and not as individuals (unless one partner has dropped out of therapy). I recommend that the therapist wait for both parties to arrive. The therapeutic task should not be manipulated to allow one partner to be seen alone if the other partner is late or does not show up. Sometimes not doing therapy may be the best therapy! The therapist has an opportunity to hold onto the therapeutic frame by withstanding the anxiety of waiting and the tolerance of not knowing, and by not trying to relieve the problem quickly.

The therapist needs to show empathy for the waiting partner but must clarify at the onset that both partners are coming for therapy as a couple because of a marital problem and not for individual therapy. The therapist might say, "We all have to tolerate a certain amount of frustration and uncertainty, including myself. Before you came we weren't even sure if there was to be a session because your presence is of great importance here and we couldn't start without you" (bonding with the narcissist via the grandiose self).

If the therapist colludes with or relieves the frustrated partner or the problem too quickly, then the problem can be neither seen nor addressed. The partner who behaves in the relationship as the waiting one, the placating one, again goes along with the absent or late partner. The therapist might say, "We need to let your husband know that his presence is very important, and it would not be the same without him. Now, if I see you alone, then you are no longer coming for conjoint therapy but for individual help, and that is something you need to think about [addressing the borderline tendency to act impulsively]. You can take your time deciding what kind of help you would like from me. I will be more than happy to wait until you decide." This opportunity to reschedule needs to be offered to the patient.

The dynamics that occur in the waiting room are often very subtle, and the therapist's own sense of attunement will be a guide for the various problematic issues that arise. More important than what creative route the therapist chooses to manage these difficulties is the depth of the therapist's understanding of the situation. The therapist who is aware that a commitment has been broken and that others have been let down or kept waiting is in a better position to begin the work. The therapist and the patient(s) have now had an experience together, one that will most likely become the main thrust of the treatment.

Case History

Ideally, the first session should be aimed at getting as detailed a history as possible. The first session offers a unique opportunity to obtain a fairly structured family background. Basically, the history should include any suicidal ideation, drug or substance abuse (including alcohol abuse), child abuse, psychotic episodes, head injuries, organicity, and hospitalizations. Not to get a history is, I believe, a technical mistake. With more regressive couples, or with couples whose partners have less impulse control, an initial history may be difficult to obtain and will have to be teased out in later sessions.

If during the history the partners continually interrupt, then I interpret how difficult it is to wait (as it was in the waiting room), and ask if this happens in the relationship—where nothing gets completed and no one ever gets fed. The purpose of taking a history is threefold. First, it is not the history per se that is of ultimate importance, but rather the process itself. One gets a chance to see who initiates, who takes control, who interrupts, and so on. Second, the history further helps to establish the boundaries and make clear who the doctor is and who the patients are. Taking a history makes the patient feel safe and secure because it indicates to the patient that the therapist is thorough, solid, and complete. Third, the information patients reveal helps the therapist understand something of their backgrounds and how they happened to meet and come together. Some of the more general questions I use are:

1. What is your full name?
2. Are your parents still alive? If not, what were the causes of death?
3. Do you have siblings? Where did you stand in the family? (Eldest? Youngest?)
4. How long have you been married? Have you had any previous marriages?
5. Do you have children? Boys or girls? How old are they?
6. Where did you meet your spouse?
7. What attracted you to her or him?
8. What qualities does your spouse have that you value and appreciate?
9. I'm going to ask you a very specific question. Before you answer, I'd like you to think carefully about it. Don't rush; take your time. Why are you here?

10. What does it feel like to be here?
11. How do you think I can be helpful to you?

Often couples will ramble on in the attempt to answer the questions. Commonly, they interrupt one another. Given the appropriate circumstances, I might say to the borderline wife, "Do you always interrupt your husband when he is speaking? Ooops! You're doing it to me now!" In a loving and caring way, I might add, "I know it's so hard to wait your turn. We just had an experience in the waiting room together, didn't we?" (bonding through mutual experience of the moment).

Initially, the responses tend to be free-associative and tangential. I try to focus on only one point. Question 10 is usually the most baffling. At this point I require very specific responses. I will say, "Let me ask the question again; perhaps you did not understand." In a very caring way I will inquire, "What does it feel like to be here?" The other partner may interrupt with a comment such as, "That's the same thing that happens at home; I can't get a response. We have this same kind of communication problem at home." I then acknowledge how valuable information and insight are. "Already we are getting to see that what happens at home is happening here, and this can be very helpful for us" (beginning of couple transference). I then take the opportunity to remind the partners how important it is to wait and to tolerate some frustration because doing this will allow something valuable to develop. "Now we can see we are already beginning to get somewhere, and that feeling forced or being left out can, in fact, interfere with knowing how we are *feeling*" (undifferentiated feeling states).

This process models how important it is to stay with one point, to maintain a focus and not get lost in "the dance." I tell the couple that "I have to focus; otherwise we all get lost and go round and round in a circle, never getting anywhere. If that happens there won't be a 'me' here to help us focus. Perhaps why you are here is that you are not sure what you are feeling, and if you lost contact with your feelings, it is impossible to relate to one another."

It is important to focus more on the process itself than on the question. Commonly, one or both partners will get angry, suggesting that we go on (wanting the quick fix). This discussion frequently leads to exposure of the difficulty the partners experience in holding onto their own feelings and ideas within themselves or their relationship. One partner might say, "I can't hold on when he pressures me. I give up too soon!" The therapist who gives up too soon is colluding with the couple, and with the partners' tendency to go along without ever achieving any understanding—and thus becoming embroiled in the dance.

Educating the Couple

The therapist has the responsibility of informing the couple about the expectations of treatment. The therapist must make sure that the couple is comfortable with the therapist. The idea that the therapist may have some special skills or experience that the partners don't have can be useful and effective: "If I were to go to you for legal counsel or investment counseling, I would assume that you would have some skills that I don't have, and I would have to rely on you and your experience. Now you are here to rely on my experience; you are assuming that I have some skills that you don't have. While you are here, you are going to have an opportunity to have a new experience" (preparing the couple for the "drama").

Part of educating the couple is allowing the "mess" to unfold. "Initially you may feel confused and uncertain about what is going on here, but in times things will get clearer. So right now it might be hard for you to be aware of what you need, simply because you are both going around in circles [living in the "mess" through blaming, projecting, and evacuating instead of thinking] and have been for quite some time." The therapist must educate the couple by indicating that "for a while, it is okay for us to stay in the mess together, so that all three of us may have an experience together. Meanwhile, I'll have to tolerate some waiting, some confusion, and some uncertainty until I get the information I need [the history]." I also tell the couple to feel free to ask me questions.

Example of the "mess": The Swindler and the Spender. A husband said, "All I get is shit. The other day my wife phoned me and called me an asshole. She screamed at me for not taking her shopping. Then I found out that she was using the credit card to the max. I can't stand it anymore! When this happens, all I want to do is walk away." To this husband, I might respond: "Yes, it does seem like a terrible thing to see a mess. I don't mind seeing the mess or the shit here [couple transference] because I know that if I can see it, then we have a chance to correct it. Already I'm beginning to see why nothing ever gets cleaned up or dealt with. There does seem to be some avoidance when there is a problem to face. This keeps things from getting accomplished. I believe you feel it is such a terrible thing to look at the problem you and your wife are having. But if we don't look at it we won't be able to see the healthy side, and all you'll see is the failed, 'shit' part."

The omnipotent and submissive features in narcissistic and borderline couples must be addressed from the onset. Since the narcissist's grandiose self frequently cannot tolerate needing anything, the narcissist will feel put down by the therapist's "needs." Common responses are to experience the therapist as controlling, needy, greedy, and "money hungry." Part of educating the couple might include saying, "Yes, I am taking care of my needs, but I think there is some confusion here. You may be worried that if I take care of my needs, I'm not going to be available to help you take care of your needs, when, in fact, it is the other way around. If I didn't take care of my needs, I wouldn't have the opportunity to take care of yours because I wouldn't know how. Again, I think that's precisely why you are here. It's perfectly normal and natural to have needs and expectations" (responding by interpretation).

To the submissive part of the borderline I might say, "It's interesting that you didn't respond to my requests or ask me any questions, and that you depended upon your husband to supply all the information. Do you always go along with what others say or wish?" (responding by entering the internal world).

When I ask each partner specific questions at the initial interview, frequently one will try to take control. In the case of Vera and Jeffrey, for instance, the borderline wife waited until her husband was in the bathroom to ask if she could tape the session. Part of educating the couple is to help them learn that this is a conjoint session, and that in this case we needed to pose the question directly to her husband. Within the context of educating the couple, I then had an opportunity to discover why the wife was not able to talk about her needs in the presence of her husband.

Ground Rules

The structure and formation of the conjoint treatment setting vary from therapist to therapist. One therapist may provide an open structure, allowing free association and open expression, while another may feel more comfortable providing a more closely structured methodology. As far as I know, there are no data as to which approach is more effective. For me, a systematic approach is necessary, and it seems to be effective in establishing the appropriate boundaries from the outset while creating a sold therapeutic framework.

Typically, couples with primitive pathological mental defenses and disorders have lifestyles that are chaotic and fragmented, leaving the partners desperately seeking some kind of order and structure. I have found that a systematic method sets a solid therapeutic framework. There must be, I believe, an organized, efficient "mommy" who is warm, practical, and understanding and who does not appear sloppy or disorganized. Patients respond more readily to a sturdy, empathic therapist who is both sustaining and containing and who can withstand complaints. This setting can further facilitate the capacity to provide a safe holding environment in which to work.

The importance of the therapist/mother as the container becomes more vital in a conjoint setting because the control issues revolve around persecutory anxiety, shame, guilt, confusion, and fantasies of separation. Ground rules need to be set:

"We must recognize that coming here is a commitment and a big responsibility for all of us. I will be committing myself to you and to this relationship, but in order for us to work together I must tell you about the ground rules. I request that you come here at least once a week for at least the next six sessions to determine if we are able to work together. I require at least 2 weeks' notice if you cannot make the session. Also, if I go away, I will give you plenty of notice. If there is an emergency or something urgent comes up, of course I will take that into consideration. But ultimately it will be up to my discretion to decide what an emergency is. If you need to change the hour, and another time is available, I will be happy to accommodate you. But you must know that this time will be set aside just for you, and you are both responsible. After 6 weeks, we will have an opportunity to reevaluate. How does that sound?"

I also let the partners know about one more important ground rule concerning telephoning me between sessions, which involves the issue of confidentiality. "If either of you needs to call me, you may feel free to do so; however, I do need to let you know that this is a joint experience and whatever happens here is to be known by all of us. Any information you disclose to me is subject to be shared, at my discretion. I think this is an important thing for you to know."

Ordinarily, along with addressing issues of commitment, I set ground rules for payment, insurance, and other housekeeping matters. But I may wait until another time to deal with these details. I use my sensitivity and attunement to decide what is appropriate in each situation.

When the initial interview is drawing to a close, it is helpful to all for the therapist to recapitulate and sum up what has transpired. Keep this summary clear and simple. Couples with primitive disorders and defenses have difficulty holding on and need absolute clarity. For example, you can say, "In this session I have had a chance to get a glimpse of part of the difficulty you are having—that of waiting. If you can't wait, then you can never get the feeding that you need. I'm concerned that you may get so impatient here that you may not be able to wait. It's going to take some time to see why you berate yourself and put yourself down. The healthy parts of you were able to come here and ask for help, and you should be acknowledged for that. The unhealthy you wants it all right away. We also discussed the ground rules, and I hope you understand that we have all made a very important commitment. Are there any questions?"

For purposes of illustrating the primary interview and to demonstrate ways of getting at the issues and coming to closure, I will describe my first session with Vera and Jeffrey.

Case Example of the Initial Session:
Presenting Issues: Vera and Jeffrey

Vera and Jeffrey had been involved in an ongoing relationship for 3 years. Vera had two teenage children from her previous marriage that were currently living with her ex-spouse. In this session I attempted to stay in contact at all times with the partners' affective interactional states.

The first session was less structured for the couple than were later sessions, primarily because I sensed that both partners needed to vent their feelings and that being overly structured would divert the expression of pent-up rage and anger. The need in this session was to evacuate, using the therapist as the "toilet breast." My attunement suggested the instantaneous choice of a "being" mommy rather than a "doing" mommy.

Three emerging themes are depicted in this case: (a) blurred boundaries regarding who is responsible for what, (b) the issue of the "bullshit" session, in which "shit" is tossed around, versus a productive "feeding session," which elicits ideas that are suitable for thinking and developing understanding, and (c) circular behaviors from which partners cannot extricate themselves.

I tentatively diagnosed Vera as the borderline and Jeffrey as the narcissist. Although Jeffrey had many borderline features (inclination to violence, drinking, drugs), his primary anxiety seemed to center around his strong need for recognition and appreciation. When faced with narcissistic injury to the nascent self, his primary defenses were guilt, introjection, and withdrawal. Although she attempted to struggle with her entitlement wishes, Vera was still too split off from her needs to be considered narcissistic. Her primary defenses were attacking, blaming, splitting, projection, and projective identification.

Jeffrey called to say he was going to be late, and Vera was asked to wait. He finally arrived. As soon as I greeted them in the consultation room, Jeffrey needed to use the bathroom. My first thought was that Jeffrey possibly needed to evacuate (the therapist's preconception), but I was cautious not to formulate an idea.

Vera (the borderline wife) was seated while Jeffrey (the narcissistic husband), who indicated that he was having a "male problem" and needed to urinate quite frequently, went to the bathroom. While Jeffrey was in the bathroom, Vera asked me if I would mind if she recorded the session. I let her know that if this were an individual session, the choice would be between her and me, but that since this was a conjoint session, we would have to take this up with her husband. She responded that she wanted to tape the session because it was hard for her to remember things (borderlines' lack of evocative memory). Jeffrey returned and sat in the chair next to Vera. I turned to Vera and suggested she ask Jeffrey if she could tape the session.

Vera:	Do you mind if I tape the session?
Jeffrey:	Well, I guess it's all right. No, maybe not!
Therapist:	Sounds like you have some mixed feelings about it.
Jeffrey:	I do.
Th:	We may have to pay attention to that.
Jeffrey:	No, I decided not to allow you to tape it.
Th:	Sounds like you made a wise choice—you paid attention to something inside of you.
Vera:	That's okay; we don't need to.

I noted with some suspicion how easily Vera gave up her needs. I then asked each partner the case history questions outlined early in this chapter. I watched each individual very carefully. I observed that Jeffrey become very impatient with Vera, and that when it was Jeffrey's turn to respond, Vera looked very uncomfortable, as if she couldn't stand waiting for her turn. Jeffrey, although he seemed to have an easier time waiting for his turn, looked very angry and very annoyed. Both looked suspicious of me.

Vera complained that although she loved Jeffrey's warmth and his friendly ways, she resented his drinking and violent temper. Jeffrey's complaint was that Vera was too bossy and picked on him, didn't listen to him, and didn't value or appreciate him. Vera declared that just as soon as she brought up an issue or something that bothered her, Jeffrey would bring up issues of his own (the narcissist's disregard for others and excessive feelings of entitlement). Each partner felt invaded and intruded upon.

Vera free-associated to a time when they met in front of a revolving door. I didn't say anything but thought that the revolving door was like the dance of the couple, the endless circle from which the partners were unable to extricate themselves. No wonder Vera needed the tape recorder; this couple was trying to deal with too many issues. Perhaps this was why they were unable to get out of the circle. I realized that she was telling us something about their dynamics, that their way of relating still felt like being caught in a revolving door.

I allowed a certain amount of freedom and interchange, but when I tried to focus on one issue, Jeffrey suddenly turned on me accusingly: "Wait a minute! That's very unfair of you. I was talking, and you interrupted me!" My countertransference reaction felt as though I had been hit over the head, attacked, and reduced to a very small child who had done something very naughty. I immediately got a sense of the violent and abusive side of Jeffrey to which Vera had earlier made reference. Jeffrey bitterly complained about how rude I was, as if to say: "How dare you! Don't you realize how special I am?"

Therapist: I'm terribly sorry. I certainly didn't intend to interrupt.

Jeffrey: That's what's happened my whole life. Even when I was a child my mother interrupted me as if what I had to say wasn't important. [This indicated some of the source of Jeffrey's narcissistic injury.]

Th: Well, unlike your mother, I do find that what you have to say very important, and you're right that no one has a right to interrupt you. [This was my response as a therapist becoming a mirroring self-object.]

Jeffrey: That's what happens a lot between Vera and me. Vera acts as if she's responsible for me.

Th: [to Vera, with an empathic and knowing look] Now I know what it feels like to be attacked. But if we both get into the battle, this session will become a terrible mess, good enough for the "garbage" or the "toilet" [I used their words and associations], and this would not be a productive session.

[Here Jeffrey interrupted me.]

Th: [looking at Jeffrey] That's the very thing you got mad at me for. [Jeffrey caught himself.] You are both entitled to have real and legitimate needs. For you, Jeffrey, no one is allowed to interrupt you when you are speaking—not Vera, not me, not anyone— and if I did, I certainly do apologize. [I did not interpret at this point that the reason people interrupt him is because he never stops talking.] Now that's what you are entitled to, but you are not entitled to become physically violent or abusive with your wife.

[turning to Vera] You are also entitled to get your needs met. I think it is very difficult for you to get them met at this point because you want it all now, like a demanding little girl who wants so much but is never heard. You too, Vera, have a right to your needs, and no one is allowed to hit you or use any form of physical force. Even if you do "push buttons" you still have to realize that no one has a right to touch or get violent. You are responsible for holding on to your own mind and your own "tape."

Closure

In closing with Jeffrey and Vera, I said: "I will feel we have accomplished something and that I have earned my fee today if only we can understand something about how important your needs are, and that this is an area where we need to work. Speaking of needs and the fee, I would like to know which one of you is going to be responsible for payment for this session."

These comments and the partners' responses closed the session. "When would you like to meet again? I recommend we meet for six sessions to see how we work together and at least sort out some of the issues. How does that sound to you? Would next week at this time work out? Yes, good. I will have a chance to explain more about this procedure, you will have a chance to think about some of these ideas, and we will review some of the ground rules. Please, if you have any questions next time, feel free to ask. Remember, if you call me, anything you say will be open for discussion, at my discretion. So you might want to think about that for the next week. Goodbye."

Thus the curtain opens and the drama begins.

SIX-POINT TREATMENT STEPS

1. The therapist must see the couple together before transition into individual therapy to form a safe bond and to caution the partners not to move into individual work until they are ready to separate (separating too early can induce a "rapprochement crisis").

    Example: A new couple was seen conjointly and soon after individually. The wife appreciated that I saw her, and we agreed to see her husband. She had a dream that she went into a woman's house but ended up getting raped by a man, who urinated and "came" all over her. Both had their clothes on. Her associations were with parents who would do things behind her back and a mother who forced her to eat contaminated chicken. I pointed out how unconsciously she felt the treatment was threatened by my seeing her husband alone.
2. The therapist must be aware that couple interaction can diminish individuality.
3. The therapist must be aware that each partner experiences anxiety differently, and that these qualitative differences must be respected.
4. The therapeutic alliance must be joined with the partner who is predominantly narcissistic because the tendency to "flight/flee," seek isolation, and withdraw can pose a serious threat to treatment. The borderline

must be provided empathic responses while the bonding with the narcissist is being accomplished.

   Example: A narcissist husband is mortified to find out about the many affairs his borderline wife is having. I try to be empathic toward her (the borderline) by attempting to "understand" how she may need many "daddies" to make up for the loss of her dead father. The husband leaves, never to return, likening my "empathic stance to confirmation/validation" of her behavior. I soon learned how important it is to bond first with the narcissist (the damaged, vulnerable self).

5. The more primitive the couple, the more structure, simplicity, and clarity they need. Secure the frame, but do not expect immediate results. It may take time to develop clear treatment boundaries. As the resistance unfolds, weave it into the relationship and gradually into the "couple transference" (fears of being trapped, annihilated, betrayed). The deep unconscious wisdom system appreciates the sound frame as a clear reference point and offers strong support for the therapeutic work.

6. When individual treatment occurs in conjunction with conjoint treatment, the same basic guidelines apply. The work must focus on conflicts related to the relationship under the umbrella and guidelines of conjoint treatment.

THREE PHASES OF TREATMENT

I have observed three distinct phases that couples move through. These phases are based on the theoretical constructs of Klein (1957) and Meltzer (1964–1965) describing three stages of development. They are similar to the various positions through which the infant moves (paranoid–schizoid to the depressive) in relation to its experiences with the mother and later to the environment. Within these three positions, there is continual movement back and forth from states of fragmentation to those of wholeness and integration. The effort of the therapist is to gradually wean the couple away from the relationship to a stage of self-development.

   To elucidate the movement away from circular, painful, and destructive behaviors, I have applied Meltzer's (1967) paradigm of *geographical confusion*. The three-phase format for treatment described in this section is superimposed on theoretical principles related to how couples move from one treatment phase to another as determinants of psychological progress.

   Meltzer (1967) discussed movement from one psychic space to another, stressing the importance of geographical confusion, particularly to adult borderline patients and the more severe psychopathological borderlines. I attempt to apply ideas from Meltzer's geographical positions to specific developmental stages through which couples move. I believe Meltzer's descriptions of skin boundary and adhesive identification visually and graphically illustrate how one individual can virtually live inside the mental space of another object. In treatment, these three phases, which can occur concomitantly and can overlap, are based on (a) fusion, (b) separation, and (c) interaction. The concepts of Freud, Mahler, Kohut, Klein, Fairbairn, Winnicott, Bion, and Bowlby are integrated and evaluated to help determine psychological development. Concepts from self-psychology, which are most useful in conjoint psychotherapy, help the therapist understand issues of the merger and fusion in the collusively bonded dyad—particularly in Phase 1, the blaming/attacking stage—that mirror the pain of a "no self" or a "mindless self" that this fusion brings about.

In the initial phase, Meltzer (1967) included intense massive projective identification, intolerance of separation, omnipotent control, envy, jealousy, deficiency of trust, and excessive persecutory anxiety. This phase of parasitic bonding is one in which the individual needs to maintain close physical contact with the partner to hold together part of the self and form an area of life space inside the self that can contain the objects of psychic reality. This is the process Meltzer termed *adhesive identification*. The intolerance to separation manifests itself in absolute dependency on an external object. In this initial phase, one object lives inside the external object in order to maintain a sense of cohesion; however, although boundaries are blurred, it is a two-part functioning. In treatment of couples, this is equivalent to what occurs between the partners when they are immersed in states of fusion. In the early stage, described in more detail later, interpretations are withheld. They are upstaged by therapeutic techniques of involvement, attunement, understanding, mirroring, and containment. Although interpretations take a back seat for the moment, they are recorded for future reference. This requires a certain capacity on the part of the therapist to contain, hold information, deal with very few central issues, and not spill out or evacuate as the patients do.

In Phase 2, the two objects begin to separate and live side by side. Meltzer distinguished between "real love" and the initial possessive jealousy that appears as a part object. Meltzer assured us that progress is almost always achieved if the analyst can persevere when geographical confusions are in the forefront of the transference and when almost endless patience and tolerance are required.

I believe Klein's ideas to be most useful in Phase 2, especially her ideas of splitting, projection and projective identification, and the good breast/bad breast versus the toilet breast concept. Bion's notion of the contained and the container, as well as his theories on linking and thinking, are also very important in this phase.

Grotstein (1984a) metaphorically and symbolically suggested that the borderline seems to cling adhesively to the surface of the mother's body as well as to other surfaces, as an exaggerated attempt to get a sense of contact and, therefore, of skin definition. The borderline experience tends to move to and from the mother's skin, whereas the narcissist tends to appreciate the mind, the capacity for introspection, and response to interpretation. The therapeutic task in this phase, then, is to gradually wean the borderline away from living emotionally inside the narcissist, and the narcissist away from idealized external objects.

Tustin (1981) suggested that autistic and childhood psychotic illness results from premature disruption of primary at-one-ness with the precocious experience of twoness. Development of reliance on another object is a slow process. I concur that emergence from this state not only requires careful scrutiny and understanding of developmental theories but can be very trying on the therapist's anxiety level.

Phase 3 is more interactional (symbiotic bonding), with the partners showing more understanding that each has the right to subjective experience. The couples are more aware of the collusional bond and strive toward healthier symbiotic ties. Prior to this, the sense of separateness has been an undeveloped idea, a nonexistent thought. Separateness is a preconception relating to a sensory-perceptional notion that an undeveloped part of the self is missing. If one is pervasively projecting inside another object, one cannot tolerate separation. Separateness is the nonpossessed object (paranoid–schizoid position). The inner world cannot tolerate the frustration of the feeling of nonexistence and thus strives to seek out others through bonding in a clinging, unfulfilling manner. In this phase there are fluctuating movements between the paranoid–schizoid position and the depressive position.

Phase 1: Borderline Lives Within the Mental Space of the Narcissist: A State of Oneness

In this phase the borderline partner is living emotionally inside the mental space of the narcissist (see Figure 8.1). It is a state of "oneness," a fusion/collusion with the other whereby there is no differentiation between self and other (paranoid–schizoid position). It is a shame/blame phase, with each one blaming the other for all the shortcomings in the relationship (who is right, who is wrong, finding fault, getting even, retaliating). There is much stonewalling, blaming, and shaming. Each partner shows little awareness of the inner forces that invade the psyche. Instead, there is a preponderance of primitive defenses such as splitting, projection, and projective identification.

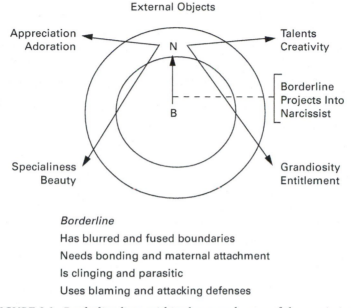

Borderline

Has blurred and fused boundaries

Needs bonding and maternal attachment

Is clinging and parasitic

Uses blaming and attacking defenses

FIGURE 8.1. Borderline lives within the mental space of the narcissist.

There is no tolerance for separateness; instead, omnipotence, control, envy, jealousy, projection, and other primitive defenses become the replacement for intimacy and closeness. The borderline partner might say, "If she loves me, then I know I am deserving. When she's gone, I feel like a nothing! I can't live without her." In this phase couples are heavily engaged in blaming and attacking behaviors and defenses. An intervention might be, "It must be very painful to feel attacked all the time and to feel that no matter what happens you are the one to blame."

During Phase 1, the borderline is living in fear inside a vacuum with "no thoughts" (beta elements), with the psychotic part of the personality communicating feelings through projection and blame. In this state of isolation, one cannot relate to others, and one drains and taxes other persons as one forcefully tries to invade. In Phase 1 the borderline derives gratification from the fantasy of the narcissist's availability. The paradox is that the narcissist is never available except for self-interest. There is no differentiation between self and other, as in, "If I'm good, Mommy is there. If I'm bad, Mommy leaves me." Good and bad objects are split off so that integration between the good and the bad cannot take place and defenses get in the way of sorting out what is coming from within and what is being projected from without. In this geographical position (as Meltzer would term it), the borderline is preoccupied with not having mommy all the time.

Toilet Breast

The borderline partner cannot make use of Mommy's breast as a container that has the capacity to hold the baby. In Phase 1, the therapist often serves as a "toilet breast" (Klein's concept, 1948). There must be an object that will contain the depth of the projection and the evacuation of painful effects (beta elements).

The therapist, like the mother, can be used by the couple (child) as a toilet breast or bad breast. These functions occur mostly in the initial stage of conjoint treatment, when the dysfunctional partners are unable to break out of their circle and need help "cleaning up" (toilet training). Part of the "dirt" is initially projected onto the bad breast therapist, who is perceived as an inadequate and unavoidable source. In this phase, the therapist must show considerable empathy with the messy, dysfunctional parts of the self in order to achieve some sense of mastery and growth.

Excessive demands, such as constant telephone calls, are other ways of using the therapist as a toilet breast. The therapist might interpret, "You keep calling me because there is a part of you that does not feel contained. For now, it is important to know that I am available to you as much as I can possibly be. It's important to acknowledge that you do need help from me, and that is the healthy part of you that can express your real feelings. I am glad that the vulnerable and healthy you can express needing me. It is the attacking, withdrawing, demanding, and blaming you that is messy. The mess is okay for now, but only until we can clean it up or wean you gradually away from this destructive part" (toilet-training the patient). The therapist, used interchangeably as breast and toilet, might explain, "I don't mind being used in this way because it helps me understand things better so we can start sorting things out here."

The concept of the toilet breast is exemplified in the case of the borderline wife who was not able to pay for her individual sessions. It became clear that the narcissistic husband was in charge of the family medical bills and expenses. Instead of taking up the issue with the husband, who was essentially the breadwinner of the family, the borderline wife attacked the therapist as being greedy, selfish, and money-hungry. The therapist responded, "I think you are seeing me as a 'money doctor', and if I am a money doctor/mommy, then you feel I am a bad mommy/therapist. It seems hard to imagine that a 'mommy' has needs. It is hard for you to see that I can also be a caring and loving doctor/mommy/me, but, in fact, this bad doctor/mommy/me can also be the caring, loving me! Maybe you feel that you are being greedy if you ask your husband for help" (bonding with the greedy/needy part of the borderline and transforming greed and need into a digestible thought).

Within these pre-Oedipal relationships, the kleinian technique of referring to the self as the "mommy/doctor/me/therapist" is very effective. Eventually, this kind of approach in primitive relationships may lead to further understanding about projections, skin boundaries, and definitions: "So you are not letting me know how bad I am for having needs. So there is a greedy 'me/you' and it is hard to see how the caring part of me can care for you. The greedy-you part is now like the greedy-me part." The therapist/mother must then be available to help the partners in the couple/infant configuration discharge their anxiety into the toilet breast so that the good breast therapist/mommy can emerge.

Phase Two: Awareness of Twoness (Transitional Space)

Emergence of Separation

This phase marks the emergence of "twoness," a tentative awareness of two separate emotional states, a sense that the therapist can be useful. There is more tolerance for ambiguity and budding insights into unconscious motivations (internal objects), and other compelling forces. It is the beginning of bonding with the therapist as a new reparative object and a "weaning" away from living emotionally "inside" the object—a move toward mutual interdependence. As the therapist emerges as a new self object, there is an opening of a new therapeutic space (transitional space). Some therapeutic bonding and assurance of the therapist's emotional availability mark the beginning of this phase. It is a hopeful stage, with a burst of new energy and feelings of excitement. There is a profound shift away from blaming/attacking and "doing," to that of feeling/thinking and "being." (See Figure 8.2.)

Phase 2 is still a twilight zone, but there is an awakening of the partners' ability to rely on the therapist as someone who can protect them from the tendency to abrogate their experience. There is a developing awareness of life other than through the partner. In this stage of "twoness," there still is very little differentiation between self and other: "My needs are your needs." This is quite different from Phase 1, in which there is little awareness of having a life or of needing.

In this state of twoness, the narcissist, although still deriving pleasure from the external world, needs constant affirmation, adoration, and approval, and begins to be aware of a consistent denial of needing another object. There is awareness that external gratification, overstepping boundaries, and blaming really do not develop a sense of self.

In Phase 2, the therapist is able to point out more of the projective processes and begin to wean the partners away from their blaming and

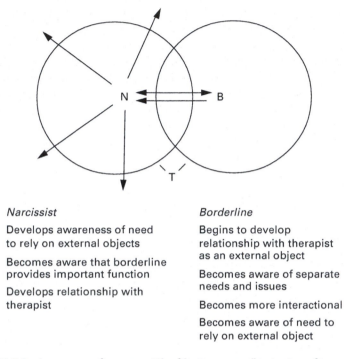

Narcissist	Borderline
Narcissist	*Borderline*
Develops awareness of need to rely on external objects	Begins to develop relationship with therapist as an external object
Becomes aware that borderline provides important function	Becomes aware of separate needs and issues
Develops relationship with therapist	Becomes more interactional
	Becomes aware of need to rely on external object

FIGURE 8.2. Awareness of twoness: The filtering stage (beginning of interaction).

attacking defenses. The therapist might say, "You are now projecting onto your (borderline) wife your own feelings of guilt because you can't tolerate facing something within yourself. You're afraid to have your own feelings or to feel vulnerable."

Parasitic Bonding Versus Healthy Dependency

Many countertransferential issues emerge in Phase 2 as the borderline begins to sense, although in a hazy manner (a preconception of an idea), that needs are healthy. In this stage we begin to differentiate between the forming of a healthy alliance (transitional use of the therapist) and a parasitic alliance with the therapist (the therapist being used as a confusional object). I cannot stress how important this distinction is. As an example of confusional use, the borderline partner might say, "Now we can get a divorce! You see I tried everything, even therapy, and it didn't work."

It is not uncommon that in Phase 2 one spouse will drop out. In the case of Vera and Jeffrey, Jeffrey became violent with Vera, and Vera terminated the relationship. Vera's integration and realization of her splitting mechanisms made her aware that the warm Jeffrey she loved was the same Jeffrey who was violent and emotionally unavailable. This enabled her to let go of the parasitic bond. She realized she could not force him to change but had to accept him as he was (the depressive "realistic" position). Even though Jeffrey no longer attended the sessions, we still dealt with these concepts in the ensuing conjoint sessions. Vera had to face that the Jeffrey she loved was the same Jeffrey who beat her up. "The reason you tolerate this 'beating-up' part is because there is an internal beater inside of you that continually berates you and puts you down. So if there is not an outside beater there is an inside one. Then you need the other part of Jeffrey to love you and relieve and reassure you because you beat yourself up." Vera indicated that there were still things about Jeffrey she loved and admired, including his insight and awareness. The work that followed led us to understand how the persecutory part of herself (the beaten-up part) tended to get stuck in clingy, unhealthy relationships.

In order for integration to take place, the beaten-up, persecutory part of the borderline needs constant feeding and nourishment. When one gets rid of an intolerable part within the self, the self never gets the nourishment it needs. The unnourished self becomes clingy and forms parasitic relationships with others. The borderline partner might say, "If only he would see how I'm hurting, he would then love me" (bonding with pain). The therapist must bond with the healthy aspects in order to allow a strong dependency relationship to develop, which then leads to growth and better object choices. Often patients will express concern about becoming too dependent on the therapist and want to "do it" by themselves. However, using the therapist as a healthy transitional object can occur when one or both of the partners recognize that they need help and can transfer the healthy, "needy" aspects of themselves. Unhealthy, parasitic relationships lead to hiding, fears, darkness, persecutory anxiety, clingyness, and emptiness. Being clingy is not the same as being needy.

Through expressions of psychosomatic illness, victimization, phobias, suicide ideation, sexual addition, and other split-off affective areas of experience, one may project massively onto the other.

Eventually the couple comes to realize that one partner cannot be the ultimate provider for the other, the rescuer, the reliever of persecutory anxiety, or the one to make up for all losses and deprivation. The partners learn that in order to attain any gratification in the relationship, one has to risk, to ask for what one needs, and not relieve the other person of responsibility.

In Phase 2, considerable support is needed during the weaning process. The therapist might say, "What you did this time was different. You did not take in the bad feelings. Even though what he said seemed perfectly rational and logical, you knew something didn't sound right, and you paid attention to your feelings. You did not run to the bank to take out a loan for him merely to relieve him of his anxiety. Instead, you waited while allowing your husband an opportunity to develop his own inner resources, which he did!"

Phase Three: Awareness of Two Emerging Separate Mental States (Dependent and Interdependent)

This phase marks the beginning of the depressive position, the boundary of two emerging individuals, separate yet bonded, connected and interactional. It is the ability and willingness for reparation to occur, the desire to "repair" the damage, to embrace guilt, mourn, and to express remorse and sadness. It is a time whereby each partner comes to terms with uncertainty, ambiguity, and healthy dependency needs. It is a time to heal and listen nondefensively to one another's hurts. This phase represents a diminution of repetitive negative projections. This is the thinking and healing phase in which the experience of "being" becomes the replacement for the act of "doing." There is an added dimension, a richness, a facing of individual issues, and a window of opportunity for further psychotherapy treatment. The couple begins to live psychically "outside" the object as two separate, yet connected, states emerge. Healthy dependency needs are recognized as each partner begins to respect the needs of the other. (See Figure 8.3.)

There is an emergence of separateness—the realization that one can live outside the other's self, within the domain of owning one's thoughts, a better use of transitional objects and transitional space. One can begin to tolerate the state of separateness, deal with truth, and ultimately face one's own fate or destiny (alpha function).

In this phase, both partners become more aware of inner conflicts (internal objects) and show more tolerance of the other partner's needs, thoughts, and feelings that are in contrast to their own. More time is spent talking about fears, individual concerns, and issues focusing on "the relationship," as well as on real concerns related to external events hitherto denied or repressed. In this final phase there is more room for introspection, fantasy, dreams, play, creativity, and the desire for further intrapsychic exploration. In taking more responsibility for the past, the partners exhibit a stronger level of anxiety containment and demonstrate an ability to wait and face their own faults and deficits. It is during this phase that some couples drop out or only one partner remains in treatment.

During Phase 3, the therapist is experienced more as a feeding/containing/waiting mommy. There is increased interaction with the therapist as a reparative object capable of providing a new experience and as a vehicle to thinking and linking new ideas.

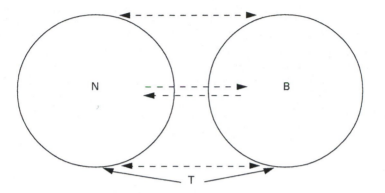

Borderline becomes more narcissistic.

Narcissist develops manic defenses against borderline.

Borderline expresses rage (better than passive-aggressive tendency to express feelings of betrayal covertly, rather than overtly).

More awareness of need for treatment.

Better and less confusional use of healthy transitional objects.

Encouragement and praise are received for taking more responsibility for behaviors.

Patient has developed appreciation for thinking over "doing" and "acting."

The "understanding" player takes a more vital part.

FIGURE 8.3. Boundaries of two separate, yet connected and bonded, individuals.

The therapist spends longer periods of time addressing individual issues rather than dyadic issues. The therapist will find that while there is discussion with one partner, as if that partner were in an individual session, the other partner is actively involved and listening. Often, sessions in this phase are reflective and introspective, and it is during this time that one, or perhaps both, partners may request individual sessions, which can be desirable and recommended. At this juncture, the couple may also want to drop out quickly because "all is well," which leaves us dealing with the quick fix, or the "flight into health." It must be clarified for the couple that progress has been made, but that taking some steps forward is not the same as a cure or integration (Mason, personal communication, 1988). They may have acquired some tools, but may not yet have the skills to use them. It must be explained to both partners that when one partner terminates, the other may carry on, and that conjoint treatment may continue even with one person not present, as long as the focus remains on the relationship and transference interpretations are made within that framework.

While the partners' behaviors improve and insights develop, they still need help to understand how they happened to get in the situation requiring therapy in the first place! They may have symptom relief, but symptom relief does not take the place of structural change. The therapist has the task, then, of helping the couple face the past as well as the future. It is in this stage that the partners need to be reminded that forgetting the past is like cutting off a part of themselves; they need the past in order to survive. Some liken this experience to a marital Holocaust: "We must not forget!" Two separate individuals with separate needs are emerging—two individuals who are aware of uniquenesses and differences yet who maintain a bond and are connected through their mutual desire to grow and develop. In Phase 3 there is some awareness, though perhaps only a glimpse, that each partner needs the other to play out their drama and ensure that there is a benefit in working things through. There is awareness that one partner stirs up unresolved conflictual issues in the other, and that to destroy the other is tantamount to destroying a part within oneself. The partners learn that to destroy, attack, or get rid of something is not the same as trying to understand something about themselves. What happens in Phase 3 is not to be confused with conflict resolution or with "working through."

During Phase 3 there is massive denial and often a tendency to develop manic defenses. Therapeutic failure may result in those who turn to the quick fix or deny the help they received. Omnipotence and devaluation—as in "We went for treatment but it didn't help!" or "We did it all on our own!"—must be interpreted at all times. For example, to one husband who told me he would like to stop because he couldn't afford the treatment, I responded, "And yet all along, while you have said you can't afford the treatment, you have been paying regularly for the past two years. I think what you are saying is that you may feel you can't afford to face some of the painful feelings you are having. Now that you have acquired some tools from me, you feel that you can do it all by yourself." The partner who drops out often has a sense of failure because there has been no quick fix. There is frequently a great deal of frustration and resistance in this phase. The partner might say, "It's better!" The therapist can help with this dilemma by responding, "I think that's exactly what happens in the relationship. As soon as there is some difficulty or frustration, there is the impulse to give in or give up. Now it is happening here. But I am not going to give up because I know that if I can hold on, something constructive may happen."

Phase 3 gives rise to more interaction around issues of loss and separation, and healthier use of transitional objects to fill in empty space, the black hole, the void. There is less taking in of the projections of the other and more awareness that the projection stimulates an unresolved internal part of the self.

Past histories, genetic material, and archaic associative responses often emerge during Phase 3, paralleling mistreatment and transcending the couple experience. There is an amazing replication of archaic anxiety about how the partners were mistreated as children, and some recognition of similar mistreatment is extended to external objects. Each partner begins to take more responsibility for the past and to recognize that what has been done now constitutes a history. The partner recognizes that the memories of these injuries cannot be dissipated or remedied quickly.

It must be clarified that during this phase defenses against mourning and facing feelings of sadness and pain become evident; however, if feelings of sadness and pain are ignored, part of the self does not heal or develop. Entering the depressive position is the facing up to losses rather than developing defenses against them. Often, conjoint treatment ends at this time. One or both of the partners may decide to continue for more intensive treatment either with the same therapist or with another. Phase 3 can be a transitional phase, and it plays itself out depending upon the needs of the couple and the capacity of the therapist to deal with both partners individually.

These three phases of conjoint treatment are neither a means to all ends nor a quick cure; rather, they provide a transition or preparation for more intensive treatment. A strong therapist can help couples through periods of resistance to treatment and help the partners avoid disrupting treatment too early—before the individuals are able to face, stand up to, and be accountable for their own behaviors. The therapist must be prepared not only to interpret fears but to anticipate manic defenses that precede the patient's entering the depressive position. The therapist's own anxiety regarding the wish to cure can get in the way of interpreting these manic defenses, or the therapist can feel too threatened or guilty to help hold onto the treatment. "I can see that for so long you felt helpless and powerless; now what you are doing is the opposite. You either withdraw, or you say or do nothing. Now what you want to do is to do it all—even take over the treatment." Beware of the quick fix: "All is well," "I can't afford it," or "I can do it myself." Be aware that for the narcissist the issue may be omnipotent control, whereas for the borderline it may be a manic defense against the powerless part of the self.

The patient may be trying to get rid of the therapist and the treatment before the patient has integrated that part of the self. "Look, Mommy, how big I am—I can take over your job!" The only problem with taking over is that the patient does not have the tools (pre-Oedipal conflicts). "See, Mommy, Daddy, how big I am; I can wear your clothes and become you!" The problem is that although a little boy can wear daddy's pants, they won't fit.

CASE ILLUSTRATION OF TREATMENT PHASES

The case of Joe and Mary illustrates the three phase of treatment.

Phase I: A State of Oneness

Therapist: So, what brings you here?

Joe: I want to stay married!

Th: What about you?

Mary: Well, I decided to move out, become independent, and do some things on my own.

Joe: Well, then, why don't you get a divorce?

Mary: No, I'm really not ready. I don't know what I want yet. I just want to live alone for a while, go out, have fun, be independent.

Notice the "grip" Mary has, keeping Joe on hold while she seeks out others to validate, appreciate, and mirror her. Her independence is not a real independence because she is running away and not facing what she really needs to face.

Th: Well, tell me how you feel, since Mary hasn't made up her mind.

Joe: I've made up my mind. I'm going to stay married!

Th: As far as I know, it takes two partners to decide to stay in a marriage.

Joe: Well, since she can't make up her mind, then I have, and my decision is to stay married!

Mary: But I don't want to.

Joe: [threatening] Then get a divorce.

Mary: No. I'm not ready.

Joe: Then that means you want to stay married.

In this phase there exists a state of oneness between Mary and Joe. Joe is living within the mental space of Mary. He derives his sole sense of himself from whether or not Mary is available to him. Mary is the more narcissistic, not only because she is keeping Joe on hold (excessive entitlement fantasies) but because she feels she can use Joe while she remains free to seek out others. Each partner is using the other as a confusional object. Although Mary realizes that the little girl part does not really know how to be independent, her grandiose self believes independence comes from external gratification ("Look at me! I'm a big girl and can be independent.") Joe appears to be the more borderline in that he cannot think beyond his primitive needs and feels terrified at the prospect of Mary leaving him. He is clinging, possessive, and retaliatory.

Their circular arguing makes for confusion; it is as if the room were spinning. In their relationship there is no room for empathy or insight. There exists only the behavior of closed minds: blaming/attacking defenses, excessive distorted ideas of grandiose entitlement fantasies, and magical thinking, as in "I want; therefore, I shall have."

After one particular therapy session, Joe and Mary left feeling very romantic and decided to make a date. At the last minute, Mary called Joe to break the date, claiming she had a headache. That night Joe went to her house and caught her with another man. He grabbed her and shook her; afterward, she called and told me she was extremely upset over this incident. In this case, the therapist is used as a toilet breast to contain the negative, hostile attacks of Joe. The therapist becomes the preoccupied mother, worried about Joe's violent and aggressive tendencies.

Phase 2: Emergence of Separateness

In the next session, I offered full support to Mary (the narcissist), while also setting a limit for Joe (the borderline) because Joe had physically shaken her. To Mary I said, "If this ever happens again, you will have my full support in getting a restraining order; no one has a right to hit you, touch you, or shake you." I offered support to Joe by acknowledging that "Mary has no right to make a commitment to you then let you down at the last minute." I let him know he was perfectly entitled to feel angry, even if she offered him the explanation of a headache. She could have made an effort—taken a nap or some aspirin. "But, more important, if Mary didn't want to be with you she could have told you. I think what hurt you was being betrayed." I turned to Mary and let her know that she had let Joe down. This provided a new awareness, and each partner felt understood. Joe and Mary finally were able to start taking in new ideas because they felt relieved, safe, protected, and not blamed.

In this phase each partner becomes aware that the other stirs up some inner conflict. The projective processes are clarified as contributors to their confusional states. There is a sense, or a preconception, that internal conflicts are distinct and separate, whereas in Phase 1, this preconception is virtually nonexistent. The partners are also beginning to examine their behaviors introspectively. Within a few sessions, Joe began to cry and told us that his alcoholic mother had never been emotionally available to him. Mary's profound withdrawal initially took the form of massive denial about the couple's current financial situation. Mary began by expressing anger and outrage about their financial state. Joe had declared bankruptcy, and he had let her down by not paying back a house loan to her father. Her withdrawal and isolation represented her inability to deal realistically with these issues and fight for that to which she was truly entitled. Narcissists never know what they are really entitled to; they go after only their grandiose fantasized entitlements.

Mary's withdrawal had a profound impact on Joe. I told him he was now letting us know what it felt like to be emotionally bankrupt. (A transformation of beta elements into alpha function was taking place, transforming poisonous material and detoxifying the feelings into something that could be digested, something emotionally useful and helpful.) Joe's capacity to tolerate his own inner badness could now be seen from a healthier perspective. "You are letting Mary know what it feels like to be emotionally bankrupt, as you have been your whole life. This feeling is so intolerable to you that instead of owning up to it, you project it onto Mary. No one every owned up to letting you down; now it's hard to face that you have let others down."

Joe came to realize why he would not file the divorce papers.

Joe: If I file them, it looks as if I want to get a divorce, and I don't. I want to stay married.

Th: You want to stay married, and I'm trying to help you see what it takes. It's difficult to stay married because it means we have to do the work for Mary and face the difficulties and work through them. But, of course, you have a "me" here to help you, and I am not an alcoholic, unavailable mother! So you say that if you file, that's the same as wanting a divorce. But as far as I know, the act and the doing are not the same thing as wanting. Just because you file doesn't necessarily mean you want a divorce. Just because you feel like hitting your wife does not justify your doing it. You can feel like shaking her, but you're not allowed to really do it. So just because you file does not mean you want a divorce.

In this phase I had an opportunity to interpret the splitting, and I noted that all behavior did not emanate from Mary. Joe was helped to face his internal state of impoverishment, and Mary was beginning to see that her running away from Joe was really avoiding facing up to unresolved money issues with him.

In interpreting the splitting, I said to Mary, "First, there are two Marys: one who loves Joe and another who is let down and doesn't know how to deal with her disappointment. Then there is the Mary who turns to lots of other men as daddies to admire her and to make her feel special." To Joe I said, "There are two Joes: one who feels hurt and betrayed and attacks in order to get even, and one who wants to hold on like glue. Both Joes desperately want to be loved. Both are destructive because neither way makes you be loved; in fact, all you'll do with Mary is hook into her rebellious child." I completed the interpretation by showing that there was a cause and effect.

Phase 3: Interactional

Phase 3 is interactional; that is, there is more interchange between patients and therapist than in Phases 1 or 2.

Mary was worried that I would be the one to terminate the sessions, that I would threaten her, abandon her, get tired of her. She was feeling guilty that she did not show up for one of the appointments. I interpreted that she was afraid that I would withdraw, become "independent," or leave her, but that indeed it would be more likely that she would be the one to leave. She might, I said, have a hard time being able to withstand the rigors of the conjoint sessions, to stand up to me and tell me what she was feeling or thinking, or to stand up to her husband. I pointed out to her that when things got tough she was the one who tended to leave, become silent, or get so enraged she turned away and avoided the situation. I reassured her that I would not leave or withdraw from her as her mother did, but would be emotionally available to her.

Mary was projecting onto me that I would be the one who would avoid the issues or go away from her. She also let us both know how painful it felt to be left. Although neither I nor Joe had actually withdrawn from her, she needed to understand how she was projecting a part of herself onto me and onto her husband. These fears kept her being a little girl and got in the way of her taking care of her needs so that she could really learn how to stand up for herself. I interpreted, "The big girl you does not know how to defend yourself, but if you walk away or don't show up here, then you will never have a chance because you will never be able to turn to those who can help you—for example, your lawyer, accountant, or financial planner—or those who can really help you 'show up'!"

Mary was hurt and felt that I was not appreciating her. I let her know that I appreciated her but that she was not appreciating me or herself. Mary thought that by pointing out her deficits, I was putting her down. "In fact,"

I said, "I see more of a resourceful you than you see in yourself! However, if I don't point out these behaviors to you, then it will seem as though I am the one who is 'not showing up' and who is withdrawing from what is really happening. If that were the case, we would continue to go around in a circle, never putting an end to these destructive behaviors." Mary responded, "I don't know how to go after what I am entitled to with Joe because I'm scared and he makes me feel so guilty." "Ah," the therapist might add, "this is the part of you I can appreciate, the part of you who doesn't know everything, the part that can admit to being scared. Now, if you can hold onto these feelings, I think that this can lead to something very special."

In the last phase, the dynamics become increasingly clear. The role of the therapist takes on a new meaning for each of the partners. Joe became the borderline child, setting up his mommy/wife to be the all-encompassing mother. The child/baby/husband now had a mommy/therapist totally preoccupied with him because of the worry that he might become violent again. I was attempting to provide the necessary holding environment, because when the potential holding environment is threatened, as in divorce, fragmentation can occur.

When the therapist can help the borderline patient contain some of the internal feelings, there is a better opportunity to face reality and see more clearly that all the badness does not emanate from within. Borderlines can hold onto the more lovable parts of themselves when they can understand that it's what they project that is destructive and not the contents from within.

Mary's interaction with me in Phase 3 was focused on allowing herself to have more healthy dependency needs. The therapist bonds with or "feeds" the healthy, resourceful part of the narcissist, while not "feeding" the detrimental parts of the defensive structures. There is an awareness that the grandiose self is destructive and that this does not lead to a state of cohesion and integration. The therapist might say, "It's good for you to face something you don't know, because then we have a chance to learn, to develop something together, to find a way—and, ultimately, you will get to know."

THE IMPOSSIBLE COUPLE

The more primitive and destructive the couple being treated is, the more structure is needed. We have all experienced the "impossible couple." These individuals tend to lack motivation because of their impulses to act out and because their primitive defenses include massive denial, projection, and blaming/attacking behaviors. The couples I term "impossible" involve partners who are not capable of being in the same session together at the same time. For the impossible couple, it may be necessary to see each partner at a separate time and to state clearly that the process is not to be confused with individual psychotherapy but rather is a precursor to conjoint treatment. The partners need to know that when the couple "grows up" and the partners can stand to be in a room together, they will be ready for conjoint treatment. Until that time, however, it will not be feasible.

During this preliminary treatment phase, the partners must be reminded that the focus still remains on the couple problem. It may be that certain individuals are too fused or merged with one another to be treated together. Supportive, structured psychotherapy is advisable to prepare the person for contact with the other partner. When couples respond in this way there is no semblance of communication. In working with these types of couples, the therapist must keep in mind that the goal is to help the partners face one another in a conjoint setting and that the function for the therapist is to serve as a means to achieving this goal.

One of the basic elements that emerges in this particular configuration is the notion that these persons cannot tolerate another person having an idea contrary to theirs. For two or more ideas about one issue to exist simultaneously is tantamount to betrayal, abandonment, and abrogation of one's personal experience. The task is to provide the understanding that an idea does not take away anything, but in fact can even add something—that if one can stay with one's own experience, ideas can blend and truth can develop. To ensure tolerance, one might wish to suggest transitional objects. It may not even be too far fetched to provide a small teddy bear for the patient to hold while another person is stating an opposing idea or thought. Provide eye contact, a supportive smile, an empathic look, a nod, or whatever it takes to help the person hold on while another idea is being presented.

TECHNIQUES

Psychoanalytic techniques and theories are meaningless unless they are artistically, emotionally, and creatively executed. Every psychological movement, like every step of a dance, must be sensitively expressed with meaning, purpose, and conviction. The therapeutic task is to link what occurs externally with the internal life of the patient(s). Let us begin with transference and couple transference.

Directive Approaches

Directive approaches put the therapist in the position of placing strong pressures on, and issuing commands to, the patient. It is popular among family therapists, including many therapists who treat couples, to assign tasks for the couple to do between sessions. However, I personally do not assign homework or exercises.

There are advantages and disadvantages to both methods. Some therapists, for instance, will ask the couple to take turns listening to one another for 15 minutes, without saying anything. Although such tactics are used to reduce anxiety and give the patient the feeling that something is being done, they do not actually relieve anxiety because they do not lead to understanding. In fact, assigning tasks can give a false sense of doing something, and this can alleviate the therapist's tolerating a state of messiness and confusion. "Doing something" removes the need of understanding how one got into the mess in the first place. Giving assignments to the narcissist/borderline couple may give the false message that the partners are to provide for one another rather than that the therapist will provide for each. For all these reasons, I choose not to offer direct tasks.

Analogous to the concept of tasks in conjoint therapy is the idea of the person who continually initiates lawsuits and seeks legal counsel to clean up some financial mess. The attorney could help take care of the specific problem, but could serve the client in greater measure by helping the client understand how the mess was created in the first place. Telling someone what to do in a specific instance is not the same as providing structure and limit-setting.

Containment

Containment is an invaluable therapeutic tool for conjoint treatment. It takes a "container" to help patients face the intolerable unknown. Patients might ask, "Why am I so lonely? I feel it gnawing away at the depths of me. I can't stand to have anyone see me in this state." The therapist might respond, "Yet even as you say you are experiencing this intolerable loneliness, you still can function; you can walk and think, and there still is a 'you' that can make decisions." The therapist might expand on this, "I think that because you feel so lonely, you become the loneliness for all to see, as if there is no skin boundary or a you to protect, or as if that is all of you."

Because of the borderline's readiness to take in the projections of others, borderline patients seem to need containment more than empathy in order to feel safe. A therapist might say, "We are better off trying to understand what it is inside of you that makes you feel bad and that makes you identify with these projections."

The Experience of Truth

In treatment, the therapist must be aware that couples need to be understood first and should be able to vent feelings. The therapist must try to be available to both partners, to allow each to have a personal experience of the "truth," and to confirm that the therapist can understand how each can feel a particular way. One of the most valuable discoveries is that there is room for more than one truth.

Who's right? Who's wrong? They're both right and both wrong. Each partner has a personal experience of the "truth." It is the way these truths are expressed that is dysfunctional. If the therapist engages in the battle or focuses on what or who is right and wrong, then the therapist is participating in the craziness. It is up to the therapist to understand both sides, which is possible through a process that Bion (1977) referred to as "detoxification."

We ask ourselves what it is that occurs intrapsychically at the moment of discovering a psychological truth. What is the truth? Bion (1977) has offered the therapist "abandonment of memory and desire," that is, the ability to give up all memory and desire by putting aside preconceptions and theories and thus being totally available, without contamination from previous sessions, other people, or other external influences. We are interested in discovering psychological truth, and that truth can be uncovered only through experience. Bion's work offers us an invaluable tool and one most useful in couple therapy.

The therapist must protect the partners when one tries to rob the other (or to rape the other person's mind) by letting the offending individual know that no matter how absurd the other person's view may seem, that person still is entitled to have that view. It is my job to allow more than one view and to allow differing views to "room" together.

When the partners argue, the therapist must be careful not to get pulled into the battle. One may instead comment, "If I respond to this, then we all will be arguing, and there will be no treatment taking place." In these situations, I advise the therapist not to respond further: It is best to wait and say nothing. Make them curious! Make them think! Make them wait! Look at each of them for a response until they are dying to know. When the timing seems appropriate, then say something like, "I think I have it! It seems clearer to me now what the problem is. It appears that you are in a competition with each other and with me—as if one idea has to win over the others. It seems intolerable that both of your ideas can live together in the same house or in the same room, and can live with my idea." If the couple denies this is going on, I remind them of what I have heard in the session and what I have experienced. The six-point procedure described earlier in this chapter helps expand these ideas.

GENERAL CONSIDERATIONS

(See Table 8.1.)

Communication

Many theorists, and even many authors of pop psychology books on how to communicate effectively, have missed the major focus. What does it mean to teach a couple to communicate?

Communication is not merely stating what is on one's mind. To do so, in fact, can be destructive and dangerous to the self. To communicate effectively means to think through and sort out thoughts, ideas, and various confusions before expressing what is on one's mind. These feelings need to be sorted out and organized before they are expressed to a partner or any other person.

Resistance

Initial resistance to making a commitment to the treatment is commonplace and includes complaints over costs. The couple needs to be reminded of the reasons that brought them to therapy in the first place. "You mean to say there are arguments, fighting, and economic problems, and now you say you can't afford to come. I don't see how you can afford not to come!"

A couple who quit treatment after 3 months because "it didn't do any good" or because they were able to "work it out all by themselves and now are doing just fine" is evidence of the patients' denial of the feeding given to

---

TABLE 8.1
General Considerations

- Introduce each partner to his/her internal object.
- Show how they stay connected to a bad external object stirred up by archaic injuries (the V-spot).
- Be aware of the specific object(s) to which the partners are internally attached.
- Show how the tendency to attach to a bad internal object is repeated continuously.
- Show each partner that even though the attachment is painful, it is also familiar.
- Show how the attachment to a bad internal object is confusing and creates chaos, splitting, and ambivalence because the object that can be cruel and sadistic can also be loving and kind.

them in the treatment, a denial of the good breast. Bion (1961) discussed flight/fight in regressive groups, wherein a couple bonds together to fight off the enemy, that is, the therapist. The therapist needs to be aware of a quick disruption in therapy that could relate to the patient's "practicing phase" (Mahler et al., 1975); when patients are ready, they don't need to reality-test the therapeutic work.

Couples may resist therapy for other reasons, including envy, greed, or massive denial. They may envy the therapist's capacity for containment and empathy or resent other attributes the therapist may have, and thereby disavow the help they receive. Many factors may be involved when a couple terminates treatment prematurely, but termination does not necessarily represent a treatment failure, a therapeutic impasse, or an empathic failure. In fact, even if only one of the partners remains, this can be considered a positive sign.

If one partner gets angry or annoyed, it is up to the therapist to let both partners know that this is preferable to avoidance, denial, or subjugation of the self, and that the therapist is not disturbed by the anger but rather welcomes it because it can lead to more understanding. The therapist has an opportunity to become the new object and to protect the borderline from the narcissistic partner who reenacts emotional abuses similar to the ones the narcissist has experienced in the past.

CONCLUSION

Although educating narcissistic and borderline partners about the therapeutic process is complex and confusing, it is essential. Not to do so is unrealistic. These couples need to know that the problem was not formulated overnight, and that it cannot be resolved or cured instantly. Each partner needs the other to play out the drama. If one expresses how one feels, that can be evacuating. If one holds back what one is thinking or feeling, that can be withholding. If we do not express how we feel, it can go against human nature. If we try to think, to relate, and to understand, that is psychoanalytic!

This chapter has attempted to outline a more systematic treatment approach to treating narcissistic/borderline couples in order to help understand treatment successes as well as failures. That a couple abruptly terminates treatment does not always mean the treatment has been a failure; in fact, in some instances it indicates success. It is the understanding of what constitutes successes and what differentiates them from failures that allows us to be better equipped as clinicians to develop more effective treatment approaches.

Chapter 9

Final Cases

CASE 1: THE DEPRESSED ARTIST

Norm

This case illustrates how the grandiose self in the artist can infect and invade the capacity to create and paralyze the entire creative process.

A middle-aged psychologist came to treatment because he had a great desire to become a writer. Writing meant everything to him. But whenever he was around other writers, especially successful ones, he would go into an emotional paralysis. His envy of other writers caused him enormous anguish, grief, suffering, and psychological torment. At an interpersonal level, he could never find the "right" women because none of them were "good enough" to meet and match his strong internal superego demands. While bridging his feelings of externalized envy into the transference relationship with the analyst, he not only denied his envy but totally denigrated the analyst and her own writings.

Norm: It happened again. I went to the Screen Writers Guild and had to walk out. I went into a panic. There sat two well-known screenwriters. I just couldn't stand it. A few others even produced plays on Broadway. I felt so intimidated and shaky, I couldn't say a word. I knew they would look at me and think, "Gee, what a loser."

Therapist: So you think these playwrights came to observe you and did not come because they are interested in sharing their work.

Norm:	Well, when you say it like that, that is pretty grandiose of me; they still scare the crap out of me.
Th:	Why do you have to compare them to you?
Norm:	Because they're successful and I'm not. I haven't written one published piece.
Th:	I wonder if you have any similar feelings here?
Norm:	What feelings?
Th:	Of envy!
Norm:	How can I be envious of you? How can you compare what I write with what you write? You write a bunch of psychobabble. I am talking about profound emotional work. Theatre works! No, I am not envious of you, if that's what you're getting at.
Th:	Norm, you put your whole sense of self into your identification as a writer, and yet you are also a very good psychologist.
Norm:	You don't get it. I hate what I do and I want to be a writer. I hate my work. When patients talk, I sit there and count money. My social life sucks. Every time I see a woman I like, she doesn't like me.
Th:	Why are you so hard on yourself?
Norm:	Because I hate not having any money.
Th:	But your work does bring you an income.
Norm:	I know, but that is not the way I want to make a living.
Th:	Why are you so hard on yourself?
Norm:	I called my father the other day; he gave me the same response. "Hi, son. You want to speak to your mom? Are you still wasting your time writing all that crap that no one reads?" He's an old fool!
Th:	No wonder you are so hard on yourself and want to run away. You don't want others to see a very shameful and demeaning father who has undermined you and ridiculed you your entire life.
Norm:	But I'm a grown man now. I should not allow what that stupid fool says to influence me.
Th:	Yes, you are grown and have separated from your father physically, but emotionally he is still inside of you. You have internalized a persecutory, shameful, ridiculing father that repeats an old scenario, "You are a fool, wasting time!" No wonder you want to run away; no wonder it is hard for you to be around others.

[Silence]

Norm: By the way, please hold my check. I don't have enough money to pay you. Besides, I want to quit. I don't think we are getting anywhere.

Th: Now you want to run away from me. The same way you want to run away from your patients, playwrights, women you are attracted to. You may feel externally bankrupt, but you can also feel emotionally/internally bankrupt and that is the worse kind. We will have to explore how you keep yourself locked in an emotional prison, paralyzed by your fears. And then you wonder why you are not successful. As you do this, you kill the creative process. The creative process feeds on new experience, on chaos, conflict, anxieties!

Norm: This is one of your best interpretations; the other stuff you were saying is crap.

Th: Yet you think others are judging. No one is judging you; you are the judge! You are the one who has internalized a very harsh, ridiculing, internal judge/father that demeans you. Then you ridicule me the way your father has ridiculed you your entire life!

[Silence]

Th: We need to stop here. Of course, I'll hold your check, but we cannot put your life on hold. It's time to cash in and start a new drama here, a new scenario, a new script.

Norm: Bye. Thanks. See you next time.

Th: With pleasure!

CASE 2: PAS DE DEUX

Judy and Blake (see also chapter 3)

This case illustrates the "dance" that takes place between the partners in the narcissistic/borderline relationship, with one clinging while the other withdraws. This becomes a dance between guilt and shame as each partner identifies with the other's projections.

Within the first 2 weeks of meeting Judy, Blake had invaded her space. He practically moved in, demanded a key to her house, took over, and consumed her with his controlling and never-ending demands. Judy, an attractive divorced mother of two college-aged children, was a top executive for a trade magazine, and Blake was an insurance salesman with three grown children whom he had not seen or visited for 5 years. Blake displayed many traits and characteristics of a borderline personality. Initially, he displayed an exquisite false self which lent itself perfectly to Judy's unfulfilled mirrored and narcissistic needs. Judy's lack of empathy and split-off feelings further exacerbated Blake's abandonment anxieties. In their "dance," Blake stirred up feelings of guilt in Judy. The more guilt she felt, the more she withdrew. The more shame he felt, the more he would pressure, cling, control, and dominate, pushing Judy further from her real needs and feelings.

Judy:	Blake and I have been together for 6 months. I want to get married, but Blake [fusion] insists we put everything together—our house, our material goods. He even insists I change my name.
Blake:	That's the only way I will feel as though we can be a couple.
Judy:	I want to be a couple, but I am beginning to feel suffocated.
Th:	In what way?
Judy:	When I leave the room to work at the computer he comes looking for me and asks me where I've been. I am beginning to feel guilty about doing anything on my own.
Th:	Blake, Judy is telling us she feels suffocated. You want to do everything together, and Judy is saying she needs more space.
Blake:	I give her space; she is exaggerating. I am just tired of going out with all these other people, all her friends. I just want more time alone.
Judy:	Blake was upset. At our last party I had my ex-husband there, and Blake had a fit.
Blake:	I would never have my ex-wife attend anything. That relationship is over; now it is just Judy and me.
Th:	It sounds as though you are coming from a place of hurt, Blake.
Blake:	I am not hurting. I just think this is the way it should be.
Judy:	Blake's mother died when he was 8 years old. I can understand why he is so clingy, but it really gets on my nerves. Even when we sleep I feel guilty going to the bathroom.
Th:	You know, Blake, there is nothing wrong with having hurt feelings, having needs, and certainly wanting to feel close. But there is a difference between closeness and domination. Perhaps if you can help us understand more about the early loss of your mother, it might help us find a way to sort out the issues in this relationship.
Blake:	Like what?

Th:	Well, it might help us understand why you need to control Judy, to push her around, without even attempting to work out some kind of compromise.
Blake:	Like what?
Th:	Well, arrange for some quality time together—time alone whereby you would both feel gratified. Or go see a lawyer; talk to him about a prenuptial agreement, name change, etc.
Blake:	I don't want to arrange a schedule. She should just want to be with me more. Nor do I want to see a lawyer.
Th:	Now you are suffocating me. You won't even allow me to help you [couple transference]. Second marriages are not the same as first ones, and this is something you will have to face. Do you love Judy?
Blake:	Yes, very much. I would do anything for her.
Th:	But no one is asking you to do everything, just some things. So tell me, how did your mother die?
Blake:	She died of cancer.
Th:	I am sorry to hear that; it is a terrible loss.
Judy:	Then I start to feel sorry for him and pressured into going along. He knows that I want very much to get married, to get a ring. All my friends are married. It would make me feel very special. At this point I'll do anything, change my name (even though I don't want to), give up some of my friends. I know it's crazy, but that's how important it is to me.
Th:	So you both share a similar dynamic. Blake, you suffocate Judy, trying to ensure you won't lose her by clinging, hanging on, controlling her. And you, Judy, suffocate yourself [suffocating internal object] by giving up your wants and hanging on because you are so scared you won't be regarded as special without a ring [the shared couple dynamic].
Judy:	What's wrong with wanting a ring?
Th:	Nothing, but I'm not hearing anything about your love, your caring for Blake.
Blake:	Does this mean we should separate?
Th:	Now you think I am going to abandon you. I can see even more clearly that is a first reaction. It's just hard to know what to do, or to see what the "real" relationship is about, especially when there is so much fear around abandonment/separation and desire

Judy: I never thought of it that way before. You mean it is hard for us to see what is real when we are so guarded?

Th: Yes, exactly.

Blake: Thanks for that. In a way you're right. My immediate reaction was that you were going to abandon us and pressure Judy into leaving me.

Th: [Laughing] No, I wouldn't do that. I wouldn't "pressure" you. That would be suffocating you, and if I did I would be doing what you do, and then there wouldn't be a me here to help you work this through. My job is to help you confront the "real" issues. I can understand your fears and anxiety. That is to be appreciated, but the control and domination is not [therapist trying to confront the aggression while remaining available to the couple's vulnerability—V-spots—by not colluding with their mutual projections].

Judy and Blake: Thank you very much.

Th: My pleasure. See you next week.

CASE 3: TURNING TO THE EXCITING OBJECT

Lenny and Sophia

This case illustrates how eroticism and excitement become the replacement for love and intimacy as two people strive to work through their developmental issues. For Lenny, the borderline, the critical reaction is in response to Sophia's lie (the disavowal of his ability to believe it was really happening, similar to the disbelief a child feels when there is a loss of a parent). In this case the recreation of the exciting object has a twofold purpose: to resurrect Lenny's dead mother, keeping her alive as an enactment of pent-up anger toward her for abandoning him, and, second, to glom onto an exciting object to assuage inner deadness and issues around unworthiness. For Sophia, turning to external daddies constituted an enactment of rebellious fantasies against a very defensive, passive, subservient mother who allowed men to devalue her womanliness.

Lenny: She opened the door wearing an old, frumpy bathrobe. As I entered the kitchen, I sensed the wonderful aroma of Italian food. Knowing it is my favorite, she had ordered it in. As I turned my head for one instant, I got a quick glimpse of a vision so erotic I actually had to catch my breath. My mouth dropped open. There she stood without a stitch of clothing, her bathrobe draped on the floor; stark naked. She moved closer and closer to me. She kissed me—one of those long, lingering kisses that seemed interminable, as if we had attained nirvana. I had never experienced this feeling in my life.

Th: Then what?

Lenny: After dinner we went for a drive, I happened to see something sticking out of her gym bag. When she got out of the car, I quickly checked, and, sure enough, I found her lace underwear and some condoms. When I questioned her, she simply said it was the underwear that she took to the gym and had no idea how the condoms got into her bag. I didn't say anything at the time but I know her well enough to say that she does not wear lace underwear during the day. Then I went to New York on a business trip. I called several times but she didn't answer. Finally, at two in the morning she answered the phone; she sounded drunk. I confronted her this time and she said that she stayed at her grown daughter's house. Well, I knew she has not spoken to her daughter for 2 years, and that it was an outright lie. When I returned, I found my clothes had been moved around. Again I confronted her. Again she lied, yet I knew she was having an affair. That morning I went to play tennis. When I returned and began to shave, I found my razor blade had been used. This time she claimed she had used it on her legs. Again, I knew she didn't use razors, that she only had her legs waxed. When she stepped out I looked and found fancy underwear in the clothes hamper. When she came back I questioned her. I had been suspicious for a long time that she may have been having an affair with her boss.

Th: So you felt you had sufficient evidence she was having an affair and that she had been lying to you.

Lenny: Yes, but I just couldn't believe it [the borderline's tendency to disavow experience]. Now for the rest of the story. I finally hired a private detective and had her followed. At 3:00 p.m. last Wednesday, the detective saw her drive up to a man's condo. Three hours later they left, drove to a French restaurant, and then again returned to his condo. I didn't say a word; I just kept listening to her lies. When the detective told me the address, it confirmed my suspicion that she was having an affair with her boss. In fact, once when I went to see her at work, I noticed her boss got very conspicuously nervous and ran out of the room. Just knew it.

Th: So now that you have proof of the "lies" and evidence of the affair, why do you stay?

Lenny: I stay because I love her. She excites me. I'm sorry I split up with my old girlfriend. She was loyal, kind, loving, but I was bored. Sophia is hot; she is Italian, has a temper. But we have the best sex, and she sure knows how to keep a man happy. Last night after dinner, she melted chocolate and put it on my big toe and sucked it. Wow! I have never in my life experienced anything like it.

Th: So the main thing is about sex and excitement.

Lenny: No, we also have a great time together. We went to Italy. Her parents have a villa in Tuscany. It's great; we all sing and eat together. She is also a very accomplished woman; she is an architect, very creative, successful. But she needs to have lots of men admire her.

Th: Nevertheless, Lenny, this is not a relationship about love; it is about addiction.

Lenny: Addiction?

Th: Yes, this kind of excitement often becomes a cover for something you are not facing in your own life. [We go on to explore how he feels unworthy, how he has not achieved the level of success he wanted after graduating medical school, and how after his mother died when he was 3 he felt a state of internal deadness.]

Lenny: Anyway, let me continue. Finally she confessed that she was not in love with her boss, that she screwed him because she needed to excite men, that women in Italy were always subservient to men, that her mother was always weak and passive. She told herself early on in life that she would never let men get the best of her. I guess that is why she has to flaunt her sexuality.

Th: This is very important and insightful information. I guess you thought that being involved with such an exciting woman would rescue you from your inner deadness, but the opposite has occurred. The more you went along with her lies and the deceit, the more devalued you felt.

Lenny: I know, but I am so in love I cannot break away. I think and dream of her.

Th: Again, Lenny, what you call "love" is not love. I don't hear anything about love, two people giving and sharing. It is more like a tennis match: she trying to get away with her lies and you repeating an old scenario of a mommy who abandoned you. This does seem to stir up some important issues: abandonment, for example.

CASE 4: "TIT FOR TAT"

Sam and Betty

This case illustrates how couples like Sam and Betty remain stuck at the most primitive level of experience as both project their "depriving" and competitive selves onto one another. At a deep emotional level we see how the narcissistic husband, Sam, is unable to express his vulnerable self at a deep emotional level, instead projecting it onto Betty, making her the "needy," shameful one for voicing her needs. Betty, who already disavows her existence, becomes easy prey for Sam's barrage of attacks and assaults. This case also demonstrates how the therapist steers the conflict away from "the relationship," moving into a new transitional space (the couple transference), away from the "depriving couple" to that of the "depriving threesome couple." Furthermore, this case illustrates how the competitive nature of the couple circumvents love by perpetuating aggression and sadomasochism, which infect the relationship like a virus that cannot be seen by the human eye.

Betty:	He's doing it again! He never takes care of my needs! I needed his support with our daughter, and he goes off to play tennis all day!
Sam:	But that's not a need. I work hard all day, so I need time to go out and play. Then, we agreed that she would not buy a new bracelet, but she went ahead and did it anyway.
Th:	So you feel what you need is more important than what Betty needs?
Sam:	You see, Betty is a taker.
Th:	What's wrong with being a taker, Sam? [Pause] It sounds like you could use a little "taking" yourself. Maybe you worry that if you take, you will be a "user."
Betty:	I'm not a taker. Okay—I only become a taker because you don't give me anything.
Sam:	How can I give you anything when all you do is spend, spend, spend, spend [Sam disavowing Betty's needs]?
Sam:	Betty used to be an accountant, but would you believe that now she can't even balance our checkbook?

Betty: But I'm an adult, a professional woman, a mother who runs a well-organized home. And I don't need a husband to order me around. I need him to help with the kids.

Th: I don't think we're going to succeed in sorting out all the needs in this session, and certainly they are important. Betty, your desire to have nice things is just as important as Sam's need to feel supported and have time to play. But before we go any further, I think we should address the "needs" of the treatment. I noticed it has been difficult for you to be here on time, and it is essential that you be here at our agreed time so that we have the full hour to work.

Sam: I don't want to talk about this. I want to talk about things that are more important [devaluing the therapist's "needs"]. You don't understand, I've been through this before and have seen many other counselors.

Th: But, I'm not just a counselor.

Sam: [Ebulliently and excitedly] Then what are you?

Th: I'm someone who attempts to work with more in-depth issues, and not offer directive advice or quick-fix solutions.

Sam: If you don't give advice, then what good are you?

Th: [With a warm embracing voice] Now you are engaged in a competitive battle with me. This is exactly what goes on in your relationship. But I'm not interested in competing with you. I'm more interested in trying to be helpful. I think you are letting me know how it feels to be diminished, to feel helpless and ineffective. But now you are putting down my needs, and the needs of the treatment.

Betty: He fights me with everything. It's okay for *him* to need things but not for me.

Th: Being here must make you feel very anxious, so instead of us being a working couple we end as a fighting/battling couple or threesome. But I will not engage in the battle, because if I do, there won't be a me here to help you, and I do not believe I can.

Sam: But I have something to say that's even more important. [Goes on about how his wife is withholding sex and how this frustrates and drives him wild.]

Betty: This is what he does with me. He gets into this competition, "If I give you sex, then will you give me support?"

Sam: There she goes again! Why don't you tell her to butt out?

Th:	So you resort to fighting or getting into a competition like a tennis match instead of expressing your feelings and making clear what your needs are?
Sam:	But if I do express my feelings she just walks all over me like a herd of camels.
Th:	[Struggles to maintain her position with Sam] This is really important information, because it helps me understand things better. Sam, you must feel very ashamed of your feelings, and I suspect they persecute you. So rather than express them openly to your wife, you do two things. You either get into a competition with her or you become destructive and abusive. Both attempts are ways in which you try to get rid of your feelings.
Betty:	I think he is just jealous.
Th:	Betty, you may be right, but if we focus here on who has more and who has less, then we are back in the tennis match, the competition, the very thing you wish to avoid. I thought you made a valuable point at the beginning of the session, to pay more attention to your needs and the needs of the relationship. Sam, What's wrong with feeling vulnerable?
Sam:	She has everything. I would love to be in her shoes. She chooses to work, but she doesn't have to if she doesn't want to. All she has to do is take care of our three kids [his envious attacks toward a powerful/controlling mother].
Th:	Sam, I think you project onto Betty the needy and vulnerable part of yourself. So instead of paying attention to your own needs, you get rid of them by displacing them into your wife [compete, battle, attack]. You do anything to avoid facing what you need for yourself.

[Sam is silent, listening attentively.]

Th:	I think I understand why this happens, and now you are saying you don't want to be a therapeutic teammate here. You are letting me know what it feels like to have a depriving mother, a parent you couldn't count on, and now you're not going to play this "therapy game" with me [using the patient's words]. So your wife and your therapist are prohibiting you, as your mother did, from going out to play or to buy toys because the cost is too high. We are prohibited because "we" cost too much.
Sam:	That's exactly right. For God's sake, how much does a goddamn ice cream cost?!
Th:	No wonder you are enraged when your wife would like you to

	provide more time, more help, more pleasure. The anger from the past [V-spot] festers in you and spills over into the relationship. It's hard to give when you have been so deprived.
Sam:	But she always puts me down when I feel vulnerable. What do others do when they get hurt and upset?
Th:	Some sulk, some sob, some somatize, get depressed. You fight! The best thing is to openly express how you feel.
Sam:	[Becomes unduly aggressive again] Oh, okay, tell me: How can I express my anger in a different way [hands crossed as if to challenge the therapist, who is desperately trying not to identify with the aggression]?
Th:	We will deal with that next time. But let me first reassure you that I will not engage in a tennis match or a battle. My intention is not to deprive you or withhold from you, but to treat your feelings with the utmost respect so I can be helpful [therapist emerging as new self object].
Sam:	[To the therapist, smiling tongue in cheek] I think you have earned your money.
Th:	[Smiling cordially] Thank you. I hope you have found this to be helpful.
Betty:	Yes, very much. Thank you.
Th:	See you both next week.

CASE 5: WITHDRAWAL VERSUS DETACHMENT

Kathy and Mathew

This case demonstrates the difference between withdrawal and attachment. With withdrawal, one remains emotionally attached; with detachment, one withdraws all libidinal connections and ties to the object. This case illustrates how Mathew detaches and splits off from his real needs by projecting them onto Kathy. The remaining sessions consist of bonding with Mathew, helping him get in contact with the real desires and needs he craves. As long as he remains detached, he will never get in contact with his real needs, let alone his passion. This case also illustrates how archaic injuries (the V-spot) can infect and invade the relational love bond, in this instance sabotaging all pleasurable experiences.

In this session Kathy calls, very upset and on the verge of tears, saying that Mathew has canceled the trip with her to Sedona at the last minute. As she expresses her hurt and pain, she is reminded of an absent, unavailable father now recreated in Mathew. The original archaic injury, emanating from early childhood, harkens back to a father who would promise to come for her birthday but at the last minute would find something "more important."

Kathy:	Did you hear what happened?
Th:	Yes, I did.
Mathew:	I just couldn't get myself to go on the trip with her. Just the thought of going was torture. It would have been too much pressure.
Th:	So you chose to abandon your partner because you couldn't handle the pressure?
Kathy:	He does that all the time! He always sabotages our plans.
Mathew:	I didn't want to subject her to my bad moods.
Th:	So because you felt Kathy would not be able to handle your bad moods, you thought it would be best for her to spend her holiday weekend alone in a hotel [detachment]?
Mathew:	I felt as though I would explode. I couldn't handle the pressure; it became unbearable.
Th:	You feel that your "bad moods" are dangerous, and that no one would be interested in understanding how you feel. So instead of being with your intimate partner you detach from her and from your feelings.
Mathew:	Yeah, I guess so . . .
Th:	Sounds like you are detaching from us here, Mathew.
Mathew:	That's what happens all the time.
Th:	When we start each session, you detach, saying you don't know where to begin or worry that you will be a burden on me if you express how you feel [moving into the couple transference].
Mathew:	I always worry I will be a big burden, especially on Kathy.
Kathy:	So that's why you let me down and didn't show up?
Th:	I guess you also let me down, didn't call me when you were in a crisis [bonding with Kathy's experience].
Mathew:	I don't like to burden people with my problems.
Th:	As a child you felt your mother couldn't handle your moods, your feelings. In fact, I recall your telling me that your mother would often send you away to your grandmother, whom you did not like. Whenever you complained, she would ridicule and laugh at you. Although your parents didn't beat you, must have felt very deprived and abused.

Mathew: Yes, I did.

[Silence]

Th: I feel your detaching right now, Mathew.

Mathew: I am detached. I don't like to deal with these feelings.

Th: Makes sense. You may feel that I am not going to handle your
             "bad moods," that your "bad moods" will torture me. But this is
             a way of mistreating me, not seeing me for who I am; instead
             you are projecting onto me old feelings [V-spot], which you are
             now bringing into this relationship. In order to treat you and
             help you, I need you to express yourself freely and tell me every-
             thing about how you feel.

Mathew: I guess I feel the same way about Kathy—that she will not be
             able to handle my moods either.

Kathy: And that is an insult to me. I love when you tell me how you
             feel. In fact, he did the same thing on Mother's Day. He did not
             buy me a card or a present. He does not acknowledge holidays
             or vacations. It's like living with a roommate. We have no inti-
             macy. Our passionate, sizzling romance has been reduced to an
             occasional "roll over and let's do it."

Mathew: I just feel tortured by all those things.

Th: I think there are some real issues regarding intimacy and com-
             mitment, Mathew. Whenever you start to get feelings, what you
             do is detach, and when that happens you become Kathy's un-
             available father.

[Mathew and Kathy are silent and listening.]

Th: And Kathy, whenever you express your needs or feelings to
             Mathew, you become his critical, punitive mother [therapist care-
             ful to express to each one their unique dynamics]. What's good
             about today's session is that we were able to get in contact with
             some really early injuries. Our work will consist of exploring
             how these injuries interfere with seeing the realities in your re-
             lationship.

CASE 6: GUILT VERSUS SHAME

Michael and Frances

This case illustrates how a guilt-ridden, overly controlling, narcissistic husband stirs up profound feelings of shame in his borderline wife, and how

the borderline wife, in turn, stirs up feelings of guilt in the narcissistic husband. The complicity of the couple entraps them in a primitive bond.

Frances, the borderline wife, complained that her narcissistic husband, Michael, was always late and unavailable. Frances took on the role of a complaining, demanding partner. Issues of separation were viewed as intolerable, keeping her in the role of a helpless victim handicapped by her lack of impulse control and containment. She vehemently denied that her husband emotionally abused and mistreated her until she found him in bed with another woman. Until that time she had felt ashamed for mistrusting him. "I can't tell how I feel because he doesn't listen. He gets angry and hostile with me when I get angry. How can I get angry when he gets angry?" [projecting his guilt onto Frances].

Treatment for this narcissistic husband focused on the incorporation of a controlling mother who gets in the way of his pleasure and fun.

Michael: She is just like my mother. My mother would never listen to me. All she would do was yell, scream, and get in the way of my fun. That's why I need other people. I need excitement. [Turns to the external excitement because he has not found the internal excitement.] Frances drives me away by her demands.

Th: Well, now we are getting somewhere. You're looking for excitement, and you're not finding it in your relationship. So your wife is like your mother—controlling, rejecting, getting in the way of your fun—but then you also see me as someone getting in the way of your fun, setting limits, and making demands here. So when your wife gets angry you rebel, and then you can't see if your wife has a legitimate gripe or not. You see her as a screaming, yelling, complaining, and controlling mother [guilt tends to distort reality].

In the transference, the therapist became the controlling, dominant mother who ruined all the fun and got in the way of his pleasure by making demands upon him. For the borderline wife, I became the "spoiler," the mother who ruined everything.

Feeling overwhelmed by guilt, Michael dropped out of the conjoint treatment, but Frances continued on with weekly individual psychotherapy. The focus eventually shifted from shame to understanding how the internal part of herself readily took in the projections of others. Although the therapeutic interventions essentially had to justify that there was an external, abusive, cheating husband (important, especially for borderlines, who tend to easily disavow their experience), they also validated that there was also an internal one. "Yes, there does seem to be this external abusive, betraying husband who leaves you out, abandons you, makes you feel shameful; there also seems to be a part that leaves yourself out, robs you of your feelings. This is what makes you feel so ashamed and helpless."

Treatment for this borderline wife focused on her delusional fantasies about going along, being a "good girl," always being nice in order to recapture the wonderful feeling of a warm, safe, soothing womb. In the transference, I became the intruder in her symbiotic world, the "troublemaker," the "spoiler."

Frances began to notice that Michael was becoming more "turned on" to her. The therapist remarked, "Yet, your idea was that I was a spoiler, that if I didn't go along, things would be catastrophic. Now you tell me that things at home are considerably better. As we can see, this internal mother that continually tells you to be a 'nice girl' or look the other way can interfere with your judgment."

The therapeutic task was to assure her that the therapist was not merely going to stand by and make "nice-nice" as she did, as well as to reassure her that the goal was not to spoil things but to help her have a healthier, richer life.

CASE 7: TO TELL THE TRUTH

Alan and Lucy

This case brings together issues around containment and truth: when to tell the truth and when truth must be contained. It is an example of how truth could not be contained because of rage and guilt.

A couple with a 2-year-old daughter moved from the East to the West Coast. Alan, the borderline husband, could not come to the session during which Lucy, the narcissistic wife, confessed that her husband was not the biological father of the child, that he was sterile and could not conceive. Lucy confessed that she'd fallen in love with another man, become pregnant, and had the child. When I asked her why she wanted me to know this, she responded that she couldn't stand the guilt, that she was not getting along with her husband and thought he ought to know the truth. I told her, "Certainly it is appropriate to feel guilty. However, although your intention may be to reveal the truth, you are not taking into consideration what is best for your family and the welfare of your child. Rather, you are considering only that you can't stand your own guilt and now want to get rid of it." I advised that she seek her own individual treatment to deal with this issue. This treatment would focus on how Lucy had been very angry at her husband's attacking, destructive behavior and now wanted to retaliate.

Mindful of being a container for Lucy, I continued, "Yes, it's certainly important to tell the truth, but in this instance it is not clear what the truth is. First, there is no proof that your husband is not the biological father of the child, and second, you are not really interested in the truth but rather in relieving yourself of the intolerable guilt you feel and getting back at your husband. I don't see how that is dealing with the truth, especially when the main issue is what is going on between you and your husband. That apparently is not being dealt with."

CASE 8: DIAGNOSTIC DISTINCTIONS (QUALITATIVE DIFFERENCES)

Albert and Ruth

In this case, the partners demonstrate both narcissistic and borderline symptomatologies and show how narcissistic traits, states, and characteristics are not clear entities but tend to vacillate back and forth on dual tracks. Albert, the narcissistic husband, displays a grandiose self, feels overly entitled, and also exhibits many blaming and attacking defenses. Ruth, the borderline wife, exhibits many borderline features in that she has difficulty believing and holding onto her own experience. This couple has been married for 4 years and has a 2-year old child. Albert had been married three times before, and Ruth was afraid that Albert would leave her. The problem centered on the "lies" he told, which she could not tolerate. Each had a different experience of the "truth" (Lachkar, 1984).

Ruth:	Albert has trouble with the truth.
Th:	Oh, in what way?
Ruth:	Albert never tells the truth. All he does is lie.
Th:	[Turning to Albert] Is there any truth to what your wife says?
Albert:	I do tell the truth. I only exaggerate the truth.
Ruth:	That's a lie! You don't tell the truth. You lie all the time! [turning towards the therapist]. We have an apartment in Redondo Beach, and he tells everyone that we have a million-dollar home in Malibu. We have a rowboat, and he tells everyone we have a yacht. Now, do you call that telling the truth? I'm so embarrassed with my friends.
Albert:	[Starting to scream] That's why I do it! I exaggerate the truth because all you do is bitch, bitch, bitch! You don't understand me, and when you're like this I just want to run away from you.

Ruth: I can't trust him. It causes bad feelings inside me. I feel as though I'm not worth anything. He treats me like a nobody. That how I feel—like a nothing, as if I don't count. I just keep hoping he'll change.

Th: [To Albert] It sounds to me as if you are not getting the appreciation and recognition you would like, so you resort to telling her anything to please her.

Albert: [Softening] When I tell her the truth, all I get is complaints. So now I just tell her what she wants to hear. She never appreciates the things I do for her. That's when I usually take off. I go off with my friends, who value me. But then I start to feel bad, so I keep coming back.

CASE 9: DIAGNOSTIC DISTINCTIONS (FINE-TUNING AND SUBTLE DIFFERENCES}

Jonathan and Luella

This case is illustrative of the complex and ever-changing states of the narcissistic/borderline couple. In one session or at one moment, Jonathan seemed to be the more narcissistic, and at other sessions and other moments Luella seemed to be the more narcissistic. Only in time did it become clear which partner was more inclined towards narcissism.

At the outset, it was not clear which partner was predominantly borderline and which narcissistic. Upon further investigation, it seemed likely to be a mixed bill. Initially, Jonathan appeared to have many pronounced borderline features. An alcoholic, he was incapable of tolerating any frustration or of staying with issues. At the drop of a hat he would blame and attack his wife.

In addition to aggressive acting-out and destructive qualities, Jonathan had many narcissistic features. He was irate when he heard his boss had moved Jonathan's desk from the front to the back showroom in the manufacturing plant (perhaps an insult to his grandiose self). Jonathan may not have felt so much abandoned as narcissistically wounded at the notion that his boss did not appreciate him. He blurted out, "I was so upset today that I almost killed a pedestrian!" I needed to determine, in light of borderline versus narcissistic rage, if this was a reaction to this abandonment anxiety or a personal injury to his sense of specialness.

In contrast, Luella, Jonathan's wife, also became irate (borderline rage), could not stick to anything, rambled on and on without much insight or awareness, split off her needs, and used her husband as a target. She would criticize her husband and put him down in a punitive and destructive manner. For instance, Luella complained bitterly that Jonathan did not help with the dirty dishes or take out the trash. The shelf paper was still not finished, he failed to notice she changed the furniture around, and he didn't notice her new negligee or that she had lost weight. On the surface, one could surmise not only that Luella felt abandoned but that generally she was not being appreciated. She confirmed this, saying that she was concerned Jonathan would withdraw from her or would go on one of his drinking binges. Still, she seemed to be more preoccupied with being recognized and appreciated than with being abandoned.

I empathized with Jonathan's feelings of not being appreciated by his boss and suggested that it might be important to take up this issue with this boss. Jonathan responded defensively that he had already dealt with his boss, explaining that his friends "from the next room talked to him." I told Jonathan that his friend talking to his boss was not the same as talking to the boss himself. He blurted out, "The problem is not the boss; the problem is all Luella!" To this I responded, "You say that the problem is Luella, while you treat me in the same manner you do Luella: You push me away and discount me and what I say, as if you don't appreciate me either. This is sort of the way your boss acted with you. Maybe you're letting us know what it feels like when you are not being appreciated."

Jonathan shook his head as if to say, "I don't want to bother with it; it's not important anyway" (clearly indicating his devaluation of this interpretation). What I had just said was very difficult for him to digest and take inside, and I let him know I understood that. I explained that we were not communicating, that he didn't have to agree with what I said or do what I suggested, but that I was just asking for him to understand. I told him that because he had "hired" me to help him discover new parts of himself and because, in a way, he was my boss, I would talk to him directly.

Jonathan smiled and looked quite surprised. He proceeded to tell us how he wished his wife would talk to him more directly. (The borderline responds better to directness and confrontation and the narcissist to interpretation.) At this point I was still unsure which partner was the more borderline and which the more narcissistic. I simply continued to interpret the avoidance, the denial, the splitting, and the blaming, attacking defenses.

In working with Luella, I attempted to focus on her splitting off her needs. On the surface, it sounded as if she were very certain of her needs, but actually she was disavowing them by spewing out her contents, using words as confusional objects, blocking communication, and not allowing meaningful interchange and expression of affects and feelings.

I told Luella, "You either want to talk about everything, tell everything that bothers you about Jonathan, or else you want to withdraw, give up, and say nothing. The problem with trying to deal with everything is that you end up dealing with nothing. So it is all or nothing [grandiose fantasies and the splitting mechanisms]. I guess I will have to confess that I am in the same position here as you are, that I can't deal with all the issues right now. But I can deal with some of them, so both of us will have to tolerate putting some of the others on the shelf for a while until we can sort out some of these areas" [couple transference].

In the fourth session, it still wasn't clear which partner was more inclined towards borderline organization and which towards narcissism. I divided the session into three parts. In the first two, one partner interacted with me while the other sat back listening and had a chance to comment and give feedback.

As usual, Jonathan decided to start, not because he felt entitled, but because of his lack of tolerance and impulse control. In spite of this, I was impressed with how they were able to sit without interrupting. I also had to use body language and eye contact to help "hold" them in place.

Both Jonathan and Luella had difficulty holding on and waiting. Each partner needed the other because they stirred up something inside the other. Their relationship with one another stimulated a halted development that needed to grow.

In the fifth session Jonathan appeared more grandiose than before, claiming that he had an overwhelming amount of work to do, and that because of his perfectionistic qualities he felt he had to do it all.

Eventually it became clear that it was Luella, rather than Jonathan, who was the more inclined towards narcissism. Luella took on the role of a very bossy, aggressive wife whose superego functions and guilt mechanisms operated at a very punitive and restrictive level. Her grandiosity was expressed by her various attempts to do too much and to tell Jonathan all the things that were wrong this him. She would then withdraw, never reflecting on or staying with any of the issues. Jonathan, however, was at a more primitive level and had more borderline features. I came to understand Jonathan's withdrawal and blaming tendencies not as an escape to his inner world but rather as a form of evacuation to get rid of anxiety.

CASE 10: UNDERSTANDING AS A DEFENSE: TEACHING THE COUPLE TO PERFORM SELF-OBJECT FUNCTIONS

Dana and Bob

Dana and Bob had been in treatment with another therapist for a year. During that time, Dana had been encouraged to "understand" her husband's passive–aggressive behaviors. The former therapist had served not only as a self object but also as a container. For the mate of a passive–aggressive person to serve as a self object can only lead to maladaptive functioning. When Dana and Bob first started treatment with me, I let her know that it was not her role to "understand" her husband's feelings, and that in this situation her understanding was only getting in the way of her own development. I encouraged her to leave the understanding to me.

Bob had a blurred concept of boundaries and allowed an intrusive mother and sister to enter his home at any hour of the day. Dana was very "understanding" of this invasion of the couple's privacy; however, her understanding became misconstrued as weakness. During therapy, Dana was overly empathic and sympathized excessively with her husband's pain. This understanding brought on behavior on her part that colluded with Bob and ultimately led to devaluation and to his further attacks on Dana.

At this point, it was necessary for me to step in and take over the function of the strong parent imago, to be available to protect the couple from outside intruders (fantasied predators). Dana could then adjust to the role of being a wife or even a "child" with normal needs, rather than active in the defensive role of the little parent, little adult, or little therapist. I was able to focus on helping Dana see the real aspects of her role—how she was intruded upon and how her rights were violated. Bob had a right to see his family but did not have a right to invade Dana's space. When I pointed out these deficits, Dana was able to respond more positively.

Bob and Dana were in business together. The husband had many fantasies of their being business partners and working together as a team (a parasitic bond as opposed to a healthy dependency relationship). They denied that the business was failing and that they were moving into serious debt.

Dana's childhood had included continuing expectations that she function as the little adult. She had to take over many parental functions for her immature, dependent mother, and in order to achieve any sense of worthiness had to provide for her younger sisters. Dana had developed many compensatory mechanisms by becoming the pseudoparent, the good girl, the good helper, and now the good patient, which included being the good little therapist. In the marriage, she believed that it was her responsibility to make up for the losses in the business, and she felt it was entirely her fault that the business was indeed failing (persecutory anxiety).

In a combination of conjoint and individual treatment, Dana was helped to acknowledge that she was not the only one responsible for the business failure and that she covered up the problems by continually relieving her husband of his responsibility and by paying all the expenses.

Treatment consisted of trying to awaken a sleepy "couch husband." Partway through the treatment Dana said, "I'll never forget the look on his face when I told him that this time he's to be responsible for half the taxes and half the loan—that we were, after all, partners. He almost fell off the couch!" The major thrust of the treatment for Dana was to help her stand up for her rights and deal with her needs in a way that was more containing and less attacking. The dependent infantile and pseudoadult aspects of Dana's psychopathological states were illustrative of earlier needs that had been severely subjugated and now were projected onto Bob. Bob initially felt betrayed by both Dana and me. The therapeutic work consisted of trying to help Bob face issues around betrayal. Although we were able to channel Bob's talents and ambitions into more realistic goals and aims, he eventually dropped out. I continued to treat Dana.

Dana became aware that she was the one who was betrayed (busily taking in Bob's projections). She said, "I worried about betraying my husband or that I would lose him. You helped me face his anger, and he respects me more now. I am beginning to see our relationship in more realistic terms."

The therapist must be able to sustain the difficult role of containing painful feelings and affects of the patient's previous injuries—not only through words but by being able to demonstrate containment with vigor and conviction.

CASE 11: THE FALSE SELF

Fred and Mary Beth

In this case, Mary Beth, the borderline wife, was helped to understand that her false self was a means of avoiding feelings of vulnerability, sadness, and mourning. Mary Beth held the distorted view that her "true self" would lead to feelings of unworthiness when, in fact, it was the projected, split-off part of herself that invariably made her feel unworthy. The case illustrates how the interpretation of an internal, persecutory mother can help patients face their feelings of vulnerability, and how the "true self" can be experienced in new ways.

As Mary Beth, her husband, Fred, and I began our sessions, Mary Beth said she was in "the worst state" but that I shouldn't worry because "soon these terrible feelings will pass and then I'll be my other self again" (false self). I reassured her, "This state of vulnerability and sadness is important. But rather than allowing yourself to have these healthy sad feelings you cover them up by being a 'good girl' and trying to please others. When you cover up these feelings, you continually undermine yourself in this relationship and your ability to relate more effectively with Fred."

Mary Beth responded that she was upset because her husband said she was worthless for not contributing to the household expenses. I pointed out that she was not feeling worthless because her husband told her she was worthless. Quite the contrary, she felt worthless because she could not hold on to her own feelings (her internal household) and felt she had to live up to the expectations of others. "You need someone like a 'me' here to help you hold onto your real feelings and help you mourn and face the feelings of sadness." (The mourning process helps one get in closer contact with needs and feelings.) I explained that the same pattern was being repeated in this session. "You don't feel worthy enough to allow yourself to feel upset, to feel hurt; instead, you tend to cover up your true feelings by bringing in a false self or your 'other self' to make it appear that all is well" (the borderline's inclination towards the abrogation of the self). "That's what makes you feel unworthy. I was very impressed by what happened. Earlier, when you allowed yourself to feel the sadness, the pain, the sensitivity, and the vulnerability, Fred responded very warmly to you. When you did allow yourself to have these experiences, you felt it was tantamount to a psychological death."

I reassured Mary Beth that when she was in what she called the "worst state," she was really holding onto her true feelings and that this was preferable to being in her false-self state because there was an opportunity to grow, to develop, to understand, and to take something inside. When she was in her false-self state she did not have a chance to take in anything, and this was what made her feel worthless. Mary Beth assumed that if she allowed herself to be a needy little girl she would be abandoned or rejected by me or by her husband. Mary Beth therefore adopted a false self and became the supervisor, manager, therapist, mother, little adult, but would end up feeling worthless because the little girl part of her could not maintain those roles. I let Mary Beth know that when she was in the false-self state she was like a little girl trying on mommy's clothes, only to discover that mommy's clothes didn't fit, and in wearing them she became a caricature instead of a real person. Analogy is a useful tool to point out the absurd and delusional part of the personality.

I spoke to Mary Beth about being in her false-self state: "When this happens, you end up persecuting yourself because you give up your own needs and feelings, and then you can't see what your real role is as a wife or as a patient" (persecutory anxiety gets in the way of thinking and seeing reality).

Mary Beth responded tearfully, "My mother always told me I should put on a good front, to look and act as though I knew everything so that I wouldn't humiliate her in front of her friends. I always wanted to have my mother's approval. I would do anything at any price to get her approval, and now it makes me feel sad to have my husband see me in this way." (We know we are doing well when we get this kind of genetic association.) Fred spoke up: "Actually, I like you better this way. You seem softer, more beautiful to me, more sensitive and real."

CASE 12: THE NICE GUY: PASSIVE–AGGRESSIVE BEHAVIORS AND HOW BORDERLINES MISPERCEIVE

Arthur and Margaret

This case is an example of how the passive–aggressive creates and recreates the parent/child dyad, and how one partner continually coerces the other to take on the caretaker role.

Arthur, a borderline husband, expressed his hostility, anger, and out-rage to Margaret, his narcissistic wife, through passive–aggressive actions. He continually would "forget" to follow through with his promises and commitments. When he was asked to go to the market for his wife, he would arrive when the market was too crowded or was closed. When they had scheduled social activities or went out to dinner, he would forget his wallet and credit cards or claim they were stolen. He allowed workers to come into their home at any hour of the day or night. Even worse, businesspeople, creditors, debtors, and marshalls serving warrants would pound on their door in order to collect unpaid bills.

This enraged Margaret, who was left feeling invaded and infringed upon. She felt the "mess" was too overwhelming and complained bitterly about her rights being violated. Instead of paying attention to what she realisti-cally could do to correct the situation, Margaret would withdraw, walk away, not talk to Arthur, or refuse to have sex. He, in turn, would attack her: "All you ever do is bitch!"

Whenever Margaret would express her outrage, Arthur would act as though he were the one who was angry. I reminded Margaret of her ten-dency to withdraw, saying that I was perplexed that Arthur was turning things around, behaving as if he were the one who was angry with Marga-ret, "while as far as I know you [Margaret] are the one who is angry with him [Arthur]." (Arthur was using language as a confusional, rather than a transitional, object.) I asked Arthur what Margaret had done to make him angry with her when it was she who was telling Arthur that she was upset about her rights being violated.

Arthur, true to the role of the passive–aggressive husband, responded, "There are many things I'm upset about," and started to list all of them. Margaret, the narcissist wife, again reacted with extreme outrage and was dramatically shocked to hear complaints she had never before heard. "He only brings up these things when I am angry with him!" I reflected, "Oh, you have 'heard' these complaints before, but you 'heard' them indirectly. Now you are hearing them in a more healthy way. I think I know what may be happening." To the husband, I said, "You don't feel deserving or entitled to bring up your complaints unless your wife gives you the entrée by being angry with you." Arthur worried that he would "become his wife" or his mother (a form of identification or twinship) if he brought up any of his own issues.

I explained, "If you continue to join with your wife's complaints by voicing your complaints only when she is angry, you will never be able to turn to the internal creditors inside to help you. You do have some healthy needs, but if you keep projecting them onto others, you will continue to feel robbed. I'm so glad you are here to get help because this will give us an opportunity to develop a new line of credit." I let Arthur know how much I appreciated and valued what he was offering us. "I can hear how very much you want to be a 'nice guy', but that's not being a nice guy! It's being a sucker! In fact, it leaves you feeling not like a nice guy at all because everyone ends up getting even angrier then you. I hope that while you are coming here as the healthy big boy/nice guy, you can learn to express your feelings more directly."

Within the context of the couple transference, they both needed to know that the therapist was not going to be a "nice doctor," but rather a helpful doctor who would know the difference between being angry and being bitchy!

CASE 13: ENTITLEMENT FANTASIES

Jane and Ron

This case illustrates how the therapist tries to help the partners sort out what each is entitled to.

After 2 years of combined conjoint and individual treatment, Jane, a 43-year-old wife, became very anxious and asked me to hold one of her checks. She had prior knowledge of an interpretation made to her husband and feared that I would respond similarly to her. Her husband, Ron, had asked me time after time to hold checks until he could "make ends meet." I felt it was important to serve for a while in the capacity of a "toilet breast," and I held checks for him until I felt Ron was ready for this interpretation: I told Ron that someday these checks might grow up to become real checks, but right now they were baby checks that hadn't developed or matured. It appeared, I said, that he would like for me to "carry him" and to relieve him of his responsibility (as his wife did). I told Ron that if I continued to relieve him in this way he would not be able to understand anything about his true entitlement needs. It might momentarily make him feel special to be joined to me in this way, but it wouldn't last. In fact, if I provided for him the things to which he was not entitled, he then might not have a chance to discover that to what he indeed was entitled.

Jane was quite worried that I would offer the same response to her request to hold one of her checks. I assured her that she had different entitlement needs that were separate from those of her husband, and that with her there had never been any issue about money. She was reassured that she had been reliable, had paid on time, and that her husband's issues were distinct and separate from hers. (Her issue was not feeling deserving enough to ask for her needs. So far, "baby checks" or bad checks had not been one of Jane's needs; however, if she never asked, then she would lose out on being a baby in this instance.)

CASE 14: CONFUSIONAL, DIVERSONAL, AND TRANSITIONAL OBJECTS

Susan and Alex

This case illustrates the importance of the "transitional object" within the transitional space. There is in sharp contrast to the "diversional object," which obstructs the development and growth of intimacy and serves as the replacement to the love object.

Susan's husband, Alex, threatened to leave her if Susan continued to use her teddy bears. He saw these objects as getting in the way of their relationship, feeling that her dependency on them was destructive and made her too needy. (Susan's previous therapist also had thought that her dependency on transitional objects would cause her to regress to an infantile state.)

A self-psychological point of view focuses on the subjective meaning of a transitional object, whereas object-relations theory reinforces the importance and significance of the meaning of transitional objects via one's projections. For instance, Susan became angry when she was told that there would be a charge for missed appointments. She accused me of being a "money-hungry therapist," and said that I didn't really care about her but only about my money. I responded, "You expect me to respect your transitional objects, those that are related to your needs, and I guess you'll have to consider respecting me, too—my security blanket." To bond is to relate to the healthy way in which one uses transitional objects and to join in the experience through understanding what is being projected, transference interpretations, and countertransference (in this instance, her greed and my guilt). It is one thing to validate the couple's experience to talk about something but quite another to use the material to become immersed in the experience.

In a later session, Susan revealed that she was feeling better and was enjoying cuddling up to her teddy bears. They helped her sleep and helped bridge the times when I or her husband was away.

CASE 15: FRIENDS AS CONFUSIONAL OBJECTS

Don and Danielle

The following case illustrates the pathological use of "transitional objects," referred to as "confusional objects." Friends, time, and money are not used to bring the couple closer, but instead are meant to confuse and impede any form of intimacy.

Don and Danielle's lives consisted of going to exciting places throughout the world: nightclubs, skiing, safaris, fancy restaurants, Academy Awards dinners, and so forth. Danielle, the borderline wife, yearned to have time alone with Don. She continually felt left out and abandoned. He would take her with him when he traveled, then suddenly leave to go elsewhere with his many "interesting" friends, leaving her behind. Every time Don promised her a nice, quiet, cozy dinner for "just the two of them," they would suddenly be bombarded by his friends. Danielle was constantly puzzled as to how these friends would appear from the woodwork.

Don's friends became confusional objects, exploding and intruding into their relationship and interrupting their capacity for intimacy. (Transitional use of friends would, by contrast, fill in the lonely space.) If friends did not appear, Don would make telephone calls the remainder of the evening while she impatiently waited or stood idly by. The telephone became, as did the friends, diversional and confusional objects rather than vehicles to enhance good feelings, communication, and understanding.

I explained to Danielle that in this case it was not delusional that she was being abandoned. Indeed she was!

CASE 16: TREATMENT AS TRANSITIONAL

Karl and Lydia

If a couple enters treatment without clear awareness as to who is in need of the treatment, if there is no awareness of the problem, or if the reason for entering treatment is not for the sake of the self but is directed toward the other, treatment may be considered diversional or confusional. When there is an awareness of the necessity for the treatment of the conflict and some sense that the therapist can facilitate a transition to mental health, treatment may be regarded as transitional.

Karl, a husband and father of two children and an attorney, entered into treatment complaining of his wife's chronic forgetfulness. He bitterly complained about being let down by his wife, Lydia. Lydia responded that she was not the one with the problem but that Karl was a nag, was boring, was a constant complainer, and never would leave her alone. Initially, Karl decided that the problem was all his wife's fault, that he was problem free. Not only was Lydia forgetful, he complained, but she was always late, spent too much money, was a compulsive shopper, and constantly would lose things.

I slowly moved in by becoming the self-object for both these individuals. I allowed Karl to make use of the treatment by helping him face realistically that he was not responsible for Lydia, that she was not a child, and that there must be reasons why he felt so responsible. Eventually, Karl was able to face that he was not responsible for his wife's forgetfulness, lateness, and so on. Karl could not deal with Lydia realistically because of his own guilt. In taking care of his own needs Karl felt he would be "abandoning" and "betraying" his wife. Eventually, Karl began to recognize that he had his own issues to deal with and started to face the difficulties surrounding his guilt. Karl would go to the party in his own car when Lydia was not ready. If she was unable to find the address, Karl faced that it was not his responsibility to be Lydia's caretaker. He cane to realize that it was ultimately more loving not to relieve Lydia with a quick fix, which would only cover up the real issue. In this illustration, forgetfulness is clearly confusional in that Lydia blocked all methods of communication. Entering into treatment might be viewed as transitional, with Karl using his wife as a transitional object. The patient may have a preconception that treatment could be helpful; or, as Tustin might say, he brought in his "bibby."

Making use of the treatment as a transitional object occurs when there is bonding to the therapist as someone helpful (a good breast), as opposed to the perception of the therapist as a toilet breast. An emerging problem cannot be dealt with realistically unless the therapist is willing to be part of the interaction to bond with the healthy parts of the patients. The therapist who has bonded with the healthy parts of patients can truly facilitate real relief from anxiety. In this "transitional" case, relief came about through a differentiation between a "me" and "not-me" with Karl's recognition that he was not responsible for his wife's behavior. This not only led to a healthy emotional separation, but facilitated the bonding with the therapist so that healthy treatment could become a transition to development and growth. The movement from using the treatment as diversional to using it as transitional occurs when there is bonding both with the therapist and with the need for treatment.

CASE 17: ADDICTIVE LOVE: THE ALBATROSS

Mark and Sandy

This case illustrates the attachment to a bad internal object and shows how the borderline will stay forever loyally and painfully bonded. It also points out how the borderline's archaic injuries (V-spot) tend to revolve around early abandonment and annihilation anxieties.

Mark: I seem to feel this low again. Sandy is back in my life and she is calling me.

[Therapist remains silent.]

Mark: I seem to hang on her words like they are everything, like when she says, "I love you." I want to believe these words, yet I know she is away with Bob again.

[Therapist is listening attentively.]

Mark: I know she is with him because I go by her house and check if his car is still there or if she has moved out. I see it, just as I suspected [borderline's inability to rely on experience and the need to keep checking because he can't count on his mind].

Th: Sounds as though you are doubting yourself and you need to check up to make sure that what you know is so, that you need to check up on yourself. How is it that you can't trust what you know? Every time you have gone by her house in the past you know you have seen Bob's car there.

Mark: I guess I can't understand how she always rejects me and loves me at the same time. It affects me so deeply. She is like my mother. She rejects me and accepts me. When I am with her, she is loving, warm, and responsive. But when I call her a few days later, she is cold, aloof, and withdrawn, as if a wall goes up. I say to her, "Hey, wait a minute. This is Mark speaking!" But it really doesn't matter so much [borderline tendency to disavow the experience and the hurt]. She reminds me of my mother; she rejects and accepts me at the same time.

Th: You must be feeling very hurt and confused. Maybe you're worried that there may be something wrong with you.

Mark: Well, I am hurt and confused. My mother said she loved me but didn't show it. I knew she had her own problems with my father, and she felt frustrated.

Th: How old were you?

Mark: Around 3.

Th: That's when your first sibling was born. That's when you felt displaced by her. Until this time you had a chance to have a special relationship with your mother, until your sister came along.

[Mark seemed too embarrassed to cry, but shook his head and became very tearful.]

Th: It must have hurt then the same way it hurts now with Sandy, feeling that something is wrong with you, that you are being replaced.

Mark: Well, I guess I was different then. I was just too sensitive to cope with my sibling.

Th: You seem to think there is something wrong with being sensitive and different, or that to have needs and feelings is wrong and makes you the outcast. And then there is a Sandy who now confirms this view.

Mark: I remember in school, I used to get a checkmark for every time I talked too much, and my mother would punish me.

Th: Too bad she couldn't see your talking as ambition, excitement, and enthusiasm—as an opportunity to develop your personality, rather than something to be put down for. Or that you may have had something important to say.

Mark: Yes, that's true. I feel as though it's still there.

[Therapist remains silent.]

Mark: I feel like a masochist. I feel so impotent. I keep going back to the pain. There are many who do accept me, but I keep going back to those who reject me.

Th: I guess it's hard to take in and need others, to be fed by them internally, when you believe there is something wrong with you. The only problem is that as long as there is a Sandy out there to stir up these painful feelings, then you don't have to face your needs or to face the part in you that needs to understand something about yourself. (Sandy projects onto Mark, and Mark identifies with the projection.)

Mark: She is like the devil and the god. She has the power to save and relieve me. She is like an albatross around my neck. I just can't let go of the fantasy. I just love her. I love the way she looks, the way she feels, the way she smells. There simply is no other woman.

Th: [Attempt at transference interpretation] Yes, but as you idealize her, you leave yourself out. If she is either the devil or the god, then there is no you. She then has everything and you have nothing. You also leave me out, as if I don't count, as if I am impotent and insignificant, and that understanding your mind doesn't count. The only thing that counts is if Sandy loves you, accepts you, or rejects you. That's pretty simple, but it doesn't help us understand why you get into this addictive state. Perhaps you do so that you don't have to face the issues that brought you here in the first place.

CASE 18: THE AFFAIR

Lauren and Jim

The following case illustrates how the borderline forms an attachment to the "unavailable" man, and how issues around abandonment, betrayal, envy, and other archaic injuries are enacted again and again.

Lauren, a narcissistic, married female physician, fell in love with Jim, a married engineer. They were in their mid-40s, each had children, and each had been married for about 10 years. They had been seeing each other on and off for approximately 1 year. Lauren and her present husband had been in combined conjoint and individual treatment.

In the initial phase of the affair, Jim called Lauren at least three times each day and said he would "go out of his mind" if he didn't see her. During the course of their relationship, the frequency of Jim's calls and the time he spent with her gradually diminished. He would explain that he was busy working or had become preoccupied with work and family. On Thanksgiving Day, the lovers arranged to see each other briefly before both families were to gather at their respective homes for dinner. Jim called a few minutes before they were to meet, saying he couldn't meet with Lauren because he was having his entire family over and there was a very special aunt coming whom he hadn't seen for a long time. On another occasion, Jim canceled their date, claiming that he was overloaded with work, and when he worked that was all he could think about. On still other occasions, he spent time with his daughter, of whom he was deeply fond. Lauren became extremely hurt, injured, and enraged by this unavailability, which she perceived as a rejection. Her rage led to feelings of envy of her lover, his family, his daughter, his work, and even his aunt. Lauren couldn't image that Jim could get excited by events or persons other than her. She wished that events in her own life could fulfill or satisfy her, but her envy and primitive rage were overwhelming.

Although Lauren had many narcissistic features, including the need to turn to the external environment to get the excitement she craved, she also exhibited many borderline characteristics. "I feel as though I am a nothing." I interpreted that it was not her lover who made her feel like a nothing; it was that she needed an outside daddy/lover telling her that she was special. Because she felt like "nothing," she idealized him and was unable to see the shortcomings and limitations of her lover. The person who really was devaluing Lauren was herself. If Jim, or whoever, as lover, was made out to have everything (idealization), then by contrast she must have nothing (devaluation). That Lauren, although she also had important things in her life, had to turn to others to seek validation made her feel even more worthless.

Lauren continually complained about her mother. Her mother, Lauren reported, didn't have a life of her own and received all of her gratification from her daughter's accomplishments. I was able to bond with the part of Lauren who detested her mother for "not living her own life" and for imposing herself on her daughter's life. It became apparent that Lauren was reenacting with her love affair this scenario of an archaic experience she had with her mother. Lauren feared that, like her mother, she would not be able to have a life of her own. As her mother lived through her, Lauren became aware of how she lived through the life of her lover, and in doing so attempted to control him. How can one feel important when living inside someone else's "internal house"? Since the affair, Lauren had neglected herself, her husband, her children, and her friends and family, yet she needed someone, another daddy/lover, to stir vital issues, to move her to pay more attention to her "internal house."

In many affairs, wives, husbands, and families do come first, and often the lover feels very much left out. As the material unfolded during Lauren's twice-weekly individual sessions, her history and her background as an only child who always had been the center of attention became apparent. She mistook her lover's unavailability as a severe narcissistic injury to her grandiose self and as a threat to her exaggerated entitlement fantasies. She fantasized that his caring and preocccupation would fulfill her desire to be the number 1 child that she always wanted to be. Her idealization of her lover and the subsequent devaluation of herself resulted in misperceiving the "reality" of their situation (devaluation and idealization get in the way of thinking).

Although I did not see Jim, I felt that some understanding of Jim's dynamics would be useful in helping Lauren see the introjections and projections. I speculated that Jim seemed to have a more realistic grasp of what their relationship meant. His ability to avoid colluding with her demands provided an opportunity to take a look at Lauren's intrusive nature and her sense of boundary and space.

I speculated that Jim also seemed to exhibit many borderline and narcissistic features. His behaviors of intense passion were followed by subsequent withdrawal and isolation; this vacillation demonstrated that Jim leaned more towards narcissistic features. His excessive caution, his withdrawal from Lauren, and his isolation represented Jim's fears of being hurt, touching on a part of himself that panicked whenever his passions and infant needs were stimulated. Jim's desire to hold onto himself and the boundaries was interpreted by Lauren as rejection and unavailability. It became apparent that Jim, as Lauren's lover, exhibited the many traits and behaviors he loudly complained about in his wife. He projected all the needy parts of himself onto his lover and relieved himself by working compulsively (just as his wife did with him and as he did with his own father). His internalized representation of an unavailable, passive father got in the way of confronting his wife and of showing his feelings and passion more directly. Because Jim was fused with his wife (by exhibiting the same behaviors and defenses as she), he could not separate from her, either emotionally or physically. He turned aggressively to business and the affair as ways of getting rid of his anxiety and his needs. He projected his real needs onto his wife and his lover, making them out to be the needy ones.

I tried to help Lauren understand how she relieved Jim, as she did her husband, by becoming so needy and so desperate that she could not see what parts of these men were truly available to her. Jim frequently used Lauren's spouse as an excuse to withhold intimacy. The bond between Jim and Lauren was the reenactment of his relationship with an intrusive, smothering mother. The internal relationship he held with his mother continually interfered with Jim's ability to maintain healthy relationships. The mother/son interactions as played out in the Lauren/Jim lover relationships would sway back and forth like a dance until the therapist was able to help the narcissistic Lauren understand that by escaping into a whirlwind of passion, she was losing a big chunk of herself. All the while she was idealizing her lover, she was losing out on finding the real excitement within herself. Reality is not always as exciting as fantasy and passion, but reality has the basic function of being something one can count on that can lead to self-esteem and to experiences that are meaningful and important.

The Secret

One therapeutic task is to help the patient learn to wait, that is, to teach the patient that quick-fix responses can destroy. The "secret" also must be viewed within the framework of containment: Does the therapist have the capacity to hold onto a secret, to make use of the secret in a way that is productive, without revealing it or otherwise betraying the patient? In the case of Jim and Lauren, I needed to hold the secret from Lauren's husband during weekly conjoint visits. This modeled for Lauren that the therapist had the capacity to contain her impulses and hold onto the anxiety of Lauren's husband "not knowing." I needed to demonstrate that even though there may be the desire to give in to the impulse to reveal the secret, to do so would be joining Lauren by not holding on; after all, good mommies do not reveal secrets and do not need to evacuate.

This is an issue that must be addressed for conjoint therapy, where there are conflicts between containing the secret and telling the "truth." It is not up to the therapist to tell the truth. It is up to the therapist to interpret the dynamics surrounding the affair (betrayal, envy, quick fix, approval), but not the secret. The therapist must interpret, not spill over. If the emphasis is on strengthening the internal structures, patients in time may reveal their own truths. For the therapist to reveal the secret would not only sabotage the narcissistic wife's real entitlement to come to terms with truth and reality, but would undermine the patient's potential to face his or her true self through the art of introspection. The issue of betrayal in this case is not a matter of keeping the secret—"Why didn't you tell me about my wife's affair?"—but more about what is being distorted and what is being projected. Addressing the issue of betrayal rather than the affair itself, the therapist might respond, "I did. I've been addressing the betrayal all along, how appointments were not kept, how promises and other commitments were broken, how money was not paid back! Now you are turning to me as if now I am the betrayer."

Through many transference interpretations, I was able to help Lauren face the narcissistic part of her personality. There were times when she became enraged with me and devalued the interpretations. I explained that "although my interpretations might not be 'number 1,' at least they still could be helpful. I don't need to be the 'special doctor'." I told Lauren that I could not provide everything for others, including her lover and her husband; however, I could help. Though I was not omniscient, we had a chance to do good work together and to make progress, and it was important to join together to have a meaningful therapeutic "affair."

In this case, the therapeutic task was to address the notion that Lauren was devaluing the treatment because of her envy and tendency to join with an idealized archaic object. Lauren needed to recognize that she was with-drawing from the treatment, her husband, her work, her own life, her family and friends, and was turning to a life that was filled with highly charged fantasy. She was engaged in an affair that did not "construct" a rich life for her, but rather one that led her to lifelessness and mental death and killed all the passion within her internal world.

Curtain Call

A Final Note

It has been nearly a decade since the publication of my book, *The Narcissistic/Borderline Couple*. Since then I have developed and formulated many new ideas, approaches; redefined narcissistic/borderline relations, including three different kinds of love relationships ranging from healthy, pathological, and perverse; and reintroduced and elaborated on such concepts as dual projective identification, couple transference, reverse superego, traumatic bonding, and the most recent concept—the "V-spot." The theoretical literature has been updated to expand on different kinds of attachments and psychodynamics; revising treatment points and a list of therapeutic functions; a list of definitions; as well as many new cases (what a relief to be able to reorganize the content—let alone correct previous typos).

As a psychohistorian, I have earned extra mileage applying emotional abuse to the political arena (parallels between political and emotional abuse). Seeing things from the global perspective makes the clinical work with couples so much more glaringly apparent. My book on treating the emotional abuse of high-functioning women is a direct outcome of this endeavor. After teaching at universities, psychoanalytic institutes, conferences, and writing extensively on marital and political conflict, numerous publications later, I felt compelled to write this 2nd edition. One of my greatest pleasures arose when a couple (both psychologists) suddenly called, after not seeing them for several years, and came in like two jubilant children letting me know how well they had progressed since being in conjoint treatment. They quipped, "You know, Dr. Lachkar, we have read your articles, your books, gone through endless theoretical material you wrote, but oddly enough the most valuable was that of the 'V-spot!' My wife and I now when we have a problem we turn to each other and actually laugh, Okay what part of your 'V-spot' is getting stirred up." It is such a wonderful and simple and playful term, I think everyone can relate.

New emotional strains, new viruses, new theorists, new cultures, new pathologies, new faces, yet the ever-ending entanglements remain the same, the forever dance goes on and on. Thus the curtain opens and the therapist has an opportunity to use his/her own creativity to effectuate a new experience.

Definitions

Borderline Personality
This term designates a defect in the maternal attachment bond and over-concern with the "other." Many have affixed the term *as-if personalities* to borderlines, for they tend to subjugate or compromise themselves. They question their sense of existence, suffer from acute abandonment and persecutory anxiety, and tend to merge with others in very painful ways in order to get a sense of bonding. Under close scrutiny and under stress, they distort, misperceive, have poor impulse control, and turn suddenly against self and others to attack, blame, find fault, and get even.

Containment
This a term employed by Wilfred Bion to describe the interaction between the mother and the infant. Bion believed all psychological difficulties universally dissolve when the mother's mind acts as receiver of communicative content, which occurs when the mother is in a state of reverie via her own alpha function. It connotes the capacity for transformation of the data of emotional experience into meaningful feelings and thoughts. The mother's capacity to withstand the child's anger, frustrations, and intolerable feelings becomes the container for these affects. Containment occurs if the mother can sustain intolerable behaviors long enough to decode or detoxify painful feelings into a more digestible form.

Couple Transference
Couple transference does for the couple what transference does for the individual, but is slightly more complex. Couple transference interpretations are derived from the analyst's experience and insights and are designed to

produce a transformation within the dyadic relationship. The couple transference refers to the mutual projections, delusions, distortions, or shared
couple fantasies that become displaced onto the therapist. The notion of
the "couple/therapist" transference opens up an entirely new therapeutic
vista or transitional space in which to work. It is within this space that
"real" issues come to life.

   Example: Both partners rebuff any attempt on the part of the therapist
to be helpful. Both partners are unable to allow themselves to rely on or be
dependent on others. For the narcissist it means feeling vulnerable, less
than perfect; for the borderline it means abandonment/betrayal.

Defining Narcissistic/Borderline Relationships
The narcissist and the borderline enter into a psychological "dance" and
consciously or unconsciously stir up highly charged feelings that rekindle
early unresolved conflicts in the other. The revelation is that each partner
needs the other to play out his or her own personal relational drama. These
beleaguered relationships involve developmentally arrested people who bring
archaic experiences embedded in old sentiments into their current relationships.

Depressive Position
This is a term devised by Klein to describe a state of mourning and sadness.
It is in this state that integration and reparation takes place. Not everything
is seen in terms of black and white; there is more tolerance, guilt, remorse,
self-doubt, frustration, pain, and confusion in this position. One becomes
more responsible for one's action. There is the realization not of what things
should be but they way they are, that there is a "no breast." As verbal expression increases, one may feel sadness, but one also feels a newly re-
gained sense of aliveness.

Envy
Klein made a distinction between envy and jealousy. Klein considered envy
to be the most primitive and fundamental emotion. A part-object function
that is not based on love, envy exhausts external objects, and is destructive
in nature. Envy is destructive, possessive, controlling, and does not allow
in outside intruders.

Guilt
Guilt is a higher form of development than shame. Guilt has an internal
punitive voice that operates at the superego level (an internalized punitive,
harsh parental figure). There are two kinds of guilt: valid guilt and invalid
guilt.

Internal Objects
Internal objects emanate from part of the ego that has been introjected. These objects involve an intrapsychic process whereby unconscious fantasies are split off and projected. When they are felt to be persecutory, threatening, or dangerous they are denounced, split off, and projected. Klein believed that the infant can internalize good objects as the "good breast." If the infant perceives the world as bad and dangerous, the infant internalizes the "bad breast."

Jealousy
Jealousy, unlike envy, is a whole-object relationship whereby one desires the object but does not seek to destroy it or the Oedipal rival (father and siblings, those who take mother away). Jealousy is based on love, has an Oedipal component, and is a triangular relationship whereby one seeks the possession of the loved object and the removal of the rival. Jealousy involves a desire to be part of the group, family, clan, nation.

Manic Defenses
The experience of excitement (mania) offsets feelings of despair, loss, anxiety, and vulnerability. Manic defenses evolve from the depressive position as a defense against depressive anxiety, guilt, and loss. They are based on omnipotent denial of psychic reality and object relations, characterized by massive degree of triumph, control, and hostility. Some manic defenses work in the ego.

Mirroring
This is a term devised by Heinz Kohut describing the "gleam" in mother's eye that mirrors the child's exhibitionistic display and other forms of maternal participation in it. Mirroring is a specific response to the child's narcissistic–exhibitionist displays, confirming the child's self-esteem. Eventually, these responses channel into more realistic aims.

Narcissistic Personality
Narcissists are dominated by omnipotence, grandiosity, and exhibitionist features. They become strongly invested in others and thus experience them as self-objects. In order to preserve this "special" relationship with their self-objects (others), they tend to withdraw or isolate themselves by concentrating on perfection and power.

Object Relations
Object relations is a theory of unconscious internal-object relations in a dynamic interplay with current interpersonal experience. The analysis of

internal objects is centered on the interaction of lost early-object relations, a splitting of the ego into two parts: (1) a realistic ego, a part of the person more fully aware of experiences, feelings and ideas and (2) a more regressed or split-off part of the ego where the identification with the object is so intense that one loses the self. Object relations seek to understand internal intrapsychic and internal conflict, including the patient's distortion, delusions, and misperceptions. This is a technique that analyzes projections, introjections, fantasies, and split-off aspects of the self to enhance healthier functioning in an interpersonal world.

Object relations is a psychodynamic theory that examines how one relates and interacts with others in the external world. It is a theory of unconscious internal objects that compel a person to form a specific dynamic interaction or attachment. Object relations differs from Freudian theory in that it is an interpersonal theory that helps explain why people cannot adapt even with a good and nurturing environment. Klein taught us how we relate to others through lenses reflecting the child's world as she developed the notion of projective identification. Klein believed the first form of anxiety is persecutory, that the environment does not originate the baby's primary anxieties and inner conflicts. Klein developed the idea of pathological splitting of "good" and "bad" objects through the defensive process of projection and introjection in relation to primitive anxiety and the death instinct (based on biology). Object relations is one of the most powerful theories that examines unconscious fantasies/motivations and reflects how a person can distort reality by projecting and identifying with bad objects.

Obsessive–Compulsive Personality

The obsessive–compulsive has difficulty completing tasks, becomes preoccupied with small tedious duties, has strict rules, and is obsessed with details, lists, and organization. This personality will, for example, redo a schedule or a file to the extent of overlooking major tasks and to the exclusion of others. They make unreasonable demands, including perfection, and display excessive devotion to work and productivity to the dismissal of leisure activities and family and social relations.

Paranoid–Schizoid Position

The paranoid–schizoid position is a fragmented position in which thoughts and feelings are split off and projected because the psyche cannot tolerate the feelings of pain, emptiness, loneliness, rejection, humiliation, or ambiguity. This position was viewed by Klein as the earliest phase of development. It involves part-object functioning and the beginning of the primitive superego (undeveloped). If the child views mother as a "good breast," the child will maintain warm and hopeful feelings about the environment. If, on the other hand, the infant experiences mother as a "bad breast," the child is more likely to experience the environment as bad, attacking, and persecutory. Klein, more than any of her followers, understood the primary importance of the need for the mother and the breast.

Part-Objects
The first part-object unit is the feeding experience with the mother and the infant's relation to the breast, initiating both oral–libidinal and oral–destructive impulses. Klein believed the breast is the child's first possession. But because it is so desired, it also becomes the source of the infant's envy, greed, and hatred, and therefore is susceptible to the infant's fantasized attacks. The infant internalizes the mother as good or bad or, more specifically, as a "part-object" (a "good breast" or "bad breast"). As the breast is felt to contain a great part of the infant's death instinct (persecutory anxiety), it simultaneously establishes libidinal forces, giving way to the baby's first ambivalence. One part of the mother is loved and idealized, while the other is destroyed by the infant's oral, anal, sadistic, or aggressive impulses. In clinical terms Klein referred to this as pathological splitting. Here the parent is not seen as a whole object but as a function for what that parent can provide—e.g., in infancy the breast, in later life money, material objects, etc. "I only love women who have big breasts!"

Passive–Aggressive Personality
Passive–aggressive personalities are often dependent, a product of sibling rivalry with avoidance aspects. The passive–aggressive typically procrastinates, puts things off until the last minute, feigns inefficiency, and invariably finds a plethora of excuses why things were not accomplished. They claim others make unrealistic demands on them, especially in respect to authority, and defend against commitments by ineptness, forgetfulness, devaluing the importance of the task, and devaluing the needs of others. The passive–aggressive's stories of mishaps are endless, "Gee, honey, the store was closed!" Decoded, the message is a form of projective identification that says, "Now, I'm going to show you 'wife/mommy' how it feels to be locked out/unfed!"

Persecutory Anxiety
This is the part of the psyche that threatens and terrifies the patient. It relates to what Klein has referred to as the primitive superego, an undifferentiated state that continually warns the patient of eminent danger (mostly unfounded). Paranoid anxiety is a feature associated with the death instinct and is more persecutory in nature. This implies that the anxiety that emanates from the primitive superego is more explosive and volatile than that from the more developed superego.

Projective Identification

This is probably the most influential Kleinian concept and is gaining in popularity. Countertransference is an aspect of projective identification in which the patient splits off an unwanted aspect of the self and projects it onto the therapist, and the therapist identifies or overidentifies with that which is being projected. Projective identification allows the self to experience the unconscious defensive mechanism whereby the self translocates itself into the other. Under the influence of projective identification, one becomes vulnerable to the coercion, manipulation, or control of the person doing the projecting. This is more complex in conjoint treatment because the projector also splits off an unacceptable or undesirable part of the self into the partner. The projector can then feel, "It's not me; it's him/her." With a perceptive therapist, interrogating the countertransference leads to a fruitful interpretation.

Reparation

Reparation involves the desire for the ego to restore an injured loved object by coming to terms with guilt and ambivalence. The process of reparation begins in the depressive position as one develops the capacity to mourn, to tolerate, and contain the feelings of loss and guilt.

Schizoid Personality

The central features of the schizoid are defenses of attachment, aloofness, and indifference to others. The schizoid, although difficult to treat, is usually motivated, unlike the passive–aggressive. But because of his detachment and aloofness, the schizoid lacks the capacity to achieve social and sexual gratification. A close relationship invites the danger of being overwhelmed and suffocated since the schizoid may envision a relinquishing of his independence. The schizoid differs from the obsessive–compulsive in that the obsessive–compulsive feels great discomfort with emotions, whereas the schizoid is lacking in emotional capacity but at least recognizes the need. Schizoids differ from the narcissist in that they are self-sufficient and self-contained. They do not experience or suffer the same feelings of loss that borderlines and narcissists do: "Who me? I don't care; I have my work, my computer, etc.!"

Self-Objects

Devised by Heinz Kohut, the forerunner of self psychology, this term refers to an interpersonal process whereby the analyst provides basic functions for the patient. These functions are used to make up for failures in the past by caretakers who were lacking in mirroring, empathic attunement, and had faulty responses with their children. Kohut reminds us that psychological disturbances are caused by failures from idealized objects, and for the rest of their lives, some patients may need self-objects who provide good mirroring responses.

Self-Psychology

Heinz Kohut revolutionized analytic thinking when he introduced this new psychology of the self, which stresses the patient's subjective experience and considers the patient's "reality." The patient's reality, unlike in object relations, is not considered as a distortion or a projection, but rather as the patient's "truth." It is the patient's experience that is considered of the utmost importance. Self-psychology, with its emphasis on the empathic mode, implies that the narcissistic personality is more susceptible to classical interpretations, and recognition of splitting and projects are virtually nonexistent among self-psychologist.

Shame

Shame is a matter between the person and his group or society, while guilt is primarily a matter between a person and his conscience. Shame is the defense against the humiliation for having needs that are felt to be dangerous and persecutory. Shame is associated with anticipatory anxiety and annihilation fantasies (e.g., "If I tell my boyfriend what I really need, he will abandon me!")

Single and Dual Projective Identification (As It Pertains to Conjoint Treatment)

In single projective identification, one takes on the other person's projections by identifying with that which is being projected. In dual projective identification, both partners take on the projections of the other and form an identification with a certain aspect of the self, the split-off part of the ego. Thus, one may project guilt while the other projects shame: "You should be ashamed of yourself for being so needy! When you're so needy, I feel guilty!"

Superego

The literature refers to different kinds of superegos. The Freudian view depicts an introjected whole figure, a parental voice, or image which operates from a point of view of morality, telling the child how to follow the rules, and what happens if they don't. Many theorists have confirmed the precursors of Freud's superego formation as coexisting with the "dos, don'ts, oughts, and shoulds," and representing the child's compliance and conformity with a strong parental figure. Freud's superego does into concretely refer to a little man inside a person, but rather a fantasy of an introjected, strong, prohibitive parental figure. Freud's superego is the internalized image that continues to live inside the child's life, controlling or punishing the child whenever its Oedipal wishes make themselves known. This is in contrast to Klein's primitive superego, which is more persecutory and hostile in nature, and invades the psyche as an unmentalized experience. Freud's superego concerns itself with moral judgment, with what people think. Klein's superego centers around the shame and humiliation for having needs, thoughts, and feelings that are felt to be dangerous, mysterious internal saboteurs.

Transference
Three Kinds of Transference
- Two Individual Transferences
  – Narcissistic Transference
  – Borderline Transference
- "Couple Transference"
- Withdrawal versus Detachment

Whole Objects
The beginning of the depressive position is marked by the infant's awareness of his mother as a "whole object." As the infant matures, and as verbal expression increases, he achieves more cognitive ability and acquires the capacity to love the mother as a separate person, beginning to view her as a person with separate needs, feelings, and desires. This newly acquired concern for his objects helps him integrate and gradually learn to control his impulses; thus, the budding signs of reparation. As the infant's development continues, there is a lessening of persecutory anxiety and a diminution of splitting mechanisms. Guilt and jealousy become the replacement for shame and envy. Ambivalence and guilt are experienced and tolerated in relation to whole objects. One no longer seeks to destroy it or the Oedipal rival (father and siblings, those who take mother away), but can begin to live amicably with them.

Withdrawal versus Detachment
Detachment should not be confused with withdrawal. Withdrawal is actually a healthier state because it maintains a certain libidinal attachment to the object. When one detaches, one splits off and goes into a state of despondency. Children who are left alone, ignored, neglected for long periods of time enter into a phase of despair (Bowlby). The child's active protest for the missing or absent mother gradual diminishes when the child no longer makes demands. When this occurs the infant goes into detachment mode or pathological mourning. Apathy, lethargy, and listlessness then become the replacement for feelings (anger, rage, betrayal, abandonment).

References

Adams, A., & Hill, L. (1997). The Phallic female in Japanese group-fantasy. *Journal of Pychohistory, 25*(1), 33–66.

Bacal, H., & Newman, K. (1990). *Theories of object relations: Bridges to self psychology.* New York: Columbia University Press.

Benedict, R. (1946). *The chrysanthemum and the sword: Patterns of Japanese culture.* Boston: Houghton Mifflin.

Berton, P. (1996). *The psychological dimension of Japanese negotiating behavior.* Paper presented at the Kyoto Conference 1994, sponsored by the International Research Center for Japanese Studies and The Japan Foundation.

Berton, P., & Lachkar, J. (2000, June, unpublished manuscript). *German and Japanese reactions to their acts of aggression during World War II: A psychoanalytic perspective.* Paper presented at the International Psychohistorical Conference, Amsterdam.

Bienenfeld, F. (1980). *My mom and dad are getting a divorce.* St. Paul, MN: EMC Corporation.

Bienenfeld, F. (1983). *Child custody mediation.* Palo Alto, CA: U.S. Science and Behavior Books.

Bienenfeld, F. (1986). Breaking through "impossible" barriers in child custody medication. *Conciliation Courts Review, 24,* 39–42.

Bienenfeld, F. (1987). *Helping your child succeed after divorce.* Claremont, CA: Hunter House.

Bion, W. R. (1958). On arrogance. *International Journal of Psycho-Analysis, 39,* 266.

Bion, W. R. (1959). Attacks on linking. *International Journal of Psycho-Analysis, 40,* 308.

Bion, W. R. (1961). *Experiences in groups and other papers.* London: Tavistock.

Bion, W. R. (1962). *Learning from experience.* London: Heinemann.

Bion, W. R. (1965). *Transformations.* London: Heinemann.

Bion, W. R. (1967). *Second thoughts. Selected papers on psycho-analysis.* New York: Jason Aronson.

Bion, W. R. (1968). *Second thoughts. Selected papers on psycho-analysis.* New York: Basic Books.

Bion, W. R. (1970). *Attention and interpretation.* London: Tavistock.

Bion, W. R. (1977). *Seven servants: Four works by Wilfred R. Bion.* New York: Jason Aronson.

Bowlby, J. (1969). *Attachment and loss* (3 vols.). New York: Basic Books.

Brandchaft, B., & Stolorow, R. (1984). The borderline concept: Pathological character and iatrogenic myth. In J. Lichtenberg et al. (Eds.), *Empathy II* (pp. 333–357). Hillsdale, NJ: Analytic Press.

Campbell, J. (1988). *The power of myth.* New York: Doubleday.

Carlson, J., & Sperry, L. (Eds.). (1998). *The disordered couple.* New York: Brunner/Mazel.

Dallek, R. (1991). *Lone star rising. Lyndon Johnson and his times 1908–1960.* New York: Oxford University Press.

DeMause, L. (1974). *The history of childhood.* New York: Psychohistory Press.

DeMause, L. (2002a). The childhood origins of terrorism. *Journal of Psychohistory, 29*(4), 340–348.

DeMause, L. (2002b). *The emotional life of nations.* New York: The Institute for Psychohistory.

Deutsch, H. (1942). Some forms of emotional disturbance and their relationship to schizophrenia. *Contemporary Psychoanalysis, 11,* 301–321.

Dicks, H. (1967). *Marital tensions. Clinical studies toward a psychological theory of interaction.* New York: Basic Books.

Doder, D. (1999). *Portrait of a tyrant.* New York: Simon & Schuster.

Doi, T. (1973). *The anatomy of dependence.* Tokyo: Kodansha.

Dutton, D., & Painter, S. L. (1981). Traumatic bonding: The development of emotional attachments in battered women and other relationships of intermittent abuse. *Victomology: An International Journal, 6,* 139–155.

Emde, R. N. (1987, August). *Development terminable and interminable, Recent psychoanalytic theory and therapeutic considerations. The effective core of the self: Motivational structures from infancy.* Paper presented at the International Psychoanalytic Congress, Montreal.

Endleman, R. (1989). *Love and sex in twelve cultures.* New York: Psychic Press.

Fairbairn, W. R. D. (1940/1952). Schizoid factors in the personality. In *Psychoanalytic studies of the personality* (pp. 3–27). London: Routledge & Kegan Paul.

Fairbairn, W. R. D. (1944/1952). Object relationships and dynamic structures. In *Psychoanalytic studies of the personality* (pp. 137–151). Boston: Routledge Paul.

Fairbairn, W. R. D. (1946/1952). A revised psychopathology of the psychosis and psychoneurosis. In *Psychoanalytic studies of the personality* (pp. 28–58). Boston: Routledge Paul.

Fairbairn, W. R. D. (1954). *An object relations theory of the personality.* New York: Basic Books.

Flicker, M. (1988). *Object relations and the treatment of the seriously regressed borderline patient.* Paper presented at the Los Angeles Psychoanalytic Institute.

Foster, R., Moskowitz, M., & Javier, R. (1986). *Reaching across boundaries of culture and class.* Northvale, NJ: Jason Aronson.

Freud, S. (1914). Narcissism: An introduction. In J. Strachey (Ed. & Trans.), *The standard edition of the complete works of Sigmund Freud* (Vol. 14). London: Hogarth Press.

Freud, S. (1921). Group psychology and the analysis of ego. In J. Strachey (Ed. & Trans.), *The standard edition of the complete works of Sigmund Freud* (Vol. 18, pp. 67–144). London: Hogarth Press.

Freud, S. (1923). *The ego and the id.* New York: Norton.

Freud, S. (1924). The loss of reality in neurosis and psychosis. In J. Strachey (Ed. & Trans.), *The standard edition of the complete works of Sigmund Freud* (Vol. 19, pp. 149–153). London: Hogarth Press.

Freud, S. (1940). An outline of psycho-analysis. In J. Strachey (Ed. & Trans.), *The standard edition of the complete works of Sigmund Freud* (Vol. 23, pp. 141–207). London: Hogarth Press. (Original work published 1938)

Freud, S. (1955). Totem and taboo. In J. Strachey (Ed. & Trans.), *The standard edition of the complete works of Sigmund Freud* (Vol. 13, pp. 1–163). London: Hogarth Press. (Original work published 1912–1913)

Freud, S. (1957). On narcissism: An introduction. In J. Strachey (Ed. & Trans.), *The standard edition of the complete works of Sigmund Freud* (Vol. 14, pp. 69–102). London: Hogarth Press. (Original work published 1914)

Gay, P. (1988). *Freud: A life for our times.* New York: Norton.

Giovacchini, P. (1979). *Primitive mental states.* New York: Jason Aronson

Greenfield, P., & Cocking, R. (1994). *Cross-cultural roots of minority child development.* Hillsdale, NJ: Erblaum.

Grinberg, L., Sor, D., & de Bianchedi, E.T. (1977). *Introduction to the works of Bion: Groups, knowledge, psychosis, thoughts, transformations, psychoanalytic practice.* New York: Jason Aronson.

Grotstein, J. (1980). A proposed revision of the psychoanalytic concept of primitive mental states. *Contemporary Psychoanalysis, 16,* 479–546.

Grotstein, J. (1981). *Splitting and projective identification.* New York: Jason Aronson.

Grotstein, J. (1983). A proposed revision of the psychoanalytic concept of primitive mental states. II. The borderline syndrome. Sec. 1. *Contemporary Psychoanalysis, 16,* 570–604.

Grotstein, J. (1984a). A proposed revision of the psychoanalytic concept of primitive mental states. II. The borderline syndrome. Sec. 2. *Contemporary Psychoanalysis, 20,* 266–343.

Grotstein, J. (1984b). A proposed revision of the psychoanalytic concept of primitive mental states. II. The borderline syndrome. Sec. 3. *Contemporary Psychoanalysis, 20,* 266–343.

Grotstein, J. (1985). The Schreber case revisited: Schizophrenia as a disorder of self-regulation and interactional regulation. *The Yale Journal of Biology and Medicine: VIII International Symposium on the Psychotherapy of Schizophrenia: New Approaches to Psychosocial Intervention, 58,* 299–314.

Grotstein, J. (1986). Schizophrenia personality disorder: ". . . And if I should die before I wake." In D. B. Feinsilver (Ed.), *Towards a complete model of schizophrenic disorders* (pp. 29–71). Hillsdale, NJ: Analytic Press.

Grotstein, J. (1987). *Meaning, meaninglessness, and the "black hole": Self and interactional regulation as a new paradigm for psychoanalysis and neuroscience: An introduction*. Unpublished manuscript.

Hall, C. (1954). *A primer of Freudian psychology*. New York: New American Library.

Hegel, G. W. (1821). *Hegel's philosophy of right* (T. M. Kox, Trans). Oxford: Clarendon.

Heimann, P. (1950). On countertransference. *International Journal of Psycho-Analysis, 31,* 81–84.

Iga, M. (1986). *The Thorn in the chrysanthemum*. Berkeley, CA: University of California Press.

Isaacs, S. (1943). The nature and function of phantasy. In M. Klein, P. Heinmann, S. Isaacs, & J. Reviere (Eds.), *Development in psycho-analyses*. London: Hogarth Press.

Johnson, F. (1994). *Dependency and Japanese socialization: Psychoanalytic and anthropological investigations into Amae*. New York: New York University Press.

Kalogjera, I. (1998). The narcissistic couple. In J. Carlson & L. Sperry (Eds.), *The disordered couple*. New York: Brunner/Mazel.

Kernberg, O. (1975). *Borderline conditions and pathological narcissism*. New York: Jason Aronson.

Kernberg, O. (1976). *Object relations theory and clinical psychoanalysis*. New York: Jason Aronson.

Kernberg, O. (1980). Regression in groups. In O. Kernberg (Ed.), *Internal world and external reality*. New York: Jason Aronson.

Kernberg, O. (1992). *Aggression in personality disorders and perversions*. New Haven, CT: Yale University Press.

Kernberg, O. (1995). *Love relation: Normality and pathology*. New Haven, CT: Yale University Press.

Klein, M. (1946). Notes on some schizoid mechanisms. In J. Riviere (Ed.), *Developments in psychoanalysis* (pp. 198–236). London: Hogarth Press. 1952.

Klein, M. (1948). Mourning and its relation to manic states. In *Contributions to psycho-analysis 1921–1945*. London: Hogarth Press. (Original work published in 1921)

Klein, M. (1952). Notes on some schizoid mechanisms. In J. Revieve (Ed.), *Developments in psychoanalysis* (pp. 242–321). London: Hogarth.

Klein, M. (1957). *Envy and gratitude*. New York: Basic Books.

Klein, M. (1975). Love, guilt and reparation. In R. E. Money-Kryle (Ed.), *The writings of Melanie Klein, Vol. I—Love, guilt and reparation and other works 1921–1945* (pp. 306–343). New York: The Free Press. (Original work published 1937)

Kobrin, N. (2002). The death pilots of September 11th, 2001: The ultimate schizoid dilemma. In J. Piven, C. Boyd, & H. Lawton (Eds.), *Jihad and sacred vengence: Psychological undercurrents of history Volume 3*. New York: Writers Club Press.

Kohut, H. (1971). *The analysis of the self*. New York: International Universities Press.

Kohut, H. (1977). *The restoration of the self.* New York: International Universities Press.

Lachkar, J. (1983). *The Arab-Israeli conflict. A psychoanalytic study.* Doctoral dissertation. Los Angeles: International College.

Lachkar, J. (1984). Narcissistic/borderline couples: A psychoanalytic perspective to family therapy. *International Journal of Family Psychiatry, 5*(2), 169–189.

Lachkar, J. (1985). Narcissistic/borderline couples: Theoretical implications for treatment. *Dynamic Psychotherapy, 3*(2), 109–127.

Lachkar, J. (1986). Narcissistic/borderline couples: Implications for mediation. *Conciliation Courts Review, 24*(1), 31–43.

Lachkar, J. (1989). *Narcissistic/borderline couples: A psychoanalytic perspective to marital conflict.* Unpublished paper presented to the Los Angeles Psychoanalytic Society and Institute.

Lachkar, J. (1991). *Primitive defenses in the Persian Gulf.* Unpublished paper presented at The International Psychohistorical Association, John Jay College, New York.

Lachkar, J. (1992). *The narcissistic/borderline couple: A psychoanalytic perspective to marital conflict.* New York: Brunner/Mazel.

Lachkar, J. (1993a). Paradox of peace: Folie à deux in marital and political relationships. *Journal of Psychohistory, 20*(3), 275–287.

Lachkar, J. (1993b). Political and marital conflict. *Journal of Psychohistory, 22*(2), 199–211.

Lachkar, J. (1997). Narcissistic/borderline couples: A psychodynamic approach to conjoint treatment. In J. Carlson & L. Sperry (Eds.), *The disordered couple* (pp. 259–282). New York: Brunner/Mazel.

Lachkar, J. (1998a, July). *Aggression and cruelty in cross-cultural couples.* Paper presented at the Psychohistory Congress, Paris.

Lachkar, J. (1998b). *The many faces of abuse: Treating the emotional abuse of high-functioning women.* Northvale, NJ: Jason Aronson.

Lachkar J. (2000). Emotional abuse of high-functioning professional women: A psychodynamic perspective. *Journal of Emotional Abuse, 2*(1), 73–91.

Lachkar, J. (2001). Narcissism in dance. *Choreography and Dance: An International Journal, 6,* 23–30

Lachkar, J. (2002). The psychological make-up of a suicide bomber. *Journal of Psychohistory, 29*(4), 349–367.

Lachkar, J. (2003). The "V-spot." Unpublished manuscript.

Lansky, M. (1981). *Family therapy and major psychopathology.* New York: Grune and Stratton.

Lansky, M. (1987). Shame in the family relationships of borderline patients. In J. Grotstein, M. Solomon, & J. Lang (Eds.), *The borderline patient: Emerging concepts in diagnosis, psychodynamics and treatment* (Vol. II, pp. 187–199). Hillsdale, NJ: Analytic Press.

Lansky, M. (1995). The stepfather in Sophocles's *Electra.* In S. Cath, M. Shopper, & L. Tessman (Eds.), *Stepfathers* (pp. 1–33). Hillsdale, NJ: Analtyic Press.

Levene, J. (1997). Couples therapy with narcissistically vulnerable individuals. *Canadian Journal of Psychoanalytic, 5,* 125–144.

Loewenberg, P. (1950). *Fantasy and reality in history.* New York: Oxford University Press.

Loewenberg, P. (1985, Spring). The victimization of human rights. *Bulletin of the Southern California Psychoanalytic Institute and Society, 72,* 20.

Loewenberg, P. (1987). *The Kristallnacht as a public degradation ritual.* London: Secker & Warburg, Leo Baeck Institute.

Loring, M. T. (1994). *Emotional abuse.* New York: Lexington Books.

Mahler, M. S., Pine, F., & Bergman, A. (1975). *The psychological birth of the human infant.* New York: Basic Books.

Maniacci, H. (1998). The psychotic couple. In J. Carlson & L. Sperry (Eds.), *The disordered couple.* New York: Brunner/Mazel.

Mason, A. (1981). The suffocating super-ego: Psychotic break and claustrophobia. In J. Grotstein (Ed.), *Do I dare disturb the universe?* (pp. 140–166). Beverly Hills, CA: Caesura.

Masterson, J. (1981). *The narcissistic and borderline disorders.* New York: Brunner/ Mazel.

McCormack, C. (2000). *Treating borderline states in marriage: Delaying with oppositionalism, ruthless aggression, and severe resistance.* Northvale, NJ: Jason Aronson.

Meltzer, D. (1964–1965). *Sexual states of mind. Scotland.* Adapted lectures read at The Institute of Education. London: University of London.

Meltzer, D. (1967). *The psycho-analytic process.* London: Heinemann.

Miyamoto, M. (1994). *Straitjacket society.* Tokyo: Kodansha International.

Nurse, R. (1998). The dependent/narcissistic couple. In J. Carlson & L. Sperry (Eds.), *The disordered couple* (pp. 315–331). New York: Brunner/Mazel.

Ogden, T. (1980). On the nature of schizophrenic conflict. *International Journal of Psycho-Analysis, 6,* 513.

Ogden, T. H. (1986). *The matrix of the mind: Object relations and the psychoanalytic dialogue.* Northvale, NJ: Jason Aronson.

Odgen, T. (1989). *The primitive edge of experience.* Northvale, NJ: Jason Aronson.

Perez Foster, R., Moskowitz, M., & Javier, R. (1996). *Reaching across boundaries of culture and class: Widening the scope of psychotherapy.* Northvale, NJ: Jason Aronson.

Piven, J. (2002). *Lord of the Flies* as parable of the invention of enemies, violence and sacrifice. In J. Piven, C. Boyd, & H. Lawton (Eds.), *Jihad and sacred vengeance* (pp. 132–158). New York: Writers Club Press.

Robins, R., & Post, J. (1997). *Political paranoia: The psychopolitics of hatred.* New Haven, CT: Yale University Press.

Roland, A. (1988). *In search of self in India and Japan.* Princeton, NJ: Princeton University Press.

Rosenfeld, H. (1987). The narcissistic patients with negative therapeutic reaction. In H. Rosenfeld (Ed.), *Impasse and interpretation* (pp. 85–104). London: Tavistock.

Rothstein, A. (1998). *Psychoanalytic technique and the creation of analytic patients.* New Haven, CT: International Universities Press.

Scarf, M. (1987). *Intimate partners.* New York: Random House.

Scharff, D., & Scharff, J. S. (1987). *Object relations in family therapy*. Northvale, NJ: Jason Aronson.

Schwartzman, G. (1984). Narcissistic transferences: Implications for the treatment of couples. *Dynamic Psychotherapy, 2*(1), 5–14.

Segal, H. (1964). *Introduction to the works of Melanie Klein*. New York: Basic Books.

Seinfeld, J. (1990). *The bad object: Handling the negative therapeutic reaction in psychotherapy*. Northvale, NJ: Jason Aronson.

Sharpe, S. A. (1981). The symbiotic marriage: A diagnostic profile. *Bulletin of the Menninger Clinic, 45*(2), 89–114.

Slavik, S. (1998). The passive-aggressive couple. In J. Carlson & L. Sperry (Eds.), *The disordered couple* (pp. 299–312). New York: Brunner/Mazel.

Slipp, S. (1984). *Object relations: A dynamic bridge between individual and family treatment*. New York: Jason Aronson.

Solomon, M. (1985, July). Treatment of narcissistic and borderline disorders in marital therapy. Suggestions toward an enhanced therapeutic approach. *Clinical Social Work Journal, 13*(2), 141–156.

Solomon, M. (1986). The application of self-psychology to marital therapy. *Clinical Social Work Journal*, 141–156.

Stein, H. (1978). Judaism and group fantasy of martyrdom: The psychodynamic paradox of survival through persecution. *Journal of Psychohistory, 6*, 1–209.

Stolorow, R., & Lachmann, E. (1980). *Psychoanalysis of developmental arrests, theory and treatment*. New York: International Universities Press.

Strean, H.S. (1980). *The extramarital affair*. New York: Free Press.

Strean, H.S. (1985). *Resolving marital conflicts: A psychodynamic perspective*. New York: Wiley.

Tuch, R. (2000). *The Single Woman–Married Man Syndrome*. Northvale, NJ: Jason Aronson.

Tustin, F. (1981). *Autistic states in children*. Boston: Routledge Paul.

Volkan, V. (1979). *War and adaptation*. Charlottesville: Universities Press of Virginia.

Waldinger, R. J., & Moore, C., et al. (2000). *Mountain out of molehills: How borderline individuls read their partners' emotions*. Judge Baker Children's Center and Harvard Medical School, Byn Mawr College.

Willi, J. (1982). *Couples in collusion. The unconscious dimension in partner relationships*. Claremont, CA: Hunter House.

Winnicott, D. W. (1953). Transitional objects and transitional phenomena in a study of the first not-me possession. *International Journal of Psycho-Analysis, 34*(2), 89–97.

Winnicott, D.W. (1965a). Ego distortion in terms of the true and false self. In *The maturational process and the facilitating environment: Studies in the theory of emotional development* (pp. 140–152). New York: International Universities Press.

Winnicott, D. W. (1965b). *The maturational process and the facilitating environment*. New York: International Universities Press.

Yi, K. (1995). Psychoanalytic psychotherapy with Asian clients: Transference and therapeutic considerations. *Journal of Psychotherapy, 32*, 308–316.

Index

approval, 60
from cross-cultural perspective, 135–139
deprivation, 43–44, 60, 105, 193–196
distancing, 91–92
needs and, 58–60
object relations and, 61–63
privation, 43–44, 105, 110
superego and, 61
psychoeducation, 155–156
psychohistory, 123–126

quick fix, 28, 91

rage, 75–76, 140–141, 146–149
real relationship, 115–117
regression, 114
reparation, 85, 87–88, 170, 228
repetition compulsions, 29
retribution, 86
Robbins, Jerome, 6
Robins, R., 125
Roland, A., 143
Rosenfeld, H., 7, 8

sacrifice, 77–78, 128–129
same-sex couples, 55–58, 131
Saudi Arabia, 144
"saving face," 135
scapegoating, 115, 117–118, 124, 127, 134
Scarf, M., 119
schizoid personality, 12–13, 74, 228
schizophrenia, 7
Segal, H., 84, 85
Seinfeld, J., 7
self, 131–132
"false," 21, 34, 131–132, 143, 206–207
grandiose, 2, 41, 42, 74, 142
individual vs. group, 139
as mommy/doctor/me/therapist, 167
sacrifice and, 77–78
"true," 21, 28, 131–132, 143
validation of, 41
self-persecution, 50
self-psychology, 15, 16, 31, 95, 105, 163. See also Kohut, H.
for cross-cultural couples, 132
defined, 229
empathy, 15, 87, 94–95, 102–104, 106, 110, 134, 143–146, 162

mirroring, 15, 18–19, 32, 89, 94–95, 101–103, 106, 145, 225
for narcissists, 103
object relations vs., 17–18
self objects, 17, 42–43, 52, 63–66, 93–96, 204–206, 228–229
weaning, 99
separation-individuation, 43, 84, 86–87, 137, 171. See also cross-cultural couples; treatment
shame, 8, 34, 187
culture and, 135
defined, 229
in groups, 127
guilt vs., 72, 198–200, 224
oneness and, 164
Single Woman-Married Man Syndrome, The (Tuch), 109
Slipp, Samuel, 90
socialization, 134
society. See also cross-cultural couples
psychohistory and, 123–126
role of, 122–123
traumatic, 127–128
Solomon, M., 52
splitting, 19, 20–21, 86
in groups, 117
pathological, 62, 226
Stein, Howard, 125
Stolorow, R., 16, 49, 65
superego, 61, 135, 136, 221
of borderlines, 7, 58
defined, 229
of narcissists, 5, 59
persecutory, 34, 58
symbiotic bonding, 164. See also bonding

task orientation, 115–116
tatamae (hidden self), 143
Tavistock Institute of Human Relations, 115
terrorism, 124–125
therapeutic bonding, 109–111. See also bonding
therapeutic environment, 22–23
therapists
anxiety in, 119
as containing mothers, 52, 156–157
female, 142
focus of, 38–39